SUPPORT FOR SECESSION

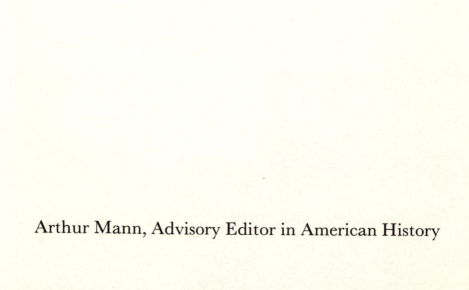

Arthur Mann, Advisory Editor in American History

SUPPORT FOR SECESSION

LANCASHIRE AND THE AMERICAN CIVIL WAR

MARY ELLISON
Epilogue by Peter d'A. Jones

The University of Chicago Press · Chicago and London

The University of Chicago Press, Chicago 60637. The University of Chicago Press, Ltd., London. © 1972 by The University of Chicago. All rights reserved. Published 1972. Printed in the United States of America. International Standard Book Number: 0–226–20593–2. Library of Congress Catalog Card Number: 72–80158.

TO MY CHILDREN

CONTENTS

PREFACE

This book is an attempt to radically reassess Lancashire's reaction to the American Civil War. The use of hitherto unscanned press sources has helped to make it possible to correct the lingering misconception that during the Civil War which tore America apart between the springs of 1861 and 1865 cotton-starved Lancashire refused to support the Confederacy. There was in fact a supreme determination to aid the South with at least moral backing while the North was viewed with a mistrust that deepened with the intensity of Lancashire's distress. This study seeks to investigate how and why this happened, to discover the role of social and economic factors and political and religious affiliation in influencing reactions to the war. Simultaneously I have tried to evaluate the relative significance of economic deprivation and moral conviction in forming attitudes towards the emancipation of the slaves. Even where practical aid was given, such as in running the blockade, motives for doing so were often unexpectedly complex. The myth of Lancashire's support for the Union during the Civil War has long needed explanation and refutation. It is to be hoped that this book goes some of the way towards providing both.

I am indebted for help and advice on the completion of this work to my Ph.D. supervisor, Professor H. C. Allen, and have benefited enormously from the criticisms and ideas of Henry Pelling, who suggested the topic. I am also grateful to Dr. Christine Bolt and Mr. Jim Potter who read and constructively commented on the manuscript in its embryonic state. The research was greatly facilitated by the cooperation and assistance of the librarians at the British Museum Reading Room and Newspaper Library; the Public Record Office; the Library of Congress; University College of London Library; University of Liverpool Library; the Co-operative Society Library, Manchester; the Cotton Exchange, Liverpool; Chatsworth House Library; the Athenaeum Library, Liverpool; John Rylands Library, Liverpool; Brown Library, Liverpool (including Liverpool Record Office); Manchester Central Library; Preston Record Office; and Ashton-under-Lyne, Barrow-in-Furness, Blackburn, Bolton, Bury, Burnley, Fleetwood, Lancaster, Oldham, Preston, Rawtenstall, Rochdale, Southport, Warrington, and Wigan Public Libraries. Final revisions suggested by members of my reconstruction seminar, by Professor Peter d'A. Jones of the University of Illinois, Chicago Circle, and by Professor Arthur Mann of the University of Chicago have greatly improved the work. For the remaining errors and inadequacies I am entirely responsible.

ix

SUPPORT FOR SECESSION

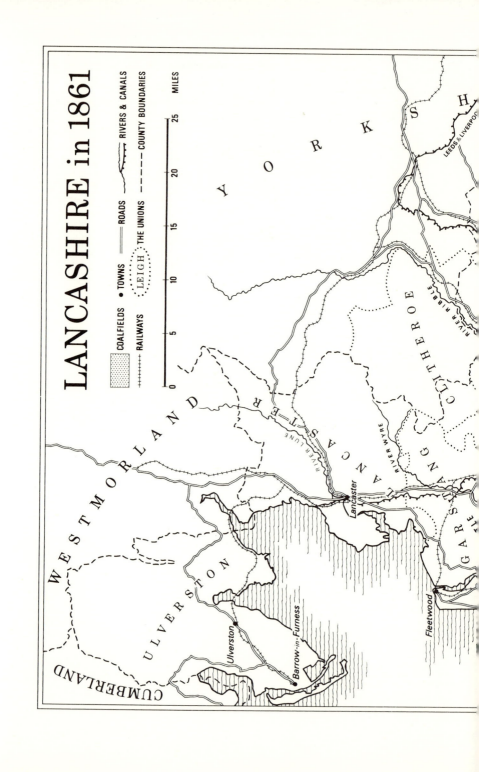

LANCASHIRE in 1861

COALFIELDS
RAILWAYS
TOWNS
ROADS
RIVERS & CANALS
COUNTY BOUNDARIES

LEIGH THE UNIONS

MILES

0   5   10   15   20   25

CUMBERLAND

WESTMORLAND

ULVERSTON

Ulverston

Barrow-in-Furness

Y O R K S H

LANCASTER

RIVER LUNE

RIVER WYRE

RIVER RIBBLE

CLITHEROE

GARS

Fleetwood

LEEDS & LIVERPO

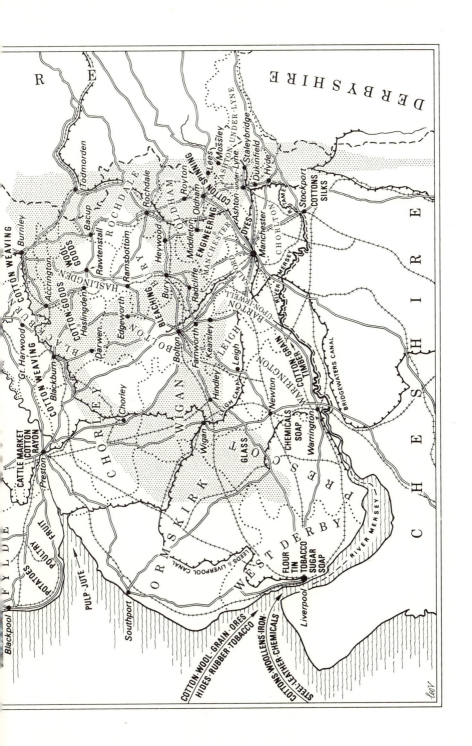

1

COTTON IN CRISIS

O dear! if Yond' Yankees could only just see
Heaw they're clammin' an' starvin' poor weavers loike me,
Aw think they'd soon settle their bother, an' strive
To send us some cotton to keep us alive.

SAMUEL LAYCOCK[1]

Extreme deprivation gave Lancashire a basic involvement in the outcome of the American Civil War. The violent upheaval generated by the war could hardly have been without global repercussions. It was inevitable that at least the steady flow of commerce would be disrupted. The calm surface of international trade was troubled by the ominous ripples of a self-imposed Southern embargo on its own cotton and a Northern blockade of Southern ports. Only in Lancashire did the ripples become waves that engulfed the entire cotton industry and left in their wake a morass of destitution. During 1862, the second year of the war, the lack of cotton was so acute in Lancashire that the majority of mills were unable to function. Unemployed operatives were forced to choose between starvation and charitable relief. Many sought to avoid this choice by urging that some kind of aid be given by Britain to the South to help establish Confederate independence and so facilitate the renewal of the flow of cotton to Lancashire.

The war was unquestionably shattering in its impact on the county. The combustible mixture of ideological complexities and tough economic repercussions detonated an explosion of sympathy for the Southern cause wherever unemployment was extensive. The basic significance of the destitution of the cotton workers lies in the fact that there was almost an exact match between the most searing distress and the strongest support for the Southern states. The impact of this support was muffled by the myth of the operatives' passivity and preference for neutrality, a myth created by the misconceptions of Richard Cobden, John Bright, and William Gladstone and strengthened by one unrepresentative Manchester meeting. Cobden and Bright were mistakenly regarded as unique spokesmen for the area and for cotton since Cobden had set up as a calico printer in Manchester in his early twenties and was M.P. for Rochdale from 1859 to his death in 1865, while Bright was a partner in the wealthy

1. "Th' Shurat Weaver's Song," in John Harland, ed., *Ballads and Songs of Lancashire Ancient and Modern.* Corrected, revised and enlarged by T. T. Wilkinson (London, 1875), p. 506.

5

Quaker cotton-spinning family firm in Rochdale as well as M.P. for Birmingham. With their campaigns for free trade and an extended franchise both men had won reputations as champions of radicalism and the interests of the workingmen. The success, with the repeal of the corn laws in 1843, of their battle for free trade gave them a status and authority that led them to be erroneously respected as interpreters of working-class opinion. Both men not only committed their allegiance to the North but falsely assumed that Lancashire's cotton operatives leaned in the same direction. The actual evidence proves that the cotton interests of the county were united in seeking official British assistance for the abortive struggle of the Confederacy for independent life.

The existence of the myth can be more readily understood when it is realized that violence was rejected as a means of expressing sympathy for the South. On his rare and fleeting visits to Lancashire during the war, William Gladstone, the chancellor of the exchequer and a Liverpudlian by birth, was impressed by the patience and passivity of the often starving operatives. He made the simple mistake of assuming that this behavior represented agreement with government policy, rather than a passive resistance to it that masked a determined but nonviolent form of protest. Demands for pro-Confederate intervention were encased in orderly public meetings and carefully worded public petitions that were sent to the government. Whether dispatched to the Commons or sent personally to Lord Palmerston, the prime minister, or to Lord Russell, the foreign secretary, such petitions were ignored with an almost amazing consistency. Simultaneously the national press overlooked the massive number of spontaneous meetings in support of the South and noted only the organized few that were attended by such noted Northern sympathizers as Cobden and Bright.

The view that the Radical elements in Lancashire gave uniquely steady support to the North[2] owes much to the way in which Richard Cobden and John Bright have been regarded as typical of this area and of Radical England as a whole. Confusion existed among Radicals at the start of the war because of the insistence of the North on the primacy of

2. J. R. Pole, *Abraham Lincoln and the Working Classes of Britain,* (London, 1959), p. 28; John W. Derry, *The Radical Tradition: Tom Paine to Lloyd George* (London, 1967), p. 226; Halvdan Koht, *The American Spirit in Europe* (Philadelphia, 1949), p. 138; early secondary authority was given to the idea by Donaldson Jordan and Edwin Pratt, *Europe and the American Civil War* (Cambridge: Mass., 1931).

maintaining the Union rather than on abolishing slavery.[3] Cobden and Bright, however, committed their sympathies to the North at an early stage in the war, and it has been mistakenly claimed that most radicals followed them once Lincoln's emancipation proclamation was issued.

Both Cobden and Bright had an enthusiastic admiration for the institutions and government of the United States. They felt that the ideals of democracy and equal opportunity held sacred there could well be adopted by Britain.[4] On 17 July 1848 Cobden wrote to Combe about the general excellence of life in America: "can such intelligence, civilisation, and moral and material well-doing be elsewhere found?" Bright commended the freedom and equality of the American way of life to Rochdale audiences on several occasions.[5] The one serious flaw was the protectionism that the North displayed in its predilection for high tariffs; this made Cobden hesitate before espousing the Northern cause. Both considered that the antislavery impulses of the North were indicative of a desire to establish the supremacy of free labor. John Bright no doubt did much to make a few workingmen in England see in the Southern Confederacy an attitude which would degrade labor to the chattel of the capitalist.[6] Goldwin Smith, the pro-North Oxford history don and friend of John Bright, went further and suggested that "The American Slave-owner proposes to put an end to the freedom of labour all over the world."[7] There were, however, few either among the middle-class radicals or the workingmen themselves who took this threat seriously. Some of the Lancashire operatives indeed referred to the possibility with utter disbelief. Bright frequently proclaimed that the North must succeed in the interests of "humanity."[8] At public meetings in Lancashire it was often wryly remarked that the interests of humanity demanded, rather, that the South be aided to victory and cotton released to the unemployed workers.

Cobden and Bright were less in harmony with the Lancashire work-

3. Charles Francis Adams, Jr., *Charles Francis Adams* (London, 1900), pp. 156–57; G. D. Lillibridge, *Beacon of Freedom* (Pennsylvania, 1955), p. 111; Henry Pelling, *America and the British Left* (London, 1956), p. 8.

4. Elizabeth Hoon Cawley, ed., *The American Diaries of Richard Cobden* (Princeton, 1952), p. 31.

5. John Bright, *Speeches on Questions of Public Policy*, ed. J. E. Thorold Rogers (London, 1868), 1: 173, 232; *Rochdale Spectator*, 7 December 1861.

6. G. M. Trevelyan, *The Life of John Bright* (London, 1913), p. 306.

7. Goldwin Smith, *Does the Bible Sanction American Slavery?* (Oxford, 1863), p. 84.

8. W. Robertson, *The Life and Times of John Bright* (London, 1883), p. 396.

ers than with the government; the "economic risk of war with the Union was the dominant consideration expressed . . . in the letters of John Bright and Richard Cobden." [9] Cobden's two main objectives for most of the war were "the improvement of international law as it affects commerce in time of war, and the limitation of expenditure upon unneeded schemes of national defence." [10] Cobden's own economic interests were also involved since he was one of the prominent foreign stockholders of the Illinois Central Railroad Company,[11] as well as various other Northern companies. Bright simultaneously may have been to some degree influenced by the profits steadily accumulated by his more influential Birmingham constituents through the sale of "hardware" to the North.

That these men did influence some Lancashire admirers as well as those elsewhere cannot be doubted, but it is equally certain that their ideas and sympathies were rejected by an enormous number from all classes, creeds, and towns in Lancashire. Bright's views on the war set up a barrier between him and many democratic workingmen.[12] These views certainly did not represent the feelings of all Radicals, and it is a mistake to assume, just because of Bright and Cobden's attitudes, "the whole-hearted support of radical England" for the North.[13]

A majority of the editors of the Lancashire local press were staunch Radicals and most of them were equally firmly pro-Southern in sympathy. Many notable Radicals in and out of Lancashire were "Southerners." John Arthur Roebuck, the Sheffield M.P. who was an ebulliently radical parliamentarian, persistently urged recognition of the South and intervention, or at least mediation, on her behalf.[14] William Shaw Lindsay, the powerful merchant and shipowner with investments in Liverpool and Bir-

9. M. P. Claussen, "Peace Factors in Anglo-American Relations 1861–1865," *Mississippi Valley Historical Review*, 26 (March, 1940):517; N. McCord points out disagreement with them in Lancashire in "Cobden and Bright in Politics, 1846–1857," in Robert Robson, ed., *Ideas and Institutions of Victorian Britain* (London, 1967), pp. 94, 112.

10. John Morley, *The Life of Richard Cobden*, 1-vol. edition, (London, 1903), pp. 837–38.

11. Ibid., pp. 684–88; Harry H. Pierce, "Foreign Investment in American Enterprise," *Economic Change in the Civil War Era*, ed. D. Gilchrist and W. D. Lewis (Charlottesville, Va., 1965), pp. 49–50.

12. Frances Emma Gillespie, *Labour and Politics in England 1850–1867* (North Carolina, 1927), p. 160.

13. E. D. Adams, *Great Britain and the American Civil War* (New York, 1900), 2: 305.

14. Robert E. Leader, ed., *Life and Letters of John Arthur Roebuck* (London, 1897), pp. 74, 295.

kenhead, was the other most active proponent of aid to the South in Parliament. He was not only a radical but a close friend of both Cobden and Bright.[15] Joseph Barker, though born in Leeds, was known as one of Lancashire's most convinced radicals. While in the United States between 1851 and 1860, he became closely associated with Lloyd Garrison and the antislavery movement. He was one of the most eloquent and persistent pro-Southern lecturers in Lancashire and he gave up his co-editorship (with Charles Bradlaugh) of the Radical newspaper, the *National Reformer,* in 1861 and devoted his time to furthering the Southern cause. Other Radicals actually lost faith in American democracy through the North's attempt to crush the South; the "first doctrine of Radicalism, they said, was the right of a people to self-government." [16]

Even John Watts, a keen supporter of the North and a committed Manchester reformer, admitted that

> there was not wanting men who saw, or thought they saw, a short way out of the difficulty, viz., by a recognition on the part of the English government of the Southern confederacy in America. And meetings were called in various places to memorialise the government to this effect. Such meetings were always balanced by counter meetings, at which it was shown that simple recognition would be a waste of words; that it would not bring to our shores a single ship-load of cotton, unless followed up by an armed force to break the blockade, which course if adopted would be war; war in favour of the slave confederacy of the South, and against the free North and Northwest, whence comes a large proportion of our imported corn.[17]

The exaggerated estimate of the frequency of antirecognition meetings was perhaps to be expected from so strong a Northern advocate. The young Henry Adams must have been as eager to discover sympathy for the North when he visited Manchester in November 1861 with the specific intention of unearthing "the attitude of the various Manchester interests to the North and to find out whether there was a party there determined to challenge the North's blockade." [18] He questioned a number of influential Manchester men and came to the conclusion that "so far as the

15. John Bright, *Diaries,* ed. R. A. J. Walling, (London, 1930), pp. 311, 325; Morley, *Cobden,* pp. 685–86.

16. John Watts, *The Facts of the Cotton Famine* (Manchester, 1866), p. 105.

17. Ibid., p. 123.

18. Arthur W. Silver, ed., "Henry Adams, 'Diary of a Visit to Manchester,' " *American Historical Review,* 51 (1945–46): 76.

cotton interests of Manchester are concerned our Government will have two months more full swing over the South. At the end of that time, a party will arise in favour of ending the war by recognising the insurgents, and if necessary breaking the blockade or declaring it ineffective." [19] Thomas Dudley, the United States consul at Liverpool, was still more disillusioned: "It was very evident from the commencement that the South not only had the sympathy of the people of England, but that the English stood ready to assist them in every way they could. I speak now of the great mass of the English people." [20]

James Spence, as a Liverpool-based financial agent of the Confederacy, could be regarded as somewhat biased when he judged that the feeling in Lancashire, which he thought had been pro-North, had by 1862 "entirely changed." But he was strongly supported by the fact that at this stage the bulk of the local press was firmly in favor of the Southern cause. At the end of 1862 and throughout 1863 a number of large and vociferous meetings were held in support of recognizing the South. Many of the speakers at these meetings and a high percentage of the editors of the local newspapers shared with Spence a belief which, even if deluded, was certainly genuine that "slavery can never be abolished in the States except by the will of the Southern people." [21] This belief was swept along into the more fantastic regions of supposition by the conviction that an independent South would actually abolish slavery and integrate the freedmen into its society.

There was a deep and widespread abolitionist feeling in Lancashire that mistrusted the motives of Lincoln and the North as far as slavery was concerned. The Emancipation Proclamation was rejected as nothing more than a military maneuver that hypocritically and ineffectually freed the Southern slaves while leaving those in the North in bondage. It has been suggested that most Radicals shook off such doubts and were unstinted in their approval by 1863.[22] This view is not supported by the editorials at the time and reports of meetings in the press which indicate that suspicion burrowed into the minds of the majority of Lancashire's radicals right up

19. In ibid., p. 82.

20. T. H. Dudley, *Three Critical Periods in Our Diplomatic Relations with England During the Late War.* Reprinted from *Pennsylvania Magazine of History and Biography* (April 1893), p. 3.

21. James Spence, *Recognition* (London, 1862), p. 21; S. B. Thompson, *Confederate Purchasing Operations Abroad* (North Carolina, 1935), pp. 7, 22–23.

22. G. D. Lillibridge, *Freedom,* p. 117; J. R. Pole, *Lincoln,* p. 28.

to Lincoln's death, when the president's obituaries were the first grudging expressions of praise or approval. Nor do the newspapers of this area bear out Professor Beloff's findings for most of the country about "the pro-Northern sentiment of the radical and working-class press." [23]

Far more accurate is Sheldon Van Auken's supposition that there was "little evidence to support the assertion that, either before or after the Emancipation Proclamation, there was any solid or vigorous support of the Union cause among the working men" of Lancashire. [24] Dr. Royden Harrison has shown in several articles that there was among English workingmen a considerable amount of support for the Confederacy, [25] but he has suggested that it might be possible to attribute the existence of radical pro-Southern sympathies to a suspicion of Bright and Cobden and their support for the United States that was felt by some of the older and least progressive Chartists. [26] A full perusal of the Lancashire newspapers would seem to prove that the amount of allegiance given by radicals to the South was too extensive and deep-rooted to be accounted for in this way. Few of the Radical editors or speakers who supported the South had ever been Chartists, and some of them were friends of Cobden and Bright, whereas two of the most persistent advocates of the North, Ernest Jones, who had settled in Manchester in 1861, and the itinerant lecturer Henry Vincent, were both ex-Chartist leaders who spent much time in Lancashire attempting to convert the operatives.

The large body of working-class and Radical opinion in Lancashire that was in favor of mediating on behalf of or recognizing the South cannot be dismissed as fitting any one pattern. Radical and working-class support in Lancashire for Southern independence was too large and too diverse to be simply explained in any terms other than those relating to basic survival. That this pro-Southern support had no influence on governmental policy does not mean, as has so often been presumed, that it did not exist, but that it lacked political power. "In 1861, British labour as

23. Max Beloff, "Great Britain and the American Civil War," *History*, N.S. 37 (February 1952): 44.

24. S. Van Auken, "English Sympathy for the Southern Confederacy" (B. Litt Thesis, Oxford, 1957), p. 90.

25. Royden Harrison, "British Labour and the Confederacy," *International Review of Social History*, Vol. 2, pt. 1 (Amsterdam, 1957): 78–105; idem, "British Labour and American Slavery," *Science & Society*, 15, no. 4 (New York, December 1961): 291–319.

26. Royden Harrison, *Before the Socialists* (London, 1965), pp. 40–77.

a political force was still embryonic." To claim that it prevented war "is at variance with labor's political weakness in these years; it ignores the fact that commercial and national interests did weigh heavily in the correspondence and speeches of diplomats in favor of peace." [27] Nevertheless the maintenance of official neutrality has been held by many to have been enormously influenced by the supposedly quiescent attitude of Lancashire. In 1861 Lancashire had over 400,000 cotton operatives out of a population of 2,429,440,[28] and as the supply of cotton dwindled, these operatives were slowly reduced to near-destitution.[29] Marx claimed that the unemployed operatives were "fully conscious that the government is only waiting for the intervention cry from below, the *pressure from without,* to put an end to the American blockade and English misery." [30] Because this pressure was, contrary to Marx's expectation, ignored by the government, it has been wrongly assumed that it never existed, and that "disturbances were unimportant and scarcely a single voice was raised in favor of breaking the blockade." [31]

Support for either side did not fall into easy categories according to the religious affiliations of the supporters, any more than it was determined by political inclinations. The assumption that most Radicals and Nonconformists were pro-North is not founded on fact. The reasons for the giving of sympathy were often as complex as the issues involved in the

27. Ibid., p. 522.
28. *Parliamentary Papers* (hereafter cited as *P.P.*), vol. LII (1863), pp. 79, 135. The figures for cotton operatives vary a good deal according to inclusion of fringe industries and juveniles. The *P.P.* cited above gives the number of families in Lancashire as 522,911: 1,173,424 males; 1,256,016 females (p. 79), and lists operatives over twenty by town, and these amount to over 300,000 (p. 135). The Central Relief Committee provides the most comprehensive figures, with 533,950 operatives working full-time in 1861 (see Thomas Ellison, *The Cotton Trade of Great Britain* [London, 1886], p. 95), and 490,755 "workpeople" in 1862 (see *Fund for the Relief of Distress in the Manufacturing Districts. Report of the Central Executive Relief Committee,* December 15, 1862 [Manchester, 1862], p. 1). The *Money Market Review* was more conservative in its estimate of 356,487 but does stipulate ages and sex: 152,553 males; 105,015 adults over 18; 47,438 children; 205,935 females. See "Number of Persons Employed in the Cotton Trade," *Burnley Advertiser,* 27 September 1862. Using a strict criterion for cotton operatives, the *Preston Guardian,* 21 February 1863, states ("Manufactures in Lancashire") there were 315,627 of unspecified age employed in 1861.
29. The effect of the blockade was delayed while the surplus cotton of 1860 lasted.
30. Karl Marx and F. Engels, *The Civil War in the United States* (London, 1938), p. 141.
31. Joseph H. Park, "The English Working Men and the American Civil War," *Political Science Quarterly* 39 (1924): 434.

war itself, but always had some basis in economic deprivation and social misery.

No individual party or sect had any clear policy on the war that might have encouraged a unified attitude among its followers. Amidst the solid Southern supporters there were to be found Radicals and right-wing Tories, young Liberals, and older ex-Chartists. The North also had support from adherents of both parties. Within the different religions there was a comparable variety of opinion. Anglican vicars were to be heard advocating the causes of both the North and the South; Wesleyan, Unitarian, and Quaker ministers were divided among themselves about the virtues of either side. Similarities or contrasts in the religious and political patterns of each town did not coincide with similar or contrasting reactions to the war.

Ashton-under-Lyne, with its preponderance of Nonconformists and Liberals was even more notably pro-Southern in sympathy [32] than Preston, with its strong Roman Catholic element and predominantly Tory political structure.[33] Fierce anti-Catholic feeling in Liberal Oldham in no way undermined the unparalleled support given there to Southern recognition.[34] The strength and timing of Blackburn's preference for mediation on behalf of the South can be explained only by the nature of the area's

32. Ashton had 23 Anglican, 15 Wesleyan Methodist, 11 New Methodist Connexion, 11 Independent, 10 Primitive Methodist, 5 Christian Brethren, 3 Baptist, 2 Moravian, 2 Latter Day Saints, 1 Christian Israelites, 1 New Jerusalem, 1 Presbyterian, and 1 Roman Catholic churches or chapels. Religious Returns, Census of Great Britain, 1851, H. O. 129, 474.

Thomas Milner Gibson was Liberal M.P. for Ashton between 1857 and 1868, during which time he was president of the Poor Law Board (1859) and president of the Board of Trade (1859–66). He had previously been M.P. for Manchester (1841–57) and a prominent orator for the Anti-Corn Law League. His home, however, remained on his Suffolk estate. His liberalism seemed accurately to reflect the politics of most Ashtonians, but his support of the North met with constant criticism and complaint.

33. Preston had 20 Anglican, 9 Roman Catholic, 5 Wesleyan Methodist, 3 Independent, 2 United Methodist, 2 Primitive Methodist, 4 Baptist, 1 Unitarian, 1 New Jerusalem, 1 Presbyterian, 1 Free Gospel and 1 Quaker churches or chapels (G. A. Gillett, *Commercial and General Directory of Preston* [Preston, 1869] pp. ix–xii). Preston had one Liberal M.P., C. P. Grenfell (1857–68), and one Tory M.P., Robert Assheton Cross (1857–62) and then Sir Thomas George Hesketh (1862–65), but the feeling in the town was mainly Tory (see H. A. Taylor, "Politics in Famine Stricken Preston," *Transactions of the Historic Society of Lancashire and Cheshire* 107 (September 1955): 121–39.

34. Anti-Catholic feelings were described in "The Irish in England," *Oldham Chronicle,* 25 October 1862, and *Oldham Standard,* 19 October, 1861. Both Oldham M.P.'s, John Morgan Cobbett and John Tomlinson Hibbert were Liberals and supporters of the South.

distress and not by its Conservative political structure and motley religious allegiance,[35] while the mildness of Bolton's approval of an independent Confederacy is related to its slight pauperization, not to its mixed politics and religion.[36] Only Liverpool, dominated by a Tory Anglican
reaction to Liberal Catholicism and with only an embryonic Nonconformist minority, was wholeheartedly in favor of the South;[37] Rochdale, with its Liberal Nonconformity, supported the North. These two
cases give superficial support to the idea of religious and political influence on the war issue. In fact Liverpool owed its sympathy primarily to
its deep involvement with cotton and shipping. Rochdale, with its strong
woollen interests, was the one isolated supporter of the North in the distressed cotton towns, and even there an undercurrent of pro-Southern resentment occasionally broke through the Cobden- and Bright-inspired devotion to the North. The whole idea of such religious and political
influence is thoroughly belied not only by the reactions of the large cotton
towns but by the pro-Northern feeling in the basically Tory, Anglican,
and noncotton West,[38] as well as by the vocal backing given to the South
in the small weaving communities of Liberal, Nonconformist Rossendale.
The distinctive features of towns that sought to aid an emerging Confederacy were not religious, political, or ethnic (even the existence of Irish
immigrant communities produced no uniform reaction). Nor did the class
structure, which was surprisingly flexible, spur support for South or
North. The determining factor was, with the sole exception of Rochdale,
the strength and timing of the distress caused by the war.

35. Both Blackburn M.P.'s were Conservatives, and William Henry Hornby, a
wealthy Blackburn mill owner, continued to represent Blackburn even after the 1906 Liberal landslide (see Henry Pelling, *Social Geography of British Elections 1885–1910* [London,
1967], p. 262). While mainly Anglican, Blackburn had substantial Nonconformist and Roman Catholic communities.
    36. Bolton had one Liberal M.P., the teetotal Nonconformist Thomas Barnes of Farn-
worth, and one Tory M.P., the local landowner Colonel William Gray. Of Bolton's population, 22.5% were practicing Anglicans, 19% Wesleyan, 7% Roman Catholic ("Church Ac-
commodation in Bolton," *Bolton Chronicle,* 12 April, 1862.
    37. J. C. Ewart and Thomas B. Horsfall, the two Liverpool M.P.'s, together with
John Laird, M.P. for Birkenhead, gave only some slight indication of the strength of Southern sympathy on Merseyside. For Nonconformism in Liverpool, see Ian Sellers, "Non-conformist Attitudes in Later Nineteenth Century Liverpool," *Transactions of the Historic Society of
Lancashire and Cheshire,* no. 114 (March 1962), pp. 215–39.
    38. Pelling, *Social Geography,* pp. 263–64.

The cotton famine induced by the American Civil War gave birth to destitution for large sections of Lancashire's industrial population. In December 1862, at the height of the distress, 247,230 operatives were out of work and 485,434 people were dependent on relief (see table 2).[39]

It is possible to see within this one county the differing reactions of those whose dependence on cotton made them feel personally involved in the war and those whose lives were so slightly altered by the conflict that they could either ignore it or make a detached appraisal of its progress. Inside the cotton districts themselves the timing and intensity of deprivation did not fall into a uniform pattern. While some places felt an immediate impact, others were affected more slowly and sometimes more severely. There is a natural correlation between the areas most dominated by the cotton industry and those most distressed. The scale of suffering was also partly determined by the predominance of spinning or weaving and by the type of cotton spun or woven. As might be expected, it was usually in the areas most badly hit by the dearth of cotton that the most active interest in the Civil War was to be found. The rural areas did have an interest in the war but it was of a superficial and cursory kind. The social and economic conditions of each region and the expression of concern with the war were always closely connected.

Insofar as it determined the economy of the region, the geography of Lancashire was extremely influential in deciding reactions to the war. While the sunny, fertile lowlands of the western region were obviously highly suited to the successful pursuit of agriculture,[40] the east was more likely to adapt to industry because of its combination of infertility, high

39. Watts, *Facts,* p. 227. The first figure includes child and female operatives. The worst year of the famine was 1862, as is indicated by the unprecedented heights reached by the numbers dependent on charity (guardians and relief committee) for survival in the following poor-law unions: Ashton-under-Lyne—56,363, Preston—49,171, Blackburn—38,104, Oldham—28,851, Rochdale—24,961, Bury—20,926, Bolton—19,525, Burnley—17,502, Chorlton—15,367, Haslingden—17,346, Salford—16,663, Wigan—14,959. All these areas were almost totally reliant on the cotton industry for their livelihood. Other unions were affected but less drastically: Chorley—7,527, Clitheroe—1,379, Flyde (The)—1,282, Garstang—1,026, Glossop—7,605, Lancaster—1,129, Leigh—2,722, Prestwich—4,794, Saddleworth—2,414, Skipton—2,635, Todmorden—7,590, Warrington—1,992, Barton-on-Orwell—5,912, and Manchester (whose paupers were always numerous)—52,477.

40. Wilfred Smith, *The County of Lancashire, Report of the Land Utilisation Survey,* pt. 45 (London, 1946), p. 51; James Glaisher, "Quarterly Returns—Meteorological Table, September 1862 and December 1862," *Journal of the Statistical Society of London* (1862): 549.

rainfall, and rich coal deposits. But despite the growth of industry in the
east there were still more people employed in agriculture in 1861 than in
any other county of England. The 80,822 adults earning their living off
the land [41] were mainly concentrated in the west, and catered to the needs
of industrial Lancashire. These workers and the farm owners were only
minimally affected by the American Civil War. The need to find new
markets to consume the food they produced, once the Lancashire cotton
workers were incapable of purchasing more than minute quantities, was a
problem that found a speedy solution. The expanding markets of the rest
of Britain were only too ready to absorb the surplus.

Industries began to grow where coal could be easily and cheaply obtained, mainly in the east and south of the county. The metal industries
were the first to develop, and when the cotton mills later dominated the
same areas affiliated metal and machine-making concerns almost always
flourished close at hand. The salt and chemical works around St. Helens
and Liverpool, together with their dependent industries, enabled most
towns of the southwest to remain relatively unaffected by the lack of cotton.[42]

The good natural harbors of west Lancashire's coastline had long
made possible the existence of a successful shipping industry, and in the
1860s this coast was still dotted with ports that shipped goods rather than
served tourists. The greatest of these was, of course, Liverpool: it had developed in the eighteenth century and had become a world port in the
early part of the nineteenth century. Goods from North America, particularly raw cotton, flooded in, and when the trade of the Indian Ocean
was thrown open in 1813 Liverpool started to develop the market in India
for Lancashire's cotton goods. The foundation of the Cunard Line in 1842
started the first regular service of passenger ships across the Atlantic.
Nearly a dozen docks were opened in the first half of the nineteenth century, and Liverpool almost monopolized the trade with America. The
tonnage of vessels entering in and clearing out from the port exceeded
that of the port of London. The tonnage of the three years from 1860 to

41. Frederick Purdy, "On the Decrease of the Agricultural Population of England
and Wales 1851–1861," *Journal of the Statistical Society of London* (1864): 395.
42. Churchtown, near Southport, did have some handloom weaving, which was virtually killed off by the Civil War (see E. Bland, *Annals of Southport and District: Chronological
History of North Meols, A.D. 1086–1186* [Southport, 1888], p. 125).

1862 at London was 16,733,096; at Liverpool it was 16,893,336.[43] Lancaster still carried on a considerable amount of trade but was declining in importance at this time in the face of increasing competition from Liverpool and the strong attraction of concentrating on the growing tourist trade.[44] Fleetwood, a newly emerged port, stopped importing cotton during the war, but was otherwise typical of coastal towns other than Liverpool in remaining untouched by the cotton famine.

Only in the east of the county did the dearth of cotton searingly undermine the livelihood of the inhabitants. Here the cotton industry was intensively localized because of a combination of circumstances that separately would hardly have produced such intensification. The availability of well-sited power and ports, along with the high humidity, soft water, and poor agricultural quality of the soil in east Lancashire, created favorable conditions for the growth of industry.[45] Once industry had taken root in this eastern section of the county and the factory system was under way, the rapid growth of the system was assured by the spate of "inventions" produced by Lancastrians in the eighteenth and nineteenth centuries.[46]

Almost as pertinent to any assessment of the reaction of the county to the Civil War was the geographical cleavage between the two basic functions of the cotton industry. This cleavage was apparent at the time of the war even though it was not to become rigid until some years later. Chapman has pointed out that spinning and weaving firms would naturally take different forms and fall under separate ownership for technical and commercial reasons.[47] That this did not simply lead to a tendency to set up different establishments close to one another, but to a decided concentration of spinning in the southeast and weaving in the northeast was partly due to the increasing differences in the conditions that prevailed in each area. In the southeast the population during the first half of the nineteenth century reached numbers that were beyond the capacity of the soil to support even when income was reinforced by home cotton produc-

43. Watts, *Facts,* p. 97.

44. R. Millward, *Lancashire: The History of the Landscape* (London, 1955), pp. 96–97.

45. R. K. Creswell and R. Laughton, *Merseyside* (Sheffield, 1964), pp. 3–4; G. W. Daniels, *The Early English Cotton Industry* (Manchester, 1920), p. 126; G. H. Tupling, "The Economic History of Rossendale," *Chetham Society,* 86 (1927): 162.

46. Ellison, *Cotton Trade,* pp. 14–34, 36.

47. S. J. Chapman, *The Lancashire Cotton Industry* (London, 1904).

tion.[48] This ready-made labor force supplemented by migrant cotton workers, was an incentive to the growth of the factory system, and spinning was the branch of the industry that was first in need of factory conditions. Essential also to this development was the improvement in communications that took place in the eighteenth and early nineteenth centuries. The towns of the southeast were linked by sturdy turnpike roads and a meshed network of canals and railways, whereas communications developed much more slowly in the northeast (see map).

By the 1830s and 1840s the bulk of Lancashire's cotton operatives were in the areas surrounding Manchester, and most of these operatives were employed in spinning rather than weaving.[49] By 1841, Ashton, Manchester, Oldham, and Rochdale contained 65% of the operatives in Lancashire. By the mid-1840s, 60% of the operatives of Ashton were employed in spinning firms.[50]

In the 1860s the three million spindles in Oldham amounted to one-ninth of the total number of spindles in the United Kingdom, and the techniques employed there were the most advanced then known.[51] Stalybridge was also famed for its spindles and the speed at which they moved, before they were brought to a halt by the cotton famine.[52] Worrals textile directory for 1884 stated that 67% of the spinning firms were concentrated in Ashton, Bolton, Manchester, Oldham, Rochdale, and Stockport, and 52% of the weaving concerns had gravitated to Accrington, Blackburn, Chorley, Colne, Darwen, Preston, and Todmorden.[53]

In the northeast the land could still provide a living for those who tended it and continued to weave on cottage hand looms. The largest expansion in the weaving industry came between 1840 and 1860 when power looms took over from hand looms. The majority of these power looms were ultimately established in the northeast after a period in the

48. Arthur Redford, *Labour Migration in England, 1800–50* (Manchester), p. 34.
49. Andrew Ure, *The Cotton Manufacture of Great Britain* (London, 1861), 2:392–97.
50. "Report of H. M. Factory Inspectors for the Half-Year Ending 31 December 1841," *P.P.* XXII(1842), pp. 334–55, 357–67, 370–418; "Royal Commission to Inquire into the Sanitary Conditions of Large Towns and Populous Districts" (1843), in Winifred Bowman, *England in Ashton-under-Lyne* (Ashton, 1960), p. 432.
51. Ellison, *Cotton Trade*, p. 139.
52. R. Arthur Arnold, *The History of the Cotton Famine* (London, 1865), p. 4.
53. S. J. Chapman and T. S. Ashton, "The Size of Businesses, Mainly in the Textile Industries," *Journal of the Royal Statistical Society* 77 (1914): 538.

late 40s and early 50s when the tendency was to set up combined firms in both areas.[54] Blackburn, where spinning was never a major concern, had a high percentage of mixed firms with spinning subsidiaries in the 50s, but by the 60s weaving firms dominated. By 1860 there was a proliferation of small weaving firms with less than 400 looms each.[55] Preston in May 1862 housed 27,148 looms (of which 17,007 were idle and 8,000 working only three or four days a week) and 1,267 mules (of which 604 were idle and 382 were working short-time).[56] Gillet's Preston directory for 1869 showed that Preston was the home of twenty weaving firms and seventeen spinning firms, and there is little doubt that the thirty-three combined firms [57] would by that time be concentrating on the manufacturing side of the industry. Expansion within the cotton world at this stage almost always meant a greater increase in the amount of weaving, stimulated by a leap in the demand for finished cloth. The extension of weaving in the southeast was discouraged by the high wages commanded by cotton spinners as opposed to the low wages that the weavers accepted.[58] This meant that weaving companies were not keen to establish factories in the more expensive south when they could be assured of cheap labor from the "agricultural reserve" of the north with its tradition of hand-loom weaving.

Conversely, spinning firms were likely to be set up in the north to compete with the already established and efficient southeast firms. The early nineteenth-century tendency was either to extend existing spinning or weaving firms into combined companies or to develop weaving firms in the north and spinning firms in the south.[59] The growth of a comprehensive and reliable internal railway system between 1830 and 1850 that linked the towns of north and south Lancashire greatly lessened any advantage there might be in having the two functions carried on in close proximity to each other. After 1856 the combined firm ceased to develop and gradually receded in importance while the horizontal spinning firms

54. M. Blaug, "The Productivity of Capital in the Lancashire Cotton Industry During the Nineteenth Century," *Economic History Review*, 2d ser., vol. 13 (1960–61): 361.

55. Watts, *Facts*, p. 139.

56. Ibid., p. 132.

57. C. A. Gillet, *Directory of Preston*, pp. 6–17.

58. J. Jewkes and E. M. Gray, *Wages and Labour in the Lancashire Cotton Industry* (1935), pp. 114–15.

59. J. Jewkes, "The Localisation of the Cotton Industry," *Economic History* 2 (1930–33): 97–102.

began rapidly to increase in towns in the south, such as Oldham, but declined in Preston and Blackburn. "The opportunity," according to Professor Taylor, "for such specialisation is apparent. Improved transport facilities—Lancashire's railway system was virtually complete by 1850—easier access to capital and an ever-expanding market paved the way to division in the industry, whether or not to its ultimate benefit is questionable." [60]

This separatist tendency had a most definite influence on the way in which the cotton districts were affected by the war. Northeast Lancashire was the area to suffer first and extremely harshly because of the cotton famine. This swift and acute effect was a natural consequence of the increasing dependence on the weaving branch of the industry. "It is a matter of common observation that the weaving, or manufacturing, department of the industry is always the first to feel the approach of a period of depression in trade." [61] Thomas Ellison explains that this is because it costs considerably less to put up a number of looms than it does to bring into operation an equivalent number of spindles; it also requires a much smaller amount of floating capital to work a weaving shed than it does to conduct a spinning mill of corresponding dimensions. Vulnerability was increased because weaving can also be profitably conducted on a far smaller scale than is possible in the case of spinning.[62] In Blackburn and Preston, the two towns most immediately and most acutely affected by the famine in this region,[63] there was a high proportion of small manufacturers. A further reason given by Ellison for the disadvantageous and precarious position of the manufacturer is that while the spinner has several markets where he can sell his yarn and it is unlikely that all would slacken off simultaneously, the weaver "has practically only one in which to sell his cloth. The spinner disposes of the bulk of his yarn to the home manufacturer of calico, but he also sells a not inconsiderable quantity to the Yorkshire and other manufacturers of mixed fabrics, while he disposes of

60. A. J. Taylor, "Concentration and Specialisation in the Lancashire Cotton Industry, 1825–1850," *Economic History Review*, 2d Ser., 1 (1948–49): 122.

61. Ellison, *Cotton Trade*, p. 78.

62. Ibid., p. 78.

63. By Michaelmas 1862, Blackburn had spent £21,258 and Preston £27,776 in the previous six months on poor relief. These were the highest amounts recorded at that stage, outside of Manchester and Liverpool, but were to be outstripped by Ashton-under-Lyne in the corresponding six months of 1863 when £40,609 was paid out. "Comparative Statement of the Expenditure for Relief to the Poor," *P.P.* LII (1863), p. 3.

a still greater quantity for export to Continental, East Indian, and other markets." The weaver, however, would often be forced to sell his cloth cheaply and pay high prices for his yarn. "Eventually he may be compelled to stop his looms. Thereupon will follow a diminished demand for yarn, which, if it continues long enough, will cause spinners first to reduce their prices and then to curtail their production." [64] The swift crippling of the weaving concerns was therefore part of a normal trade reaction to cut demand for a finished product in time of crisis. This was aggravated by the small, basically uneconomical size of many weaving firms in the northeast. These firms had no reserves of capital to fall back on once their never large daily profits failed to materialize. Such firms could not afford to run at the temporary loss sustained by larger rivals, and frequently went into liquidation.

The effect of the cotton famine varied also from town to town within each region according to the type of cloth spun or yarn woven. The production of fine yarn or goods required a much smaller supply of cotton than coarse spinning or fustian weaving. The pressure would be felt far more slowly and less severely by firms engaged in the former. In the southeast, "Bolton, which spins fine yarns, although almost wholly dependent on the cotton industry, suffered much less than Rochdale, where a considerable proportion of the people are engaged in woollen manufacture; because the cotton goods produced by Rochdale required a large amount of the very cotton which the American War had deprived them of." [65] The firm of McConnel and Co., which had mills specializing in fine spinning scattered throughout the southeast, was one of the very few to keep running full time through the whole of this disastrous period.[66] At Ashton, "where the bulk of the productions are coarse goods, and the population almost wholly dependent on cotton," practically all the mills had to either go on short-time or close down altogether. Dr. Watts considered that this combination explained the extreme distress in Ashton,[67] which suffered under the most acute and prolonged pauperization to be known

---

64. Ellison, *Cotton Trade,* p. 79. See also John Watts, *The Power and Influence of Co-operative Effort.* Lecture given on 6 November 1861 in Manchester Mechanics Institute (London, 1872), p. 15.
65. Watts, *Facts,* p. 253; see table 2 below.
66. John W. McConnel, *A Century of Fine Cotton Spinning* (Manchester, 1913), p. 13.
67. Watts, *Facts,* p. 254.

anywhere in Lancashire during the famine years.[68] Bury spun more fine than coarse counts, wove some muslin, and housed an enormous number of print works, which were slow to feel any impact from the war.[69] Wigan, which spun and wove differing types of yarn and cloth and had a flourishing coal mine, survived the depression rather better than most towns. Oldham had some excellent fine-spinning mills but their numbers were too few and their size too small to prevent this from being one of the hardest-hit areas.[70]

In the northeast the effect of the presence of many small weaving firms in Preston and Blackburn was added to by the fact that most of these firms manufactured heavy goods requiring excessively large quantities of cotton.[71] By May 1862 half of Preston's 27,148 looms were standing completely idle and the rest were only being worked for a part of the week.[72] Few of the 30,000 Blackburn looms that were normally devoted to the production of coarse goods ran at all in the latter half of 1862 or early 1863.[73] Although shorter-lived than in some parts of the southeast, the deprivation in both towns was very great.[74] Burnley was far less crippled by the war because of its large number of sizeable combined firms and because it quickly transferred its looms from the weaving of heavy goods to the manufacturing of fine "printing cloths."[75] It was also less dependent on the cotton industry for economic survival than either Preston or Blackburn (see table 4).

68. In November 1862 Ashton had 57,000 persons receiving relief either from the Guardian or the local relief committees; in June the following year there were still 40,000 dependent on aid. In the borough of Ashton (the above figures refer to the union) there were 11,686 operatives; in May 1863, 7,137 were wholly out of work and most of the remainder worked only part-time. Reports Relating to the Cotton Manufacturing Districts, *P.P.* LII (1863), p. 292.

69. "Report by John Kennedy, On the Employment of Children and Young Persons in Print Grounds and Miscellaneous Trades in Lancashire," *P.P.* SVI (1843), B2–3.

70. See table 2 below.

71. Arnold, *Cotton Famine,* p. 109.

72. Watts, *Facts,* p. 132; "Chronicles of Blackburn, 1 January 1862," quoted in G. C. Miller, *Blackburn: The Evolution of a Cotton Town* (Blackburn, 1951), p. 115. As early as January 1862, 5,423 looms and 532,850 spindles were idle.

73. Arnold, *Cotton Famine,* p. 216.

74. The Preston Relief Committee aided 40,627 in December 1862 and only 12,853 in the same month a year later (Fourth Report of Proceedings of the Preston Relief Committee, 1865, last sheet; see table 4 and note 72 above).

75. W. Bennett, *The History of Burnley from 1850* (Burnley, 1951), p. 101.

Survival was the most immediate problem for operatives who faced months or years of unemployment. Early in the war, short-time for all operatives, rather than full employment for some and destitution for others, was frequently recommended in the spinning towns.[76] In the northeast, out-of-work weavers rapidly became dependent on relief from the poor-law unions.[77] The existing funds soon became inadequate and in August 1862 the Rate-in-Aid Act was passed. This enabled any parish in a union which had spent more than ninepence in the pound during the last quarter of 1862 to charge the excess upon other parishes in the union. If the expenditure of the whole union had exceeded one shilling and three pence in the pound, several other unions in the same county might be called upon to contribute according to their rateable value. Under the Act, Wigan at one time subsidized the poor of Preston.[78] An amendment to the Act passed in 1863 enabled unions to borrow money from the public works commissioners to finance improvement of local amenities such as roads, sewers, and drains.[79] This scheme proved of more benefit to the health and convenience of the future inhabitants of the cotton towns than to the paupers of the cotton famine, who feared, more than welcomed, employment that would irreparably damage the sensitivity of their hands for delicate spinning and weaving operations.

Cotton operatives were proud men, and even where hard labor was not a prerequisite for relief they objected to having to plead with the guardians for subsistence. They preferred to find ways of helping themselves. In Preston, poor-law returns underestimated distress because the weavers' and spinners' own societies early in the war distributed funds amongst their out-of-work members.[80] In Padiham near Burnley, an East Lancashire Central Operatives Relief Committee was formed through the efforts of the Reverend A. Edward Verity, who was the first incumbent of

76. *Wigan Examiner,* 25 May 1861, 12 October 1861; *Oldham Standard,* 18 May 1861, 14 September 1861; *Oldham Chronicle,* 21 September 1861.

77. In the half-year ending with Michaelmas 1862, Blackburn spent £21,258 on relieving its paupers; at that stage Ashton had spent only £17,980. "Comparative Statement of the Expenditure for Relief to the Poor, Michaelmas Half-Years 1862 and 1863," *P.P.* LII (1863), p. 514.

78. *Wigan Observer,* 8 August 1862.

79. Under this public works (manufacturing districts) bill Preston borrowed £28,921, Blackburn £5,000, Ashton £31,328, Rochdale £5,659, Haslingden £2,600; other towns borrowed less sizeable sums.

80. Watts, *Facts,* p. 133.

the Anglican Church of All Saints at Habergam Eaves, near Burnley, and an ardent "Southerner." Workingmen also set up committees to aid the unemployed in Blackburn, Burnley, and Wigan, while in Ashton the Spinners and Minders Association distributed relief, and a town meeting called for subscriptions to aid the numerous destitute.[81]

Such aid, and that given generously by private individuals, could only skim the surface of the distress. Pictures of the plight of the operatives drawn by concerned or interested observers helped to attract the charitable aid that was distributed by the Mansion House and Central Relief Funds.[82]

Resentment at the inadequacy of the relief and the humiliating techniques of administering it led to strikes in Preston and Bolton in 1863 and massive demonstrations of protest in Oldham, Lees, and on a smaller scale at Radcliffe, near Bury.[83] Only in Ashton did the frustrations bred by unemployment and insufficient relief lead to violence. The angry operatives rioted for several days during March 1863 and were in turn crushed by the use of force.[84] But this solitary outburst serves mainly to highlight the preference for restraint and orderly protest that otherwise prevailed during the cotton famine.

The intensity of the distress and the way in which it was dealt with influenced when and how the desire to see the South recognized as an independent nation was voiced by individual towns. Blackburn and Pres-

81. *Ashton and Stalybridge Reporter,* 14 December 1861.

82. Edwin Waugh, *Home Life of the Lancashire Factory Folk During the Cotton Famine* (London, 1867) (this originally appeared in the *Manchester Examiner and Times* in article form in 1862); Anon., *A Few Words to All on the Present Distress of Our Brethren in Lancashire* (London, 1862); Mrs. Augustus Hare, *A True and Sad Story of 1862* (London, 1862); Thomas Guthrie, D.D., *An Address . . . in Aid of the Lancashire Relief Fund* (London, 1863); *Bolton Chronicle,* 30 August 1862; Rt. Hon. Earl of Derby, K.G., *Speech on Distress in Lancashire* (Manchester, 1862), p. 13; J. S. T., *The Cotton Famine* (London, 1863), pp. 2–3; The *Times,* 2 May 1862.

83. Thomas Banks, *A Short History of the Cotton Trade of Preston for the Last 67 Years* (Preston, 1888), pp. 8–10; Anthony Hewitson, *History (from A.D. 705 to 1883) of Preston in the County of Lancaster* (Preston, 1883), pp. 189–91; *Preston Pilot,* 25 April 1863; *Preston Chronicle,* 7 February 1863; *Oldham Chronicle,* 25 October 1862; *Oldham Standard,* 14, 21 February 1863. Attendance at schools for sewing and reading was often a condition for receipt of relief: *Oldham Standard,* 31 January, 14 February, 2 May 1863; *Bolton Chronicle,* 15 November 1862, 17 January, 9 May 1863; *Bury Guardian,* 18 July 1863.

84. *Ashton and Stalybridge Reporter,* 8 March 1862; *Ashton Standard,* 12 July 1862; *Ashton and Stalybridge Reporter,* 16 August 1862. This last meeting decided to petition Palmerston and the Poor Law Board for relief.

ton, for instance, petitioned the government to mediate on behalf of, or recognize, the South just when the operatives were starving for lack of Southern cotton. Oldham passed one of its firm resolutions for the recognition of the Southern states at the precise time (November 1862) when it was the second-most distressed area in southeast Lancashire. Interest in the question of slavery was widespread throughout the cotton districts but it fluctuated with the degree of hardship.

The slower spread of destitution in the spinning towns of the southeast enabled a deeper concern with emancipation to take root there than was at first possible in the stricken precincts of Preston and Blackburn. Bury, Bolton, and Wigan were among those towns that were deeply involved in the war but were never utterly dependent upon its outcome for economic survival; they were, consequently, able to judge the issues at stake with comparative detachment. In contrast, the consistency and vehemence with which Ashton, the most afflicted and disorganized union of all, pleaded for the recognition of the independence of the South seems to have been motivated more by the hope of obtaining Southern cotton than by a belief in the justice of the Southern cause. The South was defended most fully and most actively in the towns dependent on the renewal of the supply of American cotton for their economic viability; that this was due largely to a rationalization of material necessity can hardly be doubted.

As a trading as well as a manufacturing city, Manchester was affected by the cotton famine in a unique way. The existence of the city had encouraged the development of southeast Lancashire as the chief spinning area because Manchester was the source from which most spinners obtained their raw cotton. In the war years this provision of raw material to firms in both regions was still in the hands of Manchester merchants, and it endowed them with a very special control over the situation. There were many Manchester merchants who gained financially from the war by holding their stocks of cotton until prices rose and they could sell at immense profits. More than a few of these were in this way saved from the losses threatened by the glut of 1860–61.[85] Several spinners similarly made their fortunes by building up their supplies of thread until prices rocketed.

85. H.S.G. (H. S. Gibbs), *Autobiography of a Manchester Cotton Manufacturer* (Manchester, 1887), p. 160; Arnold, *Cotton Famine,* pp. 30–31.

This led to a continuation of the high price-value of cotton exports despite drops in quantity.[86] As Professor Brady has shown, raw as well as spun cotton was exported by such men in fairly large amounts throughout the war (see table 5).[87] It is important to realize that this did not mean that there was a surplus of cotton in Lancashire generally but only that a few merchants were more concerned with selling their goods to the highest bidder than with providing cotton and work for the Lancashire operatives.[88] Under the circumstances it was hardly surprising that such Manchester merchants favored the cause of the North and hoped for an effective blockade. These merchants were to some extent counterbalanced by other merchants and spinners who supported the South and did their utmost to keep the local mills going during the crisis. Kershaw and Company gave its allegiance to the South and ran its mills throughout the war, often at a considerable loss; it was also the first firm to grant relief to its workers.[89] The views of a number of merchants, spinners, and manufacturers fluctuated with the military progress of the war and the rise and fall of cotton prices.[90] The chief concern of the distressed operatives[91] was a return to full employment (a return that was dependent on a renewal of the cotton supply), but this was combined with a real solicitude about the fate of Southern slaves. Despite the publicity received by the one carefully arranged meeting of working-class men in support of the North and its policies[92] newspaper reports in general suggest that the weight of operative opinion usually came down on the side of the South.

86. C. R. Fay, "Manchester and the Lancashire Cotton Famine," in *Round About Industrial Britain 1830–1860* (Toronto, 1952), p. 101.

87. E. A. Brady, "A Reconsideration of the Lancashire 'Cotton Famine,'" *Agricultural History* 37 (Urbana, Illinois, 1963), pp. 159–62.

88. Anger that Manchester merchants could play the market while operatives starved was typified in *Oldham Standard*, 11 May 1861.

89. W. E. A. Axon, ed., *The Annals of Manchester* (Manchester, 1886), p. 286.

90. H.S.G., *Autobiography*, pp. 161–69.

91. As early as September 1861, 43,000 people were being relieved in Manchester (see Axon, *Annals*, p. 286); in 1862 the numbers rose to around 50,000, and from 2,000 to 3,000 unemployed operatives met in Stevenson Square to complain about relief administration in early May 1862 (see *Ashton Standard*, 3 May 1862). *Liverpool Daily Post*, 20 January 1862, considered that the war had created a health hazard in Manchester, as the figures of those taken into medical charitable institutions had increased from 984 in the last week of December to 1,317 in the second week in January; the deaths during the same time had risen from 250 to 314.

92. The meeting was held in the Free Trade Hall on 31 December 1862. It was considered in Manchester to be a forced and unrepresentative meeting, but was enthusiastically greeted in the Northern states as a genuine statement of the feelings of the country.

Liverpool, with the diversity of its interests, was able to gain as well as lose through the changes imposed by the American Civil War. A stimulus was given to the building of ships because of the number commissioned by the Confederacy and by English merchants who were determined at least to try to break the blockade. The increased emigration in 1863 and 1864 from Lancashire to the British colonies and to America spurred the building of passenger ships (see table 6). In some instances trade also increased. The munitions manufactured by Birmingham and other towns in the Midlands were shipped to the Northern states from the port; extra supplies of wheat were exported to Liverpool from the North (see tables 6 and 8). Nevertheless, the chief trading activity of Liverpool, the importation of raw cotton and exportation of cotton goods, was abruptly slowed down and at times brought to a halt. Cotton porters were the most badly afflicted by this lack of work.[93] Only a few merchants profited from the general shortage of cotton by re-exporting Southern raw cotton to the Northern states for substantial gains. These were among the most ardent Northern advocates in the city. For the most part both the shipbuilders who profited from the war and the cotton brokers who lost so heavily were firm in their support of the South. It was suggested that, because these Lancashire cotton aristocrats believed the Southerners to be right and refused to either profiteer or change sides at their expense, that they were sacrificing their interests to a sense of justice.[94] The newspaper evidence indicates that the operatives of Liverpool were equally firm in their allegiance to the South. It is likely that both groups believed that their interests would be best saved by supporting the section which produced the cotton so vital to their prosperity. Thomas Dudley confirmed this when he wrote to Seward in July 1862 about the building of the Laird rams: "The feeling is deep and strong against us, and the whole town seems to take sides with those who are building these vessels." [95]

Variations in reactions to the war were a consequence of the extent to which the lives of people were directly affected by it. With the exception of Liverpool, the towns of west Lancashire were dependent on agri-

93. *Liverpool Mail,* 14 February 1863, 6 June 1863; *Albion,* 1 December 1862; *Liverpool Weekly Mercury,* 2 August 1862. The Society of Coachmakers aided those distressed in Liverpool (see *Fifty-sixth Quarterly Report of the United Kingdom Society of Coachmakers in England, Ireland, and Scotland, 1862*).

94. *Liverpool Daily Post,* 2 April 1863.

95. Charles C. Beaman, Jr., *The National and Private "Alabama Claims" and Their "Final and Amicable Settlement"* (Washington, 1871), p. 102.

culture, the tourist trade, or noncotton industries, and their economies
were in no way maimed by the war. In the west, consequently, interest in
the war was somewhat superficial and cursory, and any verdict passed on
the issues involved was almost always in favor of the North. In northeast
and southeast Lancashire reaction to the war was inevitably radically influenced by the close relationship between the future of the cotton operatives and the outcome of the War. Anxiety about the war was always
present there but it became far more intense once it was realized how
firmly the economy of the region was held in the stranglehold of the cotton famine. Through the end of 1862 and all of 1863 the concern shown
in the cotton districts was as much a desperate quest for survival as a genuine involvement in the ideological, military, or political issues of the war.
Judgment on the conflict in these districts was heavily weighted in favor
of recognizing the South as an independent nation. Mediation between
the belligerents, especially in the times and places of intense distress, was
often the vehicle for hope of a peace that would acknowledge the South.
Whenever and wherever starvation loomed near, direct recognition and
occasionally even military intervention were sought.

It was not, however, surprising that the resolutions passed at over-
flowing Lancashire meetings and the petitions sent in from the suffering
areas demanding some form of pro-Southern governmental actions were
ineffectual. The political impotence and lack of sophistication of the most
impoverished operatives deprived them of any weapon with which to ca-
jole or threaten the government into considering their wishes.[96]

Since the mass of Lancashire cotton workers had no effective way of
forming a pressure group, their wishes were passed over and then forgotten. The agitation in Lancashire was in no way allowed to influence the
British government in solving its demanding diplomatic dilemma: "how
to recognise the fact of a great international war without permanently
alienating a South which might become a great nation, or a North which
already was one." [97] Any inclination the British government had to re-
spond to the Southern appeal for acknowledgment was at first checked by
caution which was transmuted into a belief that the South might well
achieve independence without outside support, and was later overridden
by an accelerating awareness of the military superiority of the North. A

96. Universal male suffrage had not yet been even closely approached in Britain.
97. H. C. Allen, *Great Britain and the United States* (London, 1954), p. 452.

temporizing solution that became permanent was found in the form of the Proclamation of Neutrality, issued on 13 May 1861. While acknowledging the belligerency, this proclamation did not acknowledge the independence of the South and made a firm declaration of Britain's neutrality. Despite the careful wording that sparked only derision in Lancashire, the proclamation aroused such antagonism in the North that even war seemed possible.[98] Seward's aggressive reply was probably "designed to precipitate a foreign war," [99] but an immediate crisis was avoided when Lincoln and the new American minister in London, Charles Francis Adams, tempered the reply for British consumption. So well did Adams handle this delicate situation that Russell moved further away from the precipice of Southern recognition.[100]

The *Trent* affair was to constitute a far greater threat to Anglo-American peace. James Murray Mason and John Slidell had been appointed as Confederate agents to England and France respectively. They were intended to travel quickly to London so that Mason, a proslavery politician from Virginia, could press the argument that British recognition would help to terminate an unnecessary war that would cripple the cotton trade.[101] The strict blockade made it difficult for Mason and Slidell to leave from any Southern port but they eventually landed at Cuba where they embarked on the British steamer *Trent.* On 8 November 1861, the Union ship *San Jacinto* fired across the *Trent's* bows, and Captain Wilkes gave instructions for the forcible seizure of the two agents. The report of the seizure reached England on 27 November and aroused an ominous storm of resentment:

> There never was within memory such a burst of feeling as has been created by the news of the boarding of the Trent. The people are frantic with rage, and were the country polled, I fear 999 men out of a thousand would declare for immediate war.[102]

There was particular anger at the infringement of neutral maritime rights. "In the general indignation there was mingled something of a

98. F. L. Owsley, *King Cotton Diplomacy* (Chicago, 1959), p. 60.

99. C. F. Adams, Jr., *C. F. Adams,* p. 179.

100. E. D. Adams, *Britain and the Civil War,* 1: 126–27.

101. James Morton Callahan, *The Diplomatic History of the Southern Confederacy* (Baltimore, 1901), p. 133.

102. Words of an American long resident in London, quoted by E. D. Adams, *Britain and the Civil War,* 1: 217.

haughty astonishment. What! England insulted on her own grand do-
main, the sea!" [103] War was widely felt to be imminent. It was most
strongly desired and anticipated in Lancashire, but neither government
wanted war and both made every effort to avert it. Adams assured Russell
on 19 December that the seizure had been unauthorized. Palmerston,
checked by the moderating influence of Prince Albert, kept his demands
to a minimum by insisting only on the release of the prisoners.[104] Seward
announced and was largely responsible for the American agreement to
this on 27 December.[105] The general relief at the decision in Britain was
only faintly mirrored in Lancashire. There the tide of pro-Southern intervention continued to swell until it reached massive proportions in the
winter of 1862–63, but it was never powerful enough to push Palmerston
and Russell off their chosen diplomatic course. The impulse to intervene
was not to be as strong again, as far as the government was concerned.[106]

    It was just remotely possible that Lancashire's mood and activities
might have themselves goaded the Union government into war. Northern
suspicion of British impartiality reached the simmering point as news of
the building of ships for the Confederacy in British ports, particularly
Liverpool, leaked out. Charles Sumner regarded this as undeclared war
by Britain,[107] and the risk of an actual state of hostility being announced
by the North lowered over the uneasy peace. The failure to prevent the
Alabama from sailing out of Liverpool in July 1862 caused "the gravest
crisis of the whole war in the relations of Britain with the North." [108] The
anger of the North was to prove justified by the destruction this powerful
warship inflicted on the Northern fleet from the time she sailed until she
was sunk off the coast of France in June 1864.[109] The anger was intensified

    103. Louis Blanc, *Letters on England,* 2 vols. (London, 1866), 1: 209.
    104. Dudley, *Diplomatic Relations* pp. 5–6. See also E. L. Woodward, *The Age of Reform
1815–1870* (Oxford, 1962), p. 308; Herman Ausubel, *John Bright, Victorian Reformer* (New
York, 1966), p. 125.
    105. Frederick W. Seward, *Seward at Washington as Senator and Secretary of State . . .*
(New York, 1891), pp. 25–27.
    106. Kenneth Bourne, "British Preparations for War with the North, 1861–1862,"
English Historical Review 76 (October, 1961): 600; idem, *Britain and the Balance of Power in
North America, 1815–1908* (London, 1967), p. 251.
    107. Edward L. Pierce, *Memoir and Letters of Charles Sumner* (London, 1893), pp.
129–31.
    108. Allen, *Britain and the U.S.,* p. 478.
    109. Raphael Semmes, *Memoirs of a Service Afloat, During the War Between the States*
(Baltimore, 1869); James D. Bulloch, *The Secret Service of the Confederate States in Europe* (New
York, 1959), 1: 277–94.

by the knowledge that the *Alabama* was not only built on the Mersey but was manned and equipped by Liverpool [110] and had sailed despite the protests of the United States consul, Thomas Dudley. The official British policy of neutrality did not allow itself to be so deviously undermined. Scrupulous care was consequently taken to ensure that the ironclad rams, also built by the Laird brothers and intended for the Confederacy, should never provide a *casus belli;* they were confiscated in October 1863 and then bought for the British navy in May 1864.[111]

Prudence in skirting war was only to be expected from the North; little could be gained and much lost through involvement in fighting on another front. The careful reactions of the British government had more anomalous and complex causes. There seems little doubt that the sympathy of the British government lay with the South over the basic issues involved in the conflict. It was particularly felt that the right of the South to assert its independence was more defensible than that of the North to crush this independence in order to save the Union; and the legitimacy of the Northern blockade of the Southern ports was frequently questioned. That this sympathy did not entail active support was partly because after Bull Run there was a delusion that English intervention was unnecessary to ensure Southern victory.[112] Those whose faith in Southern invincibility was unsure suffered from a deeper-rooted fear of Northern military might. Intervention of any kind would probably have meant war, and the increasing strength of the Northern forces made this seem less and less attractive to Palmerston and most of his cabinet. Even under the extreme provocation provided by the *Trent* incident, war would have been engaged in only reluctantly because those in power held the disadvantages to outweigh the advantages. Economic factors played a vital role, but the argument that the loss of Northern wheat would not be compensated for by the gain of Southern cotton played a minimal part in the discussions on policy. There is little or no mention of the possible danger of a wheat shortage in any of the cabinet records or diplomatic correspondence of the period.[113] The preference for peace was more permeated by a concern for the defence of Canada and an interest in the promotion and maintenance

110. Semmes, *Memoirs,* pp. 405–12.
111. Bulloch, *Secret Service,* 1: 385–87, 424–40.
112. Van Auken, "English Sympathy," pp. 37, 134; E. D. Adams, *Britain and the Civil War,* 2: 209; Arthur Redford, *Manchester Merchants and Foreign Trade,* vol. 2, *1850–1939* (Manchester, 1956), p. 92.
113. Claussen, "Peace Factors," p. 520.

of British foreign commerce.[114] British trade actually flourished as a direct consequence of the war. Arms and munitions were sold to both belligerents and the decline of the cotton industry was balanced by increased prosperity in the woollen and linen industries. The need to obtain cotton was never considered to weigh heavily enough against the other factors making for peace. A war with the Union in order to lend a dubious protection to a supply of raw material involved a commercial risk far greater than any economic gain.[115]

The plight of Lancashire was at no time regarded as a potential political danger. This bred in the government a secure awareness that no unfortunate repercussions would come from the rejection of Lancashire's numerous and forcefully worded petitions that at least British diplomatic aid be given to the struggling cotton kingdom. This supposition was, of course, correct. Petitions continued to pour into Westminster until the end of the war, but their number and urgency abated as Southern cotton slid surreptitiously through the blockade and supplies of imperial cotton increased. Rioting was never the preferred course of Lancashire operatives, but any inclination to violence was suppressed by the force with which the Ashton riots were broken up. It was obvious to any incipient troublemakers that it would be cheaper for Britain to use troops to put down cotton workers than to risk a full-scale war against the increasingly victorious Northern army. Under the inequitable and unrepresentative Victorian political system there was little that Lancashire men could effectively do. That they nevertheless dared to do something showed a combination of naive faith in the still embryonic democratic process and a sharp desperation that was willing to experiment with any hopeful measure. The faith was to prove ill-founded and the desperation to go unanswered.

114. Beloff, "Britain and the Civil War," pp. 42–43; Robin W. Winks, *Canada and the United States: The Civil War Years* (Baltimore, 1960), pp. 118–19; E. D. Adams, *Britain and the Civil War*, p. 26; C. P. Stacey, *Canada and the British Army, 1846–1871* (Toronto, 1963), p. 252.
115. Claussen, "Peace Factors," pp. 516–17.

2

THE ROOTS OF DISRUPTION

No moral nor sentimental considerations were really in-
volved in either the earlier or later controversies which so
long agitated and finally ruptured the Union. They were
simply struggles between different sections, with diverse in-
stitutions and interests.[1]

Historians today are still far from unanimous about the causes of the American Civil War. The weight of scholarly opinion might now be understood to consider that the chief impetus for secession was the desire of the majority of Southerners to safeguard slavery by asserting their independence. That the North determined to check or extinguish slavery, rather than simply maintain the Union, is more open to debate. It is rarely held that the inequity of the American tariff system was sufficient to induce the South to secede; it is more often believed that the increasing dissimilarity between the ways of life of the two sections might have fostered the Southern wish to be a full-fledged, independent nation.[2]

These possibilities provided the basis for as much endless discussion a hundred years ago as they have done in more recent times. Jefferson Davis and Abraham Lincoln justified the actions of their peoples by diametrically opposed reasoning, and some of their followers agreed with neither. Reports of speeches made by both leaders found their way into the Lancashire press and were eagerly read by many of those whose lives were catastrophically affected by the outbreak of war across the Atlantic. To some Lancashire men it did seem that the war was a simple struggle between slavery and freedom; to others the quarrel was between free trade and protectionism, or Southern independence and Northern domination. But a perhaps surprising number were aware that the war was the outcome of a deeply complex situation which could not be explained away by attributing it to only one cause.

1. Jefferson Davis, *The Rise and Fall of the Confederate Government* (New York, 1881), 1: 6.
2. The gist of the main arguments can be found in a volume of The Problems in American Civilization series, *Lincoln and the Coming of the Civil War,* (Boston, 1959) ed. Norton Garfinkle. A more detailed analysis can be seen in Kenneth M. Stampp, *The Peculiar Institution* (New York, 1956) and *And the War Came* (Baton Rouge, 1950); Allan Nevins, *The Emergence of Lincoln* (New York, 1950); Dwight L. Dumond, *Anti-Slavery Origins of the Civil War in the United States* (Ann Arbor, 1939); Avery O. Craven, *The Growth of Southern Nationalism 1848–1861* (Baton Rouge, 1953); Robert Royal Russel, *Economic Aspects of Southern Sectionalism, 1840–1861* (New York, 1960); Thomas Pressly, *Americans Interpret Their Civil War* (New York, 1962); Harold D. Woodman, *Slavery and the Southern Economy* (New York, 1966).

Within Lancashire, analysis of the origins of disunion received different stimuli in each region and conclusions varied correspondingly.[3] The northeast cotton region, where small weaving firms were swiftly and disastrously hit by the lack of raw material, quickly blamed the war on the partisan American tariff system that penalized the agricultural South and aided the industrial North. In later years a wider view was sometimes taken in which this commercial disparity between the North and the South was seen as symptomatic of a complete divergence of interests and attitudes. Those who did consider slavery to be causally important would more often than not look at it as part of this same trend.

The essential difference between the northeast and the southeast was the far greater emphasis placed by the latter on the role of slavery. Only after searching examination and discussion was slavery rejected as the vital cause by the majority of the people in the spinning towns who expressed an opinion. By far the most frequently expounded reason for secession was the total incompatibility of the North and South in almost every sphere. Tariffs were in this area not merely sometimes but almost always seen as a mere expression of disparate interests. These variations may have resulted from the comparatively slow way in which the spinning towns of the southeast were affected by the cotton famine. The initial lack of hardship combined with an awareness that this war was one which must inevitably play a vital role in their lives enabled the situation to be viewed with a unique mingling of deep concern and relative, though short-lived, detachment. Later hardship rarely altered convictions formed early in the war. It is fairly evident that sympathy shown for the right of the South to secede was the result of economic pressure. One town in this region that was badly affected, though never made destitute, by the cotton famine, stood alone in its defense of Northern motives. In Rochdale the dominant view seemed to be that this was a war waged by the North to free Southern slaves. That the persuasive oratory of Cobden and, more particularly, Bright dramatically influenced the attitude of Rochdale has rarely been considered. Simple though it may seem, this is the root cause of Rochdale's deviation from the pro-Southern verdicts of other distressed towns on the outbreak of the war.

3. See the map of Lancashire for regional divisions used in this work. They approximate to the parliamentary divisions created in 1867 if Preston is included in the northeast and Wigan in the southeast.

Cobden and Bright were also regarded as representatives of an influential body of thought in Manchester. Here a small group of committed Liberals did believe slavery to be the cause of the war. They were supported by those merchants who had a stake in the continuance of the war with its high prices. The existence of a variety of discordant views was to be expected in a town such as Manchester that encompassed a wide range of industrial and commercial activities. These certainly can be found, but the men who considered the war to be the product of years of tension between North and South or actively sympathized with the South's attempt to gain independence were less in the public eye, though more numerous, than those who agreed with Cobden and Bright.

The reaction of Liverpool was far more complex than that of any other town or region in Lancashire. Merchants, traders, and shipowners almost always had their interests bound up in the war. To some, its continuance meant disaster while others were enabled to make unprecedented profits. For a town so dependent on trade there was a surprising lack of concern over the conflict between high tariffs and free trade. To most commentators secession was the outcome of the natural desire of the South to be independent and reach full nationhood; efforts were made to help achieve this by the Southern Club and other independence organizations, all of which eventually merged in the Southern Independence Association. There was some disagreement as to whether slavery had contributed in any way to the South's desire to be independent. Few regarded slavery as the sole important issue. In so multifarious a town as Liverpool it is exceptionally difficult to discriminate between those whose expressed views were products of detached thought and those who trimmed their beliefs to fit their pockets.

The west manufactured only negligible quantities of cotton and expressed comparatively little interest in the whole question. The smattering of analysis attempted there blamed the war primarily on the determination of the South to cling to slavery. Only a very few were aware that other reasons might have joined with this to move the South to secede. The North was generally admired for its noble attempt to exterminate the "peculiar institution."

THE NORTHEAST

In northeast Lancashire many of the small weaving firms in Preston and Blackburn were rapidly crippled by the dearth of cotton, and as distress deepened the conviction crystallized that tariffs formed the pivot of the American disagreement and the northeast's own lack of trade. This attitude was justified early in the war by the editor of the *Preston Pilot* as a refusal to ratify Northern robbery of the South's economic birthright. It was widely thought that such ill-gotten gains would not easily be surrendered:

> The North does not fight for the abolition of slavery, and if it were victorious to-morrow, the "domestic institution" would stand precisely where it does at present. They fight for what is much more dear to them, namely, their protective system, which thousands of English people now learn for the first time is the most narrow, bigoted, and restricted in the world.[4]

This exaggerated view of the true situation in America, where tariffs had been gradually reduced during the twenty years that preceded the Civil War, was a distortion that was frequently to be met with in the pro-free-trade Lancashire of the 1860s. Bright and Cobden were attacked in the columns of the *Blackburn Standard* and *Preston Chronicle* for inconsistently ignoring (in view of their campaign for free trade) the injustice of Northern protectionism and for mistakenly blaming the war on slavery.[5] Considerable weight was added to this belief in the fundamental importance of tariffs when a letter from a Burnley emigrant to the United States, attributing a regionally divisive role to tariffs, was prominently displayed in the *Burnley Advertiser*. The letter also subtly linked the Confederate stake in free trade with that of Lancashire:

> Should the South gain their independence, the first thing they adopt will be the great liberal principles of free trade, throw open their ports to the world and by that means they will bring foreign manufactured goods into competition with the goods manufactured here at the North.[6]

4. *Preston Chronicle,* 17 August 1861; see also ibid, 29 May 1861, 27 September, 29 November 1862; *Blackburn Standard,* 27 November 1861; *Blackburn Patriot,* 28 January 1865.

The *Preston Chronicle* was a Liberal newspaper, whose proprietors and editors, W. and J. Dobson, were men of independent minds and spirits, deeply concerned with the welfare of the area. The *Blackburn Standard* was firmly Conservative and attached to the Church of England; it was edited by its proprietor James Walkden, a local bookseller and stationer, who also owned the *Blackburn Patriot.*

5. *Blackburn Standard,* 11 December 1861; *Preston Chronicle,* 8 April 1865.

6. *Burnley Advertiser,* 27 September 1862. This independent newspaper was run by William Waddington with no bias.

Similar significance was hung on the tariff discord by the editor of the *Burnley Free Press* over a year later. With a certainty bred of limited knowledge he assumed that the Southern reliance on agriculture and the Northern on manufactures precluded any compromise that might seal a reconciliation.[7]

Only a few voices were raised in this area to claim that slavery was the real cause of the crisis. The editor of the *Preston Guardian* suggested early in the war that this was so but the idea was never repeated or elaborated later.[8] A local dentist, Mr. S. Payton McDowell of Syke Street, Preston, in a letter to the same paper reasoned that Northern abolitionism had made the South reel with revulsion into secession.[9] When speaking at Blackburn and Preston, Mason Jones, an exiled Irishman who was an itinerant lecturer for the Manchester Union and Emancipation Society, and had spent some months in America, was wildly denunciatory of the Southern intention to propagate slavery violently. His flamboyant arguments met with a cold reception and were dismissed by the *Preston Pilot* as "being of the most flimsy nature."[10]

The editorial which condemned Mason Jones had begun with high praise for the lectures of Joseph Barker and stated that the people of Preston were in absolute agreement with the pro-Southern sentiments he expressed.[11] Barker, who had lived in Burnley from the early months of 1862, did in fact lecture frequently in this area. His views on America and slavery were likely to be given serious consideration because he had just returned from a nine-year visit (1851–60) to the United States[12] where he had "joined the anti-slavery party and become intimately associated with Mr. Lloyd Garrison, Mr. Wendell Phillips, Mr. Wright, and other leading

---

7. *Burnley Free Press,* 2 January 1864. A Liberal newspaper begun by J. Nuttall in January 1863.

8. *Preston Guardian,* 4 May 1861. This was a Liberal organ edited by George Toulmin, a keen advocate of Social and political reform.

9. Ibid., 15 August 1863.

10. Jones was an unsuccessful parliamentary candidate for Coventry's Liberal element in 1865 (Benjamin Poole, *Coventry: Its History and Antiquities* [London 1930], p. 392; "Election Intelligence" The *Times,* 12 June 1865; *Parliamentary Debates,* 3d ser. vol. 181 (February–March 1866). He aroused a great deal of antagonism in the northeast, where he frequently lectured during 1864 (see *Burnley Gazette,* 5 March 1864; *Blackburn Patriot,* 17 June 1865; *Preston Pilot,* 1 August 1863; see also *Blackburn Times,* 5 March 1864 [a Radical newspaper owned and edited by Ernest King]).

11. *Preston Pilot,* 1 August 1863.

12. Axon, *Annals,* p. 353.

abolitionists." That someone who "had been advocating the anti-slavery cause with great zeal and ability" [13] should now build a reputation as a supporter of the South and frequently deny that slavery was the vital issue of the war must have convinced many waverers and hardened the attitudes of those whose own feelings had inclined them to this point of view. His speeches castigating the North as the sole aggressor were warmly received and his motions and amendments in favor of the Southern cause were passed at many meetings in the northeast. That "the South had no other chance to secure their liberty but by withdrawing from the Union," was a conviction that was typically acceptable to the mood of his audience.[14] Others in the region expressed a related belief—that it was a desire for independence which motivated Southern action. The Reverend William Croke Squier, a Unitarian minister of Percy Street Church, Preston, and an active member of the Preston Anti-slavery Society, had no doubt about the purity of the Southerners' aims: "They are fighting not for SLAVERY but for INDEPENDENCE." [15] Charles W. Chapman vehemently concurred with this, in a lecture in Preston for St. Peter's Working Men's Club (for which he did a great deal of work). He gave reasons for the necessity for Southern independence:

> Grievances, great, deep, and lasting, had existed for years between the North and the South. The Confederates did not wish to secede for having suffered one wrong, nor in consequence of the election of this or that individual to the presidential office; it was because wrongs had been heaped upon them, and because they could stand those wrongs no longer, that they demand separation a necessity. They had borne silently the insults and tyranny of the North; but they could bear them no longer; and they had resolved to fight and die rather than sacrifice their liberty and independence.[16]

Many editors also felt that the prime aim of the North was to crush this independence and reassert the power of the Union, leaving slavery intact.[17] S. A. Nichols, the honorary secretary of the Darwen Relief Com-

---

13. John Thomas Barker, *The Life of Joseph Barker* (London, 1880) p. 309.

14. *Burnley Advertiser,* 18 April 1863, see also ibid., 18 October 1862, 22 August 1863; *Burnley Free Press,* 18 April, 22 August 1863; *Preston Guardian,* 1 August, 18 April 1863.

15. *Preston Chronicle,* 9 May 1863. For other similar nonconformist views, see ibid., 8 August 1863.

16. *Preston Chronicle,* 3 October 1863. Charles W. Chapman was a relative of the incumbent of St. Peter's Church (since 1862) the Reverend Dawson F. Chapman.

17. *Blackburn Standard,* 17 July 1861, 23 April 1862, 17 June 1863; *Preston Mercury,* 26 October 1861; *Preston Pilot,* 22 June 1862; *Preston Chronicle,* 19 September 1863.

mittee, considered that most people in his area thought that "the North was bent upon the assertion of its supremacy."[18] This surmise was fully borne out by an overflow meeting in Darwen which carried, at a ratio of four to one, the amendment: "That this meeting regards slavery with strongest feelings of abhorrence and condemnation, and will gladly render aid and sympathy to any just efforts for its extinction, but this meeting cannot approve of making the question of slavery as [sic] a pretext for sympathising with and encouraging the Northern States of America in the cruel and disastrous war which they are now waging against the South, and in the perseverance of which they are depriving the working classes of Lancashire of suitable industry, and thus imposing upon them the most painful destitution and distress."

This was proposed by a local workingman, Mr. J. B. Deakin, who prefixed it with the deprivation-rooted judgment that this was a war waged for a commercial empire.[19] It was at times mourned that the North seemed to be undermining the whole American spirit of independence which the South was commendably trying to defend.[20]

In the northeast the distorting effect of immediate hardship made it appear that tariffs were the means whereby the North stemmed the flow of cheap Southern cotton to Lancashire. Tariffs were also felt to be an attempt to demonstrate that the South could be held in a pincer-like grip that would inflict economic and political impotence. Such rationalization left the region free to defend Southern secession with uncomplicated ardor.

THE SOUTHEAST

In southeast Lancashire controversy about the causes of disunion was pervaded by an overwhelming concern with slavery. Possibly because of the delayed effects of the cotton famine, the complexity of the situation in America was more frequently understood here than in the northeast. Judgment seemed sharpened by the deeper insight and wider vision with which the problems involved in the war were seen.

18. S. A. Nichols, *Darwen and the Cotton Famine* (Rawtenstall, 1893) p. 17.
19. *Preston Guardian.* 18 April 1863; see also *Blackburn Standard,* 22 April 1863. Similar sentiments were expressed at meetings in Burnley (*Burnley Free Press,* 11 April 1863; *Manchester Courier,* 18 April 1863; *Blackburn Times,* 5 March 1864). See chapter 3 for further evidence.
20. *Burnley Gazette,* 19 March 1864. See also *Preston Chronicle,* 19 September 1863; *Burnley Gazette,* 29 November 1862; *Blackburn Standard,* 23 October 1861, 23 April 1862.

When discussion was over and the issues were weighed, few held slavery to be the cause of the war. Only in the Rochdale of Cobden and Bright was such a belief consistently adhered to by a large proportion of the population. Initially even this town, and Cobden and Bright themselves, were doubtful about the motives of the North in waging war.[21] Bright quickly became convinced that the North intended to abolish or restrict slavery, but Cobden remained uncertain and was troubled by the possibility that to support the North might be tantamount to upholding protectionism against free trade. Within a matter of months, however, Bright, in a notable conversation, won Cobden round from his misgivings and enlisted him henceforward as an earnest champion of the North.[22] Speaking at public meetings and dinners held in their honor at Rochdale, they combined to persuade, or at least predispose, many in the town to believe that this was a war waged to free the slaves. In a lengthy speech in the Town Hall in December 1861, Bright left his audience in no doubt that he considered any question other than slavery to be inconsequential:

> It is a question of slavery—(cheers) and for 30 years it has constantly been coming to the surface, disturbing social life, and overthrowing almost all political harmony in the working of the United States.—(Cheers) In the North there is no secession; there is no collision. These disturbances and this insurrection are found wholly in the south and in the slave states; and therefore, I think that the man who says otherwise, who contends that it is the tariff or anything whatsoever else than slavery, is either himself deceived or endeavours to deceive others.—(Cheers) The object of the South is this—to escape from the majority who wish to limit the area to slavery.[23]

Such speeches would be reported in the national press, while meetings and lectures in other towns would almost never be mentioned, and this helped to perpetuate the myth that the ideas of this town were typical of the area. It cannot be disputed that they were influential in Rochdale itself. The editor of the *Rochdale Observer* put over the belief that the war had been set off by the election of an antislavery president at a time when the South was determined to cling to the institution. "This may not be the prominent issue, but it is the real one. It may not be what the belligerents have on their lips, but it lies in their hearts. When the Northerners speak

21. C. F. Adams, Jr., *C. F. Adams* (London, 1900), pp. 156–57.
22. John Morley, *Cobden*, p. 837.
23. *Rochdale Spectator*, 7 December, 1861.

of the maintenance of the Union, they mean the duty of the people to obey such laws as are enacted by the Senate, even though it should abolish compulsory servitude, and when the Southerners talk about the rights of secession they mean the wrongs of slavery." [24] This was still the view held by Alderman Moore over two years later when he said that slavery was undoubtedly "the great cause of contention between the two parties." At this meeting, which he chaired, a motion was passed stating that the war had "originated" in slavery. [25] The same attitude was echoed in other meetings at this time. [26]

Such sentiments were to be expected; what is surprising is the strong dissentient element to be found even in Rochdale. Joseph White, the editor of the *Rochdale Pilot,* considered it highly unlikely that the North was waging war over slavery because, only a few months before, President Lincoln had been assuring the people that he had no intention of interfering with this domestic institution. [27] He dismissed Bright's views as contemptible and was convinced that in doing so he was in accord with Englishmen generally. [28] A few years later, in November 1864, Cobden admitted that a great many people, friends as well as enemies, some of them his constituents, did not entertain the same opinion as he did about the American war. [29] Rather more important was the existence in Rochdale of a branch of the Southern Club. A lecture was given under its auspices on 2 December 1863, to an "exceedingly large" audience, by Thomas Bentley Kershaw, a Manchester cotton spinner who insisted that slavery was not the vital issue of the war. A motion denying this was only eventually passed amidst great confusion, though by a large majority, after most of the Southern sympathizers had left. [30] Even more unexpected was the successful proposition of a pro-Southern motion and the defeat of an amendment firmly ascribing the guilt for the war to Southern slavery at a less

24. *Rochdale Observer,* 23 November 1861. This was a Liberal and Nonconformist newspaper, owned by the "residents."

25. *Rochdale Spectator,* 27 February 1864.

26. Ibid., 12 March, 14 May 1864.

27. *Rochdale Pilot,* 8 June 1861. Joseph White was a moderate Conservative and a member of the Church of England. He consistently attacked Bright.

28. Ibid., 7 December 1861.

29. John Bright and J. E. M. Rogers, eds., *Speeches on Question of Public Policy by Richard Cobden* (London, 1903) p. 488.

30. T. T. Heywood, *New Annals of Rochdale* (Rochdale, 1931) p. 57; *Rochdale Spectator,* 5 December 1863. The *Spectator* misprints Kershaw's initials as R. B.

numerous meeting addressed by the Reverend A. E. Verity on 25 January 1864.[31]

Outside Rochdale the pronouncements of Cobden and Bright had little influence. General annoyance was expressed with Bright's assumption that Lancashire and England as a whole sympathized with the Northern cause, and the assumption was at times flatly contradicted.[32] Cobden was also regarded as mistaken about the causes of the war but was given respect for his views on other matters in a way that Bright was not. Bright was attacked for inconsistency because his encouragement of the Northern cause and campaign seemed hardly compatible with his previous policy of "peace at any price."[33] His insistence that slavery was at the root of this disruption aroused James Hudsmith, the open-minded and high-principled editor of the *Bolton Chronicle,* to sarcastic denunciation:

> Well, England is a free country: and as an Englishman Mr. Bright is at perfect liberty to ride his hobby to death if he likes. We might say, indeed, that the more erroneous and extravagant the opinions such a man embraces the better, for few men gifted with his energies and his eloquence have had the art of so making unpopular the causes which they supported. But he might, if he has the good taste or the Christian feeling, at least discern the good policy of not attributing "crime" and "infamy" to those who differ from him.[34]

The imputation that it meant upholding slavery to believe the South had a just cause for secession was continually denied.[35] The *Oldham Chronicle* was vehement in its "deep-seated abhorrence" of slavery and considered it shallow and dishonest ". . . to attempt to brand with a tolerance for slavery those who see no honest design on the part of the North to put an end to the institution, or who deny the right of any section of the Federal Republic to force unwilling States to remain in the Union."[36]

31. *Rochdale Spectator,* 30 January 1864.
32. *Oldham Chronicle,* 27 December 1862. Jonathan Hirst was the Liberal editor of the *Oldham Chronicle* who advocated reform in all spheres. See also *Bolton Chronicle,* 4 April 1863; *Oldham Chronicle,* 7 December 1861; *Oldham Standard,* 7 December 1861; *Bolton Chronicle,* 20 June 1863; *Wigan Observer,* 27 November 1863; *Oldham Chronicle,* 8 November 1862. The *Wigan Observer* was a Liberal newspaper, edited by the progressive Thomas Wall, a practicing Nonconformist and a keen Radical, who took every opportunity to further the cause of reform.
33. *Oldham Chronicle,* 11 July 1863.
34. *Bolton Chronicle,* 4 April 1863.
35. *Rochdale Spectator,* 7 December 1861; *Rochdale Observer,* 7 December 1861.
36. *Oldham Chronicle,* 8 November 1862.

James Hudsmith of the *Bolton Chronicle* was also genuinely worried about ever being thought of as proslavery; he made it clear that if he could believe that this was a war to free the slave his sympathies would be with the North, as indeed they had been for a brief spell at the start of the war. To him it was clear that "the federals cared nothing about the slaves: what they did care for was that whether slave or free, the American Republic should never be less. They fought—not for freedom—but for power." [37] Such a view was typical.[38] Other editors considered that it was hardly giving the North credit for much common sense to say that it would wage war to abolish an institution that could only be successfully wiped out by negotiation.[39]

James Paul Cobbett, the Liberal reformer, sensed the paucity of abolitionist feeling in the North,[40] and a lack of emancipatory fervor was thought by John Heap, the progressive and Liberal editor of the *Bury Times,* to be fully evident in Lincoln's own supreme caution.[41] At Oldham the Virginian chaplain to the Southern army, the Reverend George Victor Macdona, breathed life into the local refusal to believe in slavery rather than arrogance as the cause of the war.[42] It was probably because of the strong emphasis placed by Cobden and Bright on slavery that some people in this area found it necessary simply to refute the idea that slavery was at the root of the rupture, without automatically pointing out which other issues were of importance. But every possible cause was, in general, carefully examined and weighed and then balanced in the scales against slavery.

Some estimated that the balance tilted in favor of the unequal tariff system imposed by the North on an unwilling South. Ashton-under-Lyne was the place most severely hit by the cotton famine, and it is surely not coincidental that the home of the most acute distress experienced in Lancashire should attach greater importance to the tariff controversy than any other place in this region. In 1861 Edward Hobson, the editor of the *Ashton and Stalybridge Reporter,*[43] and Mr. Kirkham, at the Stalybridge Me-

37. *Bolton Chronicle,* 24 September 1864.

38. *Middleton Albion,* 13 June 1863; *Bury Times,* 19 December 1863; *Ashton Standard,* 27 August 1864.

39. *Bury Guardian* 21 September, 8 June 1861; *Wigan Examiner,* 11 May 1861.

40. *Oldham Standard,* 7 September 1861.

41. *Bury Times,* 19 December 1863.

42. *Oldham Standard,* 31 January 1863.

43. *Ashton and Stalybridge Reporter,* 29 May 1861. The newspaper advocated Liberal measures.

chanics Institute, maintained that the tariff had justifiably provoked Southern withdrawal from the Union.[44] William Aitken, an Ashton schoolmaster who had spent some years in America and had written some articles for the United States Oddfellows Society, of which he was a grand master, maintained that slavery, which he expressly condemned, was certainly not the vital question to be decided in this war. "From what he had seen of the United States, they were now divided never again to be united; they were divided in sentiment, the feelings of the North and South were as diametrically opposed to each other as light and dark. In the South their principle was free trade, whilst the North were a disgrace to a free country and especially a Republican one." [45] Almost identical suppositions were put forward by the Reverend John Page Hopps, Unitarian minister of Dukinfield, to a large and sympathetic audience at Ashton Town Hall later in the war,[46] and at a meeting in Lees, near Oldham, by Dr. Charles Shaw, a local physician, who was the chairman, and Mr. Steeple, the secretary of the Oldham Southern Independence Association.[47] The editor of the *Bolton Chronicle* was voicing opinions also held by the editors of the *Bury Guardian* and *Wigan Examiner* when he decided that this was not a war between slavery and freedom: "It has far more the features of a war between Protection and Free Trade, in which both the sympathies and interests of all the European nations must incline them to favour the Free Traders." [48]

Many believed that the great differences between the North and South had made secession inevitable: "soil, climate, associations, and occupations have been breeding divergence ever since the Union was founded. What Providence and nature have thus potently been putting asunder, it is something worse that pedantry for men of the calibre of Mr. Lincoln or Mr. Seward to attempt to join." [49] The explosion of Northern

44. Ibid., 12 October 1861.

45. *Ashton Standard,* 7 December 1861.

46. Ibid., September 1864. John Page Hopps had ministered in Sheffield until 1864 and had there made no secret of his pro-Southern sympathy. He was an ardent Liberal with a profound respect for Cobden's and Bright's views on all but this one issue. He was also active in the Cooperative movement.

47. *Oldham Standard,* 12 September 1863.

48. *Bolton Chronicle,* 14 September 1861; see also *Bury Guardian,* 8 June, 21 September 1861; *Wigan Examiner,* 11 May 1861.

49. *Bolton Chronicle,* 4 May 1861; see also *Ashton Standard,* 1 June, 1861, *Bury Guardian,* 11 April 1863; *Oldham Chronicle,* 15, 22, 29 November 1864.

violence that was intended to end the split was regarded as much worse than pedantic; it was an act of uncalled for and unconstitutional domination.[50] This was the view in several lectures like the one that Joseph Barker delivered to a highly appreciative audience at Mossley, near Oldham. At this meeting a resolution was passed denouncing the violent attempt to secure "the subjugation and extermination of the Confederate States."[51] Thomas Wall of the Radical *Wigan Observer* gave voice to the generally held, if misconceived, idea that "the struggle of today is on the one side for empire and on the other for independence."[52] With terse conviction, Jonathan Hirst of the *Oldham Chronicle* upheld a fundamental liberal belief in self-determination as the worthy cause the Southerners were fighting for:

> We contend, in common with all who are worthy of the name of reformers, that every people has a right to decide upon its own form of government. This right does not depend upon their power to escape from thraldom.[53]

Surprising sophistication marked the reaction of the southeast to the causes of the American Civil War. The perceptibly slower engulfment of this area by destitution enabled scrutiny to move beyond the glaring discrepancy of Northern and Southern attitudes to tariffs and to see a more basic disparity between two alien civilizations. Slavery was recognized as the focal point of defense in both the economies and the attitudes of the two combatants. The fight of the South for independence was increasingly seen as a symbolic battle for freedom. A fine veneer was painted over the fact that, as far as Lancashire was concerned, the most essential freedom for the South to gain would be the right to trade unhampered by legislative impediments and crippling blockades.

MANCHESTER

There was undoubtedly in Manchester a section of the influential press that believed implicitly in the justice of the Northern cause. There

50. *Ashton Standard*, 27 August 1864, 29 April 1865; *Bury Guardian*, 13 February 1864. The *Bury Guardian* was independent and claimed to be classless.

51. *Oldham Standard*, 9 May 1863.

52. *Wigan Observer*, 15 May 1863; see also *Wigan Examiner*, 11 May 1861; *Bolton Chronicle*, 24 September 1864; *Bury Guardian*, 22 October 1864; *Oldham Chronicle*, 20 December 1862.

53. *Oldham Chronicle*, 29 November 1862.

was also a sizeable group of well-respected business men who judged the North to be fighting for the abolition of slavery; this group eventually formed the backbone of the Manchester Union and Emancipation Society. Beneath this vocal and influential element there ran an important substratum of dissentient writers and editors, merchants and millowners, artisans and operatives.

The editor of the *Manchester Weekly Times* was fairly representative of the prevailing mood at the start of the war, in his complete certainty about the cause of the conflict:

> It springs from that system of slavery which philanthropists have always declared would someday produce unholy fruit. . . . It is a potent fact, that, for a long period the North has habitually sacrificed its feelings on this subject to the selfish and interested Southerners. The event which immediately led to the secession movement was simply the election of a Republican to fill the Presidential chair.[54]

Far more extreme was the *Manchester Review*'s claim that the success of the South would be synonymous with the indefinite extension of slavery on American soil, and, possibly, the reestablishment of the slave trade itself.[55]

Evidence of the sympathy of many prominent Manchester businessmen for the cause of the North is scattered throughout the Wilson papers.[56] Thomas Bazley, M.P. and vice-president of the Manchester Cham-

---

54. *Manchester Weekly Times*, 4 May 1861. See also *Manchester Guardian*, 27 April 1861; *Manchester Weekly Penny Budget*, 25 May 1861; John Watts, *Facts*, p. 104; *Cotton Supply Reporter*, 15 May 1861. The *Manchester Weekly Times* was the weekly edition of the *Manchester Examiner and Times*, which was a Liberal newspaper deeply concerned with furthering reform. It was owned by Alexander Ireland and S. W. Paulton. Goldwin Smith described it as "the most influential paper in the manufacturing North of England" (Goldwin Smith to C. E. Norton, Oxford, 5 August 1864, Goldwin Smith papers). The *Manchester Guardian* was also Liberal and pro-Reform and was noted for its stern independence; it was owned and edited by J. E. Taylor. The *Guardian* became progressively more sympathetic towards the South during the war while the *Examiner and Times* fluctuated in its allegiance. The *Cotton Supply Reporter* made few judgments on the issues involved in the war.

55. *Manchester Review*, 25 May 1861. The *Manchester Review* was established on 7 January 1860. The editor was Thomas Ballantyne, who wrote most of the articles, all of which were broadly liberal. He was, incidentally, an expert on Carlyle.

56. George Wilson was a Manchester corn merchant and starch and gum manufacturer; he was chairman of the Anti-Corn Law League to February 1846 and became Chairman of the National Reform Union in 1864. He was a close friend of Cobden and Bright; see letters to Wilson from John Bright (Wilson Papers, 1861–64, Manchester Central Library). He was also vice-president of the Manchester Union and Emancipation Society.

ber of Commerce, assured the young Henry Adams that the leading men of Manchester did support the Union.[57] Pamphlets by J. H. Estcourt, chairman of the Union and Emancipation Society, founded in 1863, and the North American Reverend Marmaduke Miller were published by the Society and blamed the war squarely on Southern slavery.[58]

Mancunians themselves were more often to be found attributing the conflict to a search for independence. Thomas Kershaw wrote a pamphlet in which tariffs and Northern lust for power were denounced as the cause of the war, and slavery was exonerated. James Paul Cobbett, the ex-Chartist, had similarly found slavery blameless in a pamphlet written several years earlier.[59] A Manchester manufacturer pointed out in his autobiography that there were "many spinners, manufacturers and merchants" who thought that the South had caused the conflict in a simple effort to gain independence.[60] When Henry Adams made his visit to Manchester in 1862, to assess its sympathies, he stayed with Mr. Stell, an American, whom he immediately questioned: "I began at once on one part of my errand by asking what was the feeling among the solid people of Manchester towards the North. My host evidently thought it not at all what it should be. He thought it was generally unfriendly and even hostile, but did not deny that the radical party, the Brights and Cobdens of Manchester, who have a large influence, are with us." [61] These unfriendly and "hostile" attitudes found mild expression in the columns of *The Manchester Guardian*,[62] and a stronger instrument in the pages of the *Manchester Courier*, the *Weekly Express* and the *Manchester Review*, which condemned

57. Silver, "Henry Adams," p. 87.

58. J. H. Estcourt, *Rebellion and Recognition* (Manchester 1863), p. 15; Rev. M. Miller, *Slavery and The American War* (Manchester, 1863), p. 4.

59. T. Bentley Kershaw, *The Truth of the American Question* (Manchester 1864), pp. 3–11, especially p. 10. James Paul Cobbett, *Causes of the Civil War: the United States* (London and Manchester, 1861), p. 4. Cobbett had once been a Chartist but left the movement when it advocated extreme measures. He was moderate in his views on most topics (see Mark Hovell, *The Chartist Movement* [London, 1925] p. 122). He was later a vice-president of the National Reform Union founded by George Wilson in Manchester on 20 April 1864 (Wilson Papers, 1864, Manchester Central Library)

60. H. S. G., *Autobiography*, p. 2.

61. Silver, "Henry Adams," p. 80.

62. *Manchester Guardian*, 25 May 1861. It is surprising that despite this, and later and stronger condemnation, Charles Sumner considered the *Guardian* to be basically in sympathy with the North (see Edward L. Piece, *Memoirs and Letters of Charles Sumner* (London, 1893), p. 164.

the contemptuous attitude of the North towards slaves and scoffed at its weak pretensions to abolitionism: "this is not a war of freedom against slavery, as Mr. Bright asserts it to be." [63] The war was rather made necessary by the incongruity of an alliance as riduculous as that of the force-reliant North with the freedom-loving South: "When oil and water chemically combine or gunpowder and fire exist in contact with an explosion, North and South may possibly live again in harmony under one Government." [64] It was to be expected that Manchester would have a variety of views; as the liberal government inspector of factories, R. A. Arnold, pointed out, it was a town that lacked homogeneity and was "too large for its opinion to be without complexity." [65] The issues of slavery and independence were here most clearly interwoven, and sympathies tended to shift with the vagaries of war and the swings of economic fortune.

LIVERPOOL

Liverpool has been recently called "the most Southern of cities," and James Spence referred to it in 1863 as "the headquarters of Southern sentiment" which had "gone for the South from the first day." [66] Although it had some of the inevitable variety of opinion to be found in any large city, Liverpool was amazingly unanimous in its conviction that this was a war fought by the South to gain its independence and by the North to maintain the Union. A few did believe that the South had seceded because it felt both its "peculiar institution" and its "states rights" to be threatened, but it was rarely held that the North was genuinely concerned to free the Negro from servile labor.

The theory that this was a war of slavery against freedom was occasionally heard in Liverpool, always expounded by lecturers or clergymen who were not natives of the city. The London Chartist, Henry Vincent, the Reverend Newman Hall, also London-based, and the Reverend William Channing, an American who had lived in Britain for seven years, insisted in their lectures that the North was fighting to free the slaves. None

63. *Manchester Review,* 7 December 1861; *Manchester Courier,* 17 January 1863, *Manchester Weekly Express,* 22 February, 1 November 1862. The *Manchester Courier* was a Conservative, Church of England newspaper with a wide circulation, owned and edited by Thomas Sowler and his son John.

64. *Manchester Review,* 4 May 1861.

65. Arnold, *Cotton Famine* (London, 1865), p. 231.

66. Van Auken, "English Sympathy," p. 93; Spence to Mason, 12 January, 23 August 1863, Mason Papers, Library of Congress.

tested the reactions of their audiences.[67] One of the few Liverpool merchants to adhere to this view was Charlton R. Hall, a member of the Liverpool Cotton Brokers Association, who, significantly, made his fortune while aiding the North—he and his partner "purchased considerable quantities of cotton for shipment to New York and Boston during the American war." [68] At a meeting in Everton during February 1863 he successfully proposed a resolution which declared: "That in the opinion of this meeting the war now raging in the United States of America originated in the institution of slavery and in the antagonism which this inevitably presents to the institution of freedom." [69] Mr. Hall's advocacy of the Northern cause can hardly be regarded as disinterested, but the fact that his proposition found favor with even a fairly small meeting cannot be discounted when attempting to assess the strength of any sympathy with the aims of the North.

The case for Southern secession was stated most clearly and succinctly by the Liverpool merchant James Spence, in his "S" letters to the *Times.* It was elucidated most comprehensively in a succession of popular pamphlets and his one book, *The American Union,* which rapidly ran into several editions. Spence started to write the "S" letters with a Northern bias, having many friends and business acquaintances and interests in the North, but, as he delved deeper into the origins of the rift, he rapidly became convinced that the South had every right to secede.[70] In the *American Union* he not only denied that slavery was the cause of the rupture but thought that "the formation of a Southern power affords a prospect of its early amendment and ultimate extinction." [71] He thought it even more ridiculous to believe that the question of the extension of slavery to new territories was of any consequence to the North because slavery already existed in all Southern states "and also the whole of the territories into which it can be carried. They object to its extension where it cannot be extended." [72] All the findings of the *American Union* found high praise in the columns of the *Albion* and the *Liverpool Mail,* where it was also pointed out

67. *Liverpool Daily Post,* 18, 19 February 1863.
68. Ellison, *Cotton Trade,* p. 218.
69. *Liverpool Weekly Mercury,* 14 February 1863.
70. Edward R. Spence, K. C., *Bar and Buskin, Being Memories of Life, Law and the Theatre* (London, 1930), p. 9.
71. James Spence, *The American Union* (London, 1861), p. 165.
72. Ibid., 4th ed. (1862), p. 111.

that Spence had begun his research into slavery with sympathetic feelings towards the Northern attitude, but had come to realize how fully this was tainted with deviousness.[73] Much later in the war, the editors of the *Albion* and the *Mail* still did not regard abolition as the central cause of the war.[74] Like Spence, T. M. Mackay, the chairman of the Liverpool Chamber of Commerce and a prominent Liverpool shipowner, averred firmly and frequently that slavery had nothing whatsoever to do with the contest—tariffs were the serious source of strife.[75] When James D. Bulloch came to Liverpool in 1861 to secure war vessels for the Confederacy, he noted that the writings of these two men led their readers to see

> that the Southern people had just cause to be dissatisfied with a Union whose protective tariff was impoverishing them, and in which they were exposed to continuous invective and abuse in respect to a domestic institution whose pecuniary profit accrued in the greater part to that portion of the country in which the abuse was coined, and from which it passed into foreign circulation.

Bulloch boldly surmised that the people of Liverpool soon disbelieved any Northern claims to be waging war for freedom and "transferred their sympathies to the maligned Southerner." [76]

J. M. Whitty of the *Liverpool Daily Post* thought it beyond doubt that most people in the city were Southern supporters, but he himself was critical of many of Spence's conclusions. Great admiration was expressed for Spence's thoroughness, clarity, and excellence of style, and he was considered to paint so fair a picture of the situation in the South that he proved it had seceded to maintain its slave system and not to evade Northern tariffs! [77] An experienced cotton merchant, Thomas Ellison, in his *Slavery and Secession in America,* showed an unusually sophisticated understanding of

73. *Albion,* 11 November 1861; *Liverpool Mail,* 7 February 1863.
74. *Albion,* 1 February 1864; *Liverpool Mail,* 2 January 1864. The agreement between the *Albion* and the *Mail* over the American war was a good example of the way in which judgment of this conflict transcended politics. The *Albion* was firmly Liberal while the *Mail* enjoyed the active patronage of the Conservative party. Despite its Tory bias, the *Mail* was supported by a large number of operatives.
75. *Liverpool Daily Post,* 22 June, 22 November 1861 (the policy of the *Post* was dictated by its forceful Liberal owner, M. J. Whitty); James Spence, *Southern Independence, An Address Delivered at a Public Meeting in the City Hall, Glasgow, 1863* (London, 1863), pp. 17–23.
76. Bulloch, *Secret Service* (New York, 1959), 2: 311.
77. *Liverpool Daily Post,* 27 November, 25 June 1861.

both the psychology and actuality of the situation. "We have the word of the Southerners themselves that it is the fear of Northern interference with slavery alone which has been the cause of the present hostile attitude of the cotton States." This fear, he felt, was groundless because the North was fighting only for the Union and not to abolish slavery.[78] Like Spence and J. M. Whitty, he thought slavery would and could only be abolished by the Southerners themselves.[79] Having pondered at length in his own editorial columns, he finally answered his own rhetorical question: "What, then, are the Americans fighting for? For dominion. The Confederates desire a republic of their own to rule over—the Federalists the restoration, one and entire, of the disrupted Union. The North is battling for a distinct idea—neither more nor less than the Union; and the Confederates are, no doubt, by this time perfectly aware of the fact." [80]

Mr. Laird, whose family firm built the *Alabama,* and who had become M.P. for Birkenhead at the beginning of the war, mocked the myth of a war fought to free slaves. To him it was waged merely to maintain the Union.[81] Spence had stressed this in an "S" letter to the *Times* and condemned the attempt of the North to crush liberty and self-government.[82] This attempt was called an outrageous military despotism by the editor of the *Liverpool Weekly Mercury,* who was full of admiration for the efforts of the South to establish an independent nation.[83] Joshua R. Balme, an American Baptist clergyman who had settled at Brownlow hill, Liverpool, was saddened that anyone should suffer from the "strange hallucination" that the North was fighting for freedom while its military despotism trampled on liberty. In his view slavery was a mere stalking horse for the subjugation of the South and would have been abolished by the

---

78. Thomas Ellison, author of the *Cotton Trade of Great Britain,* was owner of the firm of Ellison & Co. A member of the Liverpool Cotton Brokers Association from 1871, he had commenced business in 1864 in partnership with G. R. Haywood, after serving his apprenticeship with Mr. Maurice Williams (see Ellison, *Cotton Trade,* p. 556; Thomas Ellison, *Slavery and Secession in America, Historical and Economical* (London, 1861) pp. iv, 276–277.

79. Ellison, *Slavery and Secession,* pp. 237, 241, 246; *Liverpool Daily Post,* 2 July, 1 August 1861, 1 June 1863.

80. *Liverpool Daily Post,* 2 January 1862.

81. *Bolton Chronicle,* 4 April 1863.

82. The *Times,* 19 May 1862.

83. *Liverpool Weekly Mercury,* 5 October, 9 March 1861, 24 May 1862. The *Liverpool Mercury* was run by E. Smith on strictly Liberal lines; freedom in all fields was advocated.

Southerners without the shedding of blood or interruption of commerce.[84]

A letter from a Liverpool merchant to H. C. Carey of Philadelphia, pleading for the right of the South to choose its own form of government in this war for freedom, was published in the *Daily Post*.[85] It found echoes in meetings of the Liverpool Southern Club a year later. The only ends to be attained by the South were to be the achievement of its "independence and freedom as a nation." [86] It was felt by the editors of both the *Albion* and the *Mercury* that Southern secession was fully justified by political, social, moral, and commercial difficulties between North and South. It was in fact "a geographical necessity." [87] To Spence, the people of the North and South formed quite distinct communities. The climate and productions of the two regions of the country were so different as to render divergence inevitable. "Throughout all history, difference of latitude has been accompanied by difference of temperament, and has formed the natural cause of the division of men into families—into races, the limits of which are the true foundations of political geography." [88] The *Albion* claimed that the justice of the Southern cause had won Liverpool to its side, and Bright was being both ridiculous and dishonest in assuring the U.S. Chamber of Commerce that Britain believed in the North:

> In Liverpool we are not supposed to have any feelings above cotton, and, therefore, we presume our testimony would be scornfully rejected; but still, it might be observed, that if an import of cotton be our great object, the opening of the ports by the North would be the quickest means of arriving at that end. Does anyone, however, who knows Liverpool, doubt that the overwhelming balance of sympathy is on the side of the South? . . . What dictum of a statesman has been more cordially received or more warmly re-echoed than that of Lord Russell, when he declared that the North were fighting for empire and the South for independence?—and what does this mean but that the policy of the former is selfish and grasping, that of the other noble and praiseworthy? [89]

84. Joshua R. Balme, *Letters on the American Republic* (London, 1863), pp. 102, 69–70. J. R. Balme lived at 32, Sun Street, Brownlow Hill, Liverpool, and 56, Islington, Liverpool during the war. He was the author of numerous religious tracts.

85. *Liverpool Daily Post*, 27 September 1861.

86. *Liverpool Mail*, 18 October 1862.

87. *Albion*, 28 January, 19 August 1861; *Liverpool Weekly Mercury*, 17 May 1862, 17 January 1863.

88. J. Spence, *The American Union*, 4th ed. (1862), pp. 87, 88.

89. *Albion*, 12 May 1862.

This claim was strongly echoed by newspapers less wholly sympathetic to the South[90] and validated by the available evidence about the views of Liverpool on the causes of the war. A greater divergence of views was found here as well as more subtle shades of understanding. But Liverpool began by feeling that the South was justifiably defending its intrinsic right to freedom and self-government, and the progress of the war in no way undermined this belief or put out the blaze of sympathy for the Confederacy.

THE WEST

The west of Lancashire manufactured only minute quantities of cotton. The sale of its coal and agricultural products was affected by the cotton famine, but markets outside Lancashire were quickly found to absorb any surplus and stabilize the economy of the region. Interest in the causes of the conflict was consequently more detached and, unlike in the rest of the county, was confined to editorial comments made in the early stages of the war.

These verdicts almost unanimously held slavery to be responsible for the outbreak of hostilities. The editor of the *Leigh Chronicle* thought that the war was an inevitable consequence of the existence of "the curse of slavery" and seemed rather pleased that the North had come to its senses enough to attempt to purify this scourge and cleanse America.[91] The *Warrington Guardian,* the *Warrington Standard,* and the *Fleetwood Chronicle* and the *Lancaster Gazette* also claimed that this was a straight contest between slavery and abolition.[92] The *Lancaster Guardian* was rather more equivocal, uneasily wondering whether the Federals were in fact fighting for protection and empire. The Morrill Tariff was expressly condemned as harmful to English manufactures as well as to the South.[93] Lancaster was, incidentally, a part of this area to suffer distress during the war, because of

90. *Liverpool Mail,* 26 April 1862, 2 January 1864; *Liverpool Daily Post,* 9 April 1863.
91. *Leigh Chronicle,* 11 May 1861. Thomas Halliwell ran this newspaper with no political bias.
92. *Warrington Guardian,* 27 May 1861; *Warrington Standard,* 4 May 1861. A. Mackie ran the *Warrington Guardian* on ostensibly neutral lines but the paper did incline towards Liberalism; the *Warrington Standard and Times* was a bulwark of Conservatism and the Church of England, and was edited by Charles Gerrard. *Fleetwood Chronicle,* 17 May 1861; *Lancaster Guardian* (a Liberal paper) 27 April, 17 August 1861, 22 March 1862.
93. *Lancaster Gazette,* 27 April, 8 June 1861. The *Gazette* was Conservative owned and edited by George C. Clark.

its number of small weaving firms and the lessened activity in its port. A more disinterested concern with the inequality of the American tariff system was voiced by the *Ulverston Mirror*.[94] The *Southport Independent* similarly joined the minority by putting the battle between slavery and freedom into the wider context of a war over the right of secession and self-government.[95]

Despite these thought-provoking but exceptional editorials, the mood of this noncotton region was one which established slavery as the cause of the conflict more generally than anywhere else in Lancashire with the notable and solitary exception of Rochdale.

In Lancashire as a whole the war was viewed most often as a glorious struggle for independence on the part of the South and a shameful attempt at oppression on that of the North. It seemed ironic to many that any part of the America that had once rebelled against England should strike out to crush a people struggling to reach full maturity as a separate nation. Slavery was seen as symptomatic of this basic conflict: the North, both at the start of the war and through the Emancipation Proclamation of 1862, was only using abolition as a means of gaining greater political power; the main Southern objection to such antislavery schemes was that they represented the determination of one section to impose its will on the other. In the eyes of most Lancashire spectators the South did not wish to maintain the slave system indefinitely. They did wish to be free to abolish it when and how they thought best. Tariffs were similarly regarded as symbols of domination, and were isolated in the east of the county as the main cause of contention when the swift onset of real hardship made it essential to find an easy scapegoat for a catastrophe that was generally understood to have its roots in years of tension. The Marquis of Hartington, while in the United States in 1862, gave an explanation for the Northern refusal to allow the South to terminate the tension in secession—an explanation that was very much in tune with the views of Lancashire men:

> They mix up in the most perplexing manner the slavery question which they say makes theirs the just cause, with the Union question, which is really what they are fighting for. They say they cannot

94. *Ulverston Mirror,* 8 November 1862.
95. *Southport Independent,* 12 September 1861. The *Southport Independent* was edited by its owner, F. M. Jones, who favored progressive Liberal policies.

spare the South, that they cannot do without the ports and the Mississippi, and that if they once let go, they would split up into half a dozen small republics.[96]

The cotton operatives and owners were agreed that it would be no tragedy for the Union to disintegrate. What was important was that an independent and free South should be able to send its cotton unhindered to the waiting mills of Lancashire. Wherever the need was most urgent, the lack of cotton most debilitating, there it seemed glaringly obvious that some economic inequity or twist of fate must have been the cause of the war. In the towns where rationalizations filled the void that cotton left, freedom and the South were artificially made close lovers. Only those detached through economic self-sufficiency or those leaning towards the North through financial gain could see that these two were only nodding acquaintances.

96. Marquis of Hartington to his father, the Duke of Devonshire, 29 September 1862, Devonshire papers, Chatsworth. Hartington Spence Compton Cavendish, Liberal M.P. for North Lancashire, visited the North and South (this letter was from Baltimore) in 1862 and 1863. He became a firm Southern supporter during the course of his visit.

3

THE EMPTINESS OF EMANCIPATION

Have we not proofs that "The North" does not care a straw
for the liberty of the coloured man . . . ? "The Union" has
held the slave in bondage; Southern independence will effect
his freedom. "The Union" has crushed and degraded him;
Southern independence will humanise and elevate him.

EXECUTIVE COMMITTEE, MANCHESTER SOUTHERN
UNION CLUB.[1]

The most vulnerable aspect of Lancashire's support of Southern independence was slavery. With strangely coincidental flashes of brilliance the
moral dilemma was solved in all the towns and cities that clung to their
Southern allegiance by the revelation that a free Confederacy was far
more likely to be a true emancipator than the North. The reaction of the
distressed towns of east Lancashire to the troublesome question of Negro
emancipation is a superb example of the rationalization in moral terms of
a basic economic need. The towns that needed Southern cotton most urgently were the towns that were most unshakably convinced that Northern schemes for emancipation were no more than amoral weapons in the
armory of war. They were equally adamant that true abolition, incorporating integration, could and would emerge only from a free South.
The fundamental importance of the whole question of slavery was not
minimized or shirked, and slavery itself was never justified. The sole, blink-
ered judgment was the placing of faith in Southern emancipation, and
even that was eventually to seem vindicated by the South's decision to enroll blacks in its army.[2]

The response of the weaving and spinning towns to emancipation
varied in nuance and degree rather than in kind. The weaving towns of
the northeast condemned the Emancipation Proclamation as a farce
quickly and dogmatically, while the southeast was prepared to sift and
weigh the evidence before ultimately rejecting Lincoln's plans.[3] The edi-

1. In the *Bury Guardian*, 30 May 1863.
2. Negroes were enrolled in the Confederate army by "An Act To Increase the Military Force of the Confederate States" in March 1865 (see Charles W. Ramsdell, ed., *Laws
and Joint Resolutions of the Last Session of the Confederate Congress* [Durham, N.C., 1941], pp.
118–19). Lee and Benjamin were among those who had for some time advocated Negro enrollment and subsequent emancipation, but the idea originally met with opposition.
3. Lincoln issued a preliminary Emancipation Proclamantion 22 September 1862,
but it was not until 1 January 1863 that the final proclamation freeing slaves in the rebel
states was made public.

tors and operatives of east Lancashire maintained that not only was the Union the chief concern of Lincoln and the North in issuing the Emancipation Proclamation, but that this did not in fact secure abolition. It was only with the passage of the thirteenth amendment in 1865 that freedom from slavery became a constitutional reality. Even then it was a reality shunned by many in the northeast. While the faith of southeast Lancashire in Southern manumission was more slender than that of the northeast, it was still omnipresent, forming a cloud of self-deceptive justification that was not shared by later historians. However, the awareness of the weakness of Northern feeling about abolition, an awareness that was even more marked in this area, is fully validated by contemporary scholarship.[4]

The slower engulfment by distress in the southeast allowed an initial detachment to be established that was never quite lost, especially in the several towns which were at no point swamped by destitution. Influential also was the close proximity of Manchester with its proselytizing Union and Emancipation Society. The long arm of this Society did reach out to the northeast but not with the frequency or insistence to ensure that the spinning towns at least heard, even if they did not approve, sympathetic explanations of the policies of the North.

Emancipation was as emotional a problem in Lancashire's two cities as in its cotton towns, but the answers originating in Liverpool and Manchester were more subtle and complicated than those produced by the famine-stricken East. These cities appreciated the complexity of the race issue in America with a depth of perception rarely reached in the manufacturing districts. The constitutional difficulties surrounding abolition were more widely understood, and the attitudes towards both North and South were often tinged with a healthy skepticism. With this skepticism ran currents of unparalleled devotion to the emancipatory intentions of each section of the United States, devotion polarized into Manchester's Union and Emancipation Society and Southern Independence Association. These extremes found expression in pamphlets, editorials, and

4. Kenneth M. Stampp, *The Era of Reconstruction, America After the Civil War, 1865–1877* (London, 1865), pp. 45–47; John Hope Franklin, *Reconstruction: After the Civil War (Chicago, 1961), p. 12; The Emancipation Proclamation* (Chicago, 1963). See also D. E. Fehrenbacher, "Disunion and Reunion," in John Higham, *The Reconstruction of American History* (London, 1962), pp. 101–104.

meetings that overshadowed the massive indifference to the very existence of black Americans felt among those in both cities whose fate did not hang on the outcome of the war. Such detachment reached its apotheosis in the noncotton west. There noninvolvement was almost complete. There alone did the final verdict favor Northern emancipation. In Manchester and Liverpool the efforts of the dedicated Northern supporters proved no match for the entrenched suspicion of the Federal policies and the faith in Southern abolitionist intentions. More headway was made in Manchester than Liverpool, but there were never enough rank-and-file Northern supporters to make the Union and Emancipation Society any more than a half-grown body.

THE NORTHEAST

Mistrust of Northern intentions about abolition, sown early in the war in the weaving towns, was steadily maturing when Lincoln announced his emancipation plan in the autumn of 1862. The proclamation in an odd way fertilized this mistrust and rounded out the charge that the North was using the Southern slave as a pawn in the military game. The conviction that the South would initiate its own scheme for freedom was not only unshaken but reaffirmed by the proclamation with its obvious flaws.

The ranks of those who did agree with the course pursued by Lincoln and the Northern government were exceedingly thin in this area, and there was a marked lack of local leaders to direct their cause. The meetings that were held to express agreement with the North were organized and addressed by men who by no stretch of the imagination could be said to hail from the locality, and the meetings seemed contrived rather than spontaneous.

The few editors who were not actively pro-Southern were decidedly lukewarm in their approval of the North. In fact the only two editorials praising Northern antislavery feeling were to be found in the *Preston Guardian* and the *Burnley Advertiser* in the early months of 1862.[5] Letters defending the North were conspicuous for their absence or anonymity.[6] Miss S. J. Clemesha, a Preston Quaker and secretary of the local Anti-Slavery

5. *Preston Guardian,* 1 February 1862; *Burnley Advertiser,* 22 March 1862.
6. *Burnley Advertiser,* 11 February 1862; *Preston Guardian,* 4 July, 14 February, 18 April 1863.

Society, was almost alone in openly acknowledging her belief that slavery was about to crumble under the Northern onslaught.[7]

Meetings to cultivate support for Northern abolition were almost always carefully organized by agents from the Manchester Union and Emancipation Society; speakers were gathered from London and other places outside this district, and discussion was usually discouraged. Despite all the careful preparations, meetings expressly called to demonstrate approval for Lincoln's emancipation policy often ended in a show of sympathy for the South.

George Thompson was one of the antislavery orators who could at least claim some link with Lancashire, since he had been born in Liverpool, though he had never really lived there. His appeal was, however, very limited and he misrepresented the mood of Lancashire in his writings. After touring the country to further the Northern cause and visiting only one Lancashire town, Heywood, in the southeast, Thompson wrote to William Lloyd Garrison on 5 February 1863 generalizing about the "self-forgetfulness" of all Lancashire workers who were united in "their willingness to suffer all the hardship consequent upon a want of cotton, if hereby the liberty of the victims of Southern despotism might be promoted." [8] He declined to comment on the impressions he had formed by the end of a far more comprehensive tour of several northeastern Lancashire towns in 1863 where his reception was almost uniformly cool and his words were swallowed up in the whirlpool of enthusiasm for the South. In the spring of 1863 he defended Lincoln's Emancipation Proclamation in Preston and Bacup and hoped that both towns would publicly support it. So little effect did this appeal have that the chief resolutions passed in both towns made their Southern allegiance perfectly clear and demonstrated a mistrust of the North that was as intense as their dislike of slavery.[9]

Thompson's arguments in favor of Northern abolitionism acquired a new potency when he was accompanied by the Reverend Charles Wheeler Denison, the Connecticut-born chaplain to the Union relief ship,

7. *Preston Chronicle,* 2, 16 May 1863.

8. Thompson was a friend of John Bright and stayed with him in Rochdale at the end of 1861 (See Bright to Wilson, 15 November 1861, Wilson Papers); F. J. and W. P. Garrison, *William Lloyd Garrison, 1805–79,* 4 vols. (New York and London, 1889), 4: 75.

9. *Preston Chronicle,* 21 March 1863: *Preston Guardian,* 9 May 1863; *Bury Guardian,* 30 May 1863.

George Griswold. Denison's presence at a Blackburn meeting was a constant reminder to the pauperized audience that they owed at least some of their food supplies to the benevolence of Northern donors.[10] The only resolution that succeeded in supporting the Northern emancipation scheme was proposed by the Reverend Denison himself at a Thompson-addressed meeting in Preston in April 1863.[11]

The general effectiveness of George Thompson's orations at this time may well have been undermined by his ill-health after a stroke suffered in India, his advancing years, and his own suspicion that until 1864 Lincoln's utterances on emancipation were tainted by "the alloy of expediency."[12] The ring of conviction that alone might have converted the hostile weaving towns seemed to be lacking.

Mason Jones was roughly received during 1864 in the large towns which were only then beginning to recover from effects of the famine, while some of those smaller towns which had never been so austerely deprived heard him more readily. At Burnley and Blackburn he eulogized the North for its fight for Negro rights and attacked the South for its worship of slavery. To thin and unreceptive audiences no attempt was made to propose any pro-Northern resolutions.[13] Audiences in Darwen and Haslingden were somewhat less incredulous,[14] but Mason Jones was generally held in a peculiar kind of contempt.[15]

The small towns were the chosen "stumps" of many other pro-Northern orators. Dr. Massie left the safer ground of the London Union and Emancipation Society to try to convert the inhabitants of Bacup. He was markedly unsuccessful.[16] E. O. Greening, the honorary secretary and co-founder (with Thomas B. Potter) of the Manchester Union and Emancipation Society, was aided by William Andrew Jackson,[17] the black ex-

10. Denison became a delegate to the national antislavery convention in 1850, but later opted out of the movement. The *George Griswold* was a ship sent from New York to Liverpool laden with food contributed by New York merchants for the starving Lancashire operatives; it docked in February 1863. *Blackburn Standard,* 25 March 1863.

11. *Preston Pilot,* 11 April 1863.

12. F. J. and W. P. Garrison, *W. L. Garrison,* 4: 106.

13. *Burnley Advertiser,* 6, 13, 20 February 1864; *Blackburn Patriot,* 5, 12 March 1864.

14. *Blackburn Times,* 2, 23 April 1864.

15. *Burnley Gazette,* 5 March, 20 February 1864.

16. *Preston Guardian,* 9 May 1863.

17. Jackson, a thirty year-old Negro, came to England when he left the South at the start of the war. He was befriended by George Thompson, who found employment for him as an itinerant lecturer for the Manchester Union and Emancipation Society.

coachman of Jefferson Davis, and by Peter Sinclair in persuading Padiham and Haslingden audiences to pass votes of confidence in the emancipation policy of the North.[18]

The far more indigenous and solid support for the South fell into two main categories: the simple condemnation of Lincoln's Emancipation Proclamation as a hypocritical military maneuver, and a more subtle defense of the Southerners as the true potential creators of Negro freedom.

The case for condemning the Emancipation Proclamation was argued cogently by editors in the distressed town of Preston and Blackburn who were united in a singular way on this particular issue. The editors of the *Preston Chronicle* and the *Preston Mercury* had agreed in 1861 and 1862 that the North had no real interest in abolition and would accept it only as a tool to use in undermining Southern independence.[19] This was considered to be borne out by the "moral worthlessness" of the proclamation, which was an act of "military necessity" and "horrible hypocrisy," particularly worthy of disregard for its retention of slavery in the loyal states.[20] The *Preston Chronicle* and the *Blackburn Standard* were gratified by the realization that the majority of Englishmen remained unconvinced by the inconsistent orations of "certain emissaries of the North" who had been engaged to persuade people that the North was fighting for emancipation.[21] The *Preston Pilot* damned the hypocrisy of the partial emancipation and the incitement to violence as "too monstrous to think of," [22] while the *Blackburn Patriot* was angered by the lack of real concern or gain for Negroes.[23]

Correspondents of the local press, such as Charles W. Chapman of Preston, were almost apoplectic at the mere idea of crediting the prejudiced Federals with pro-Negro motives: "Why sir, they *roasted* them in New York only a few days ago, and hunted them about in that city,—I won't say with the further intention of *eating* them." [24] William Croke

18. *Burnley Free Press,* 15 August 1863; *Bury Times,* 6 June 1863.
19. *Preston Chronicle,* 17 August 1861, 21 June, 27 September 1862; *Preston Mercury,* 26 October 1861.
20. *Preston Chronicle,* 17 January 1863; *Preston Pilot,* 18 October 1862.
21. *Preston Chronicle,* 11 April, 28 November 1863; *Blackburn Standard,* 17 June 1863, 14 October 1863.
22. *Preston Pilot,* 18 October 1862.
23. *Blackburn Patriot,* 24 September 1864.
24. *Preston Pilot,* 8 August 1863; *Preston Chronicle,* 11 April 1863; *Preston Guardian,* 11 April 1863; *Burnley Advertiser,* 18 October 1862, 2 February 1863; *Preston Guardian,* 11 April 1863, *Preston Chronicle,* 11 April, 8 August 1863. The New York riots took place between 13

Squier, the Unitarian minister who had long since proved himself one of
Preston's staunchest defenders of the South, was utterly skeptical of the
Proclamation and averred that "by means of the dreadful war now waging in America, the negro is being, not emancipated, but destroyed."
Squier, J. Sutcliffe of Burnley, and Francis Robinson, a Blackburn operative, gloomily foresaw only death through battle, starvation, or maltreat-
ment for ex-slaves in the North.[25] Such emphatic condemnation of Northern emancipation policies was the recurring note in the press of the area.

Joseph Barker was one of the chief instruments through which it was
made clear that this rejection of Lincoln's proclamation was shared by
vast numbers. He evoked a response of such passionate agreement wherever and whenever he spoke against both the North and slavery that it
seems likely he was articulating clearly what many already hazily believed. At many of the meetings arranged to show the existence of support
for the North, his anti-Northern resolutions were the only ones that were
passed, because he so accurately reflected the prevailing mood. In April
1862 Barker spoke eloquently to a Burnley meeting of massive proportions. The meeting had been well publicized by Northern supporters and
was addressed by Sinclair, Denison, and Jackson, who hoped to see a vote
of confidence in the policies of the North passed. Denunciation of Northern prejudice by William Cunliffe, a local cotton operative who had visited the Northern and Southern States, led to a rabidly anti-Northern
amendment being almost unanimously passed.[26] This was defeat indeed
for the North in Burnley and an indication of the strength of Southern
feeling in that town. Further proof was garnered by Barker at later Burnley meetings, one of which passed a motion seeking peaceful abolition but
abhorring the war.[27]

In Blackburn Barker attacked the use of freedmen to provide a "free
buffer" for the white soldiers in the Northern army, as at Fort Hudson

and 16 July. They were ignited by anger at the draft but provided an outlet for the expres-
sion of general resentment against the government. In the course of the riots many innocent
Negroes were killed or maimed. (see Horace Greeley, *The American Conflict: A History of the
Great Rebellion* [Hartford, Conn., 1866]. 2: 503–7).

25. *Preston Chronicle,* 25 April 1863; *Preston Guardian,* 11, 25 April 1863; *Burnley Advertiser,* 2 February 1863; *Blackburn Times,* 10 December 1864.

26. *Burnley Free Press,* 11 April 1863; *Burnley Advertiser,* 11 April 1863.

27. *Burnley Free Press,* 18 April 1863; *Burnley Advertiser,* 18 April, 22 August 1863; *Preston Guardian,* 18 April 1863.

where 800 black soldiers were placed in the front lines and 600 were slain. "The probability was that the sufferings of the negroes who had been emancipated in the course of the war had been greater than what had been endured by the whole slave population of the Southern States for generations past." Blackburn men agreed that it was the Union rather than slavery that motivated Northern leaders, and voted to support the South despite, on one occasion, entreaties by W. A. Jackson and Ernest Jones.[28] Preston also gave Barker a warm reception when he denounced Northern abolitionist duplicity.[29]

Without hearing any notable pro-Southern speaker, Rawtenstall rejected the witness of Andrew Jackson and the pleas of Peter Sinclair at a meeting organized by the Manchester Union and Emancipation Society passing an anti-North motion and voting against an amendment of confidence in the Northern emancipation policy.[30] Rossendale, especially Bacup and Rawtenstall, was the scene of particularly spontaneous meetings denying the value of Northern emancipation edicts. The Reverend T. Lawson, a Bacup clergyman, was given a vote of approval, never matched during the forays of the Union and Emancipation Society into the area, when he argued that military strategy dictated emancipatory measures.[31] The area's rejection of Northern policy was more specifically indicated by the passage of at least four resolutions by large majorities in early 1863 refusing to accept that the war was in any way benefiting the Negro.[32] Even religious meetings were permeated by anti-Northern emotion; at Todmorden's annual Congregational meeting, on 2 January 1863, warnings were uttered against the mischievous delusions about Northern abolitionism propounded by some Manchester speakers.[33]

At a meeting in Burnley late in 1863, A. E. Verity attacked the North for its lack of any genuine interest in the plight of American Negroes, and Mr. Uttley, a local surgeon, thought that the North hated blacks far more than the South.[34] Verity and Charles W. Chapman successfully argued along the same lines at Preston in 1863, and Verity at

28. *Blackburn Standard*, 5 August 1863; *Preston Guardian*, 1 August 1863.
29. *Preston Chronicle*, 25 July 1863.
30. *Preston Guardian*, 18 April 1863.
31. *Bury Guardian*, 23 May 1863.
32. Ibid.; *Bury Times*, 25 April 1863.
33. *Inquirer*, vol. 22, 10 January 1863.
34. *Burnley Free Press*, 19 December 1863.

Great Harwood a year later found agreement with his theories that the Proclamation had proved itself totally worthless and that recognition of the South would stimulate emancipation.[35]

The belief that a gradual erosion of bondage instigated by independent Southerners was the only kind of freedom that could work, was widely held in this part of Lancashire. The idea was implanted in Burnley when the American Baptist, the Reverend J. R. Balme predicted in August 1861 that, because free labor was more productive than slave labor, the Southerner would soon initiate emancipation of his own volition.[36] The Preston and Burnley press believed that a separate South open to European influence would resolve on a gradual system of emancipation that would far more satisfactorily eradicate the hated institution than the method proposed by the North.[37]

To many the proof that the South would emancipate the slave and that it considered independence more important than slavery lay in the decision to enroll Negroes in the Confederate army. This was anticipated in 1863 *Preston Chronicle* and 1864 *Blackburn Patriot* editorials, which predicted that the slaves would soon be armed and then freed despite the great pecuniary loss to the slaveholder. By February 1865 this was felt to be imminent, and both newspapers had little doubt that the South would at last gain the universal backing it had so long and valiantly sought.[38]

At many meetings and lectures the general assumption that the South would initiate a workable system of gradual abolition was more important than denunciation of the North. Joseph Barker insisted at Preston, Burnley, and Blackburn in 1862 that any satisfactory scheme for emancipation would be introduced by the slavemasters themselves, and resolutions were passed endorsing peaceful abolition.[39] At Burnley and in the surrounding towns A. E. Verity suggested that slavery could only be ended by the spread of the Gospel in an unoccupied Confederacy, cer-

35. *Blackburn Times,* 17 December 1864; *Blackburn Standard,* 21 December 1864; *Preston Chronicle,* 18, 25 July, 3 October 1863.

36. *Burnley Advertiser,* 31 August 1861.

37. *Preston Chronicle,* 13 August 1862, 17 January, 2 February, 11 April, 8 August, 5 September 1863; *Burnley Advertiser,* 28 June 1862, 28 March 1863; *Burnley Free Press,* 2 January 1864; *Preston Mercury,* 4 May 1861; *Burnley Gazette,* 21 March 1864.

38. *Preston Chronicle,* 19 September 1863; 18 February 1865; *Blackburn Patriot,* 19 November 1864; 1 April 1865.

39. *Preston Chronicle,* 25 July 1863; *Burnley Advertiser,* 18 April 1863; *Preston Guardian,* 18 April, 1 August 1863; *Burnley Gazette,* 11 April 1863; *Blackburn Standard,* 5 August 1863.

tainly not by violence, while other local men held that recognition of Southern independence would create a situation conducive to black freedom and equality.[40] In Preston W. C. Squier forcefully reminded his fellow townsmen that he had always been a strong antislavery man and that he foresaw gradual and peaceful emancipation along the lines of that effected in the British West Indies, once the South stood alone and open to the influence of "the civilised world." At the close of this meeting a motion was passed to recognize the Confederacy, a sure indication that the majority of people in Preston considered that separation would lead to emancipation.[41]

Motives for alignment with North and South were almost always attributed, at least in part, to an altruistic concern for the future welfare of Negroes. Few openly placed their own welfare first, however much that may have been the vital unspoken or even subconscious factor. One of the few was a Preston cotton operative called Lundy, who attacked without compunction supporters of the Emancipation Proclamation.

> Talk about selling blacks and slaves in America! they ought sooner to sympathise with their fellow creatures in Preston. (Great pressing in the crowd, and cries of "Hear, hear," "Go on," and groans.) . . . Did you ever hear of slaves committing suicide through hunger? ("Never") No, you never did; you never heard of a slave doing what the watch maker did a few days since, committing suicide to end his misery, through not being able to keep his wife and children.[42]

A meeting at Over Darwen in the same month passed an amendment putting the blame for all this misery directly at the feet of the North and its misguided emancipation policy.[43] Also in April, a Bacup meeting of 1,200 in the Co-operative Society assembly room voted for an amendment proposed by Henry Maden, a local man, by "a considerable majority":

> That this meeting regards slavery with abhorrence, but cannot approve of making the question of slavery a pretext for getting up demonstrations of sympathy with the Northern States of America in the lamentable war in which Lancashire has been deprived of cotton and the present distress has been entailed upon the working classes.[44]

40. *Burnley Free Press,* 19 December 1863, *Blackburn Times,* 17 December 1864; *Blackburn Standard,* 21 December 1864.

41. *Preston Chronicle,* 28 November 1863; *Preston Guardian,* 28 November 1863.

42. *Preston Guardian,* 18 April 1863; *Blackburn Standard,* 22 April 1863.

43. *Preston Pilot,* 25 April 1863. Rioting followed this meeting.

44. *Bury Times,* 25 April 1863.

Echoes of this resolution reverberated throughout the northeast. There Northern emancipation was never seen as anything more than an amoral tool intended to prise independence away from the South and maintain the crippling cotton famine.

THE SOUTHEAST

Southeast Lancashire differed from the northeast in the somewhat greater degree of approbation for Lincoln's emancipation policy that found expression there and in the numbers who attacked the Southerners for their support of slavery. Rochdale was consistently behind the North on this issue, and in other towns such as Bury and Bolton a considerable amount of favorable comment could be found. Several local editors and speakers gave encouragement to the Northern plan, and speakers from outside the area met with a reception that did not bristle with hostility when they poured forth praise on Northern intentions. Nonetheless, in this spinning-dominated region, as in the northeast, mistrust of Northern policy heavily outweighed support for it, and faith in the intention of the Southerners to introduce their own system of abolition grew as the war progressed.

The Rochdale newspapers gave a warm reception to Lincoln's Emancipation Proclamation,[45] and wholehearted enthusiasm gushed from the *Bury Times*.[46] Temporary doubts in 1864 were quelled by Lincoln's insistence on emancipation in his re-election speeches and his annual message to Congress.[47] Cobden, in a letter to various American newspapers, which was published in the *Rochdale Spectator* in July 1864, had already insisted that the North was admirably destroying slavery.[48] John Bright was among the few who had anticipated the proclamation in his belief that the war would result in the termination of the slave system. In a letter to his wife on 27 July 1862 he considered that emancipation would soon come:

> I believe the deliverance of the whole negro race may come from this terrible strife, and that, 20 years hence, men will wonder at the

45. *Rochdale Spectator*, 11 October 1862; *Rochdale Observer*, 11 October 1862.
46. *Bury Times*, 17 January 1863.
47. Ibid., 17 September, 26 November, 24 December 1864; *Rochdale Spectator*, 19 November 1864, 22 April 1865.
48. *Rochdale Spectator*, 16 July 1864.

changes wrought out by the hurricane of passion which is now sweeping over the North American continent.[49]

Bright's delight at the publication of the proclamation was unbounded; it was for him—perhaps for him almost alone—a turning point in the war.[50]

Meetings dealing with emancipation proliferated shortly after President Lincoln had issued his proclamation, and at a number of these the speakers and their audiences expressed approval for Northern policy. Although some were spontaneous and featured local speakers, many were clearly planned and filled to ensure a show of support for the North. At such gatherings the figures of W. A. Jackson, Peter Sinclair, the Reverend Denison and other loyal members of the Manchester Union and Emancipation Society became extremely familiar.

In February 1863 a moderate-sized meeting approved W. A. Jackson's praise of Northern attitudes on abolition by passing a motion in favor of the policy of the North.[51] At Farnworth Jackson was accompanied by a group from Manchester, whose voluble presence may have facilitated the passing of a resolution supporting the Northern emancipation scheme.[52] Only a tiny audience could be mustered at Oldham in April to pass a motion proposed by James Todd, a speaker from Manchester and backed by Jackson, asserting faith in complete emancipation by the North.[53]

The mild success of these meetings was offset by the near-total failure of others. In May Jackson was heckled at Ramsbottom meetings when he declared his confidence in the North and attacked local allegiance to the South. He was called a liar, and after it was stated that no motion would be put before the meeting, a member of the crowd suggested that this was because there was no hope of it being carried.[54] This dismal failure delighted "An Operative," who wrote to the *Bury Guardian* protesting at the abortive attempt to dupe an operative audience with "rubbish," [55]

---

49. Bright to his wife, Elizabeth, 27 July 1862, Bright papers, University College Library, London.

50. Ausubel, *John Bright,* p. 136.

51. *Bury Times,* 21 February 1863.

52. *Bolton Chronicle,* 21 February 1863.

53. *Oldham Standard,* 11 April 1863.

54. *Bury Guardian,* 16 May 1863; *Bolton Chronicle,* 16, 30 May 1863.

55. *Bury Guardian,* 30 May 1863.

A very small and carefully "picked" meeting in the town in June, which *Bury Times* reporter David Thomas lambasted with rhetorical pro-Northern questions, persuaded no one that Ramsbottom favored Federal policies.[56]

In Bolton, Jackson just managed, despite opposition from several workingmen, to successfully propose a resolution which condemned the South as utterly dedicated to slavery. This small gain was weakened by the slender majority of less than 100 out of 800 and the knowledge that many present voted twice "from mere sport." [57] Lees did not even provide Jackson with a decent-sized audience, and, despite the backing of Peter Sinclair, it was obviously not thought wise to permit discussion, much less encourage a vote.[58] Sinclair was also part of a contingent from Manchester that blamed the war, slavery, and the cotton famine on the South in meetings in Bury[59] and Bolton.[60] At Lees, on 9 September 1863, he was given a dour hearing and the Southerners definitely had the best of the ensuing argument.[61]

The travels of the Reverend Denison through this region in 186: provided a constant reminder of Northern charity. He usually remained silent or made only a brief speech, but occasionally he held the stage for a sustained eulogy of the North. His most successful venture was a lengthy lecture at Little Bolton. He used a marginally more subtle form of persuasion than gifts of food when he informed his listeners that, before releasing cotton to Lancashire, the North was waiting for English approval of Northern policy expressed in public meetings. He bowed to the skepticism of his audience by admitting that Lincoln was not exactly an ardent abolitionist but compensated for this by emphasizing that the North was fighting to free Negroes while the South was determined to prolong their degradation. At the close of the meeting a resolution of sympathy with Northern emancipation policy was passed by acclamation.[62]

Mason Jones occasionally deserted his favored northeastern area to garner converts for the North in southeast Lancashire. On 1 March 1864

56. Ibid., 13 June 1863.
57. *Bolton Chronicle,* 27 June 1863.
58. *Oldham Chronicle,* 25 July 1863.
59. *Bury Times,* 4 April 1863.
60. *Bolton Chronicle,* 27 June 1863.
61. *Oldham Standard,* 12 September 1863.
62. *Bolton Chronicle,* 4 April 1863; *Oldham Standard,* 18 April 1863.

he declared at Bury that Lincoln's Emancipation Proclamation was the most glorious document issued since the Declaration of Independence. He was resoundingly applauded at the end of his speech and a favorable resolution was passed.[63] However, he met with an almost sullen reception when he praised Lincoln's emancipation scheme at cotton-hungry Ashton.[64] In the second of two lectures at Rochdale at the end of March he claimed to be quoting the actual words spoken to him by Lincoln in defense of his proclamation, in answer to criticism about the morality of freeing the slaves at such a militarily strategic time:

> The attitude of the Southern states raised slavery from its municipal or sectional character into a gigantic enemy, aiming a blow at the national heart and life, and because slavery is now aiming at secession, at the destruction of the national life, the nation gives to me, the constitution puts into my hands a sword with which to defend that life and to strike the enemy to the ground.[65]

George Thompson, in April 1863, strongly praised the abolitionist plans of the North at a small Oldham meeting and managed to stimulate a successful resolution approving Lincoln's emancipation policy. A ferocious attack on Thompson's speech was made by the *Oldham Standard* on the grounds that the slavery issue was too "grand and solemn" to be degraded by the "hired eloquence" of devious English politicians.[66]

When Ernest Jones glorified the Northern fight for freedom at Ashton he was ably supported by Hugh Mason, who assured his incredulous fellow Ashtonians that the North regarded the question of union as secondary to that of emancipation.[67] In pro-Northern Rochdale Jones claimed the Southerners wanted to extend slavery not only to the free states but also to Canada, and he linked the fate of the Negro with that of the British worker. Here a resolution supporting the "unconditional freedom" given to all bondsmen by the North was passed without any dissenting votes.[68] Shortly after this his eulogy of Northern policy was almost as well received by an audience at Bury.[69]

63. *Bury Guardian,* 5 March 1864.
64. *Ashton and Stalybridge Reporter,* 19 March 1864; *Ashton Standard,* 19 March 1864.
65. *Rochdale Spectator,* 2 April 1864.
66. *Oldham Standard,* 18 April 1863.
67. Ernest Jones, *The Slaveholders War* (Ashton, 1863).
68. *Rochdale Spectator,* 12 March 1864.
69. *Bury Guardian,* 6 December 1863.

Other lecturers could be heard speaking for the North in the area throughout 1863 and 1864. Henry Vincent gave a series of lectures in both Bury and Bolton in February and April 1864, and in each town one of his lectures concentrated on refurbishing the tarnished image of Northern abolitionism.[70] A British Mr. Jackson also rhapsodized over Lincoln's emancipation policy in Bury in May 1863, and was criticized because "he rather strove to excite the passions of his audience than to inform their understanding." [71] His failure may have influenced a change of heart; in June 1863 he presented the radically different view that it might be better for the slave to let the South secede in peace.[72] Thin audiences also marked two lectures given in Oldham by W. W. Broom of Manchester in July 1863. On the second occasion not even a chairman could be found, because the Oldham Southern Club had warned the inhabitants that the meetings were prearranged by the Manchester Union and Emancipation Society and Oldham should shun the "farcical" affairs.[73]

Emissaries to Rochdale were heard more readily than those who visited Oldham, unreceptive in its grinding distress. In October 1863 the Reverend A. Hymans, a native of Jamaica on his first visit to England, forecast that through the Civil War slavery would die. On 25 February 1864 at Rochdale, E. O. Greening was welcomed as he praised the abolitionism of the North and bitterly denounced the South.[74]

At a large Bolton meeting Manchester again provided several speakers. A resolution committing the support of the meeting to President Lincoln's policy was proposed by Thomas Evans of Manchester. Evans was promptly charged with being a paid Northern agent by Thomas Ward of Bolton but his resolution still passed.[75] At a second meeting in Bolton, 2,000 were present. Several local men and the ubiquitous W. A. Jackson spoke in support of Northern emancipation policy before two resolutions favoring the North were passed. The second resolution pointedly thanked the North for the food supplies carried by the *George Griswold*. The suspicion that there had been a certain amount of preparatory work by the Manchester Union and Emancipation Society was confirmed by the read-

70. *Bolton Chronicle,* 5 March 1864; *Bury Guardian,* 30 April 1864.
71. *Bury Guardian,* 23 May 1863.
72. *Bury Times, Bury Guardian,* 6 June 1863. *Oldham Chronicle,* 11 July 1863.
73. *Rochdale Spectator,* 17 October 1863.
74. Ibid., 27 February 1864.
75. *Bolton Chronicle,* 14 February 1863.

ing of a telegram at the meeting from the society's president, Thomas Bayley Potter.[76]

At a Northern-organized Oldham meeting in February 1863 utter confusion and laughter met the proposal that: "our sympathies are with, and are freely given to, President Lincoln and his government in their efforts to suppress this wicked and unjustifiable rebellion." Thomas Tetlow was constantly argued with when he claimed that Lincoln intended to extinguish slavery forever while Jefferson Davis aimed only to perpetuate it. The chairman declared the motion to be carried, "but it was impossible to decide as a great majority voted for both sides, and evidently regarded the whole proceedings only in the light of a very good joke." [77]

Ashton was even less disposed than Oldham to accept praise of the North. Milner Gibson told his constituents in January 1864, at a meeting in the Town Hall, that the North was fighting a battle for emancipation, but the discordant note which this hit in the town was shown by the qualification of the normally routine vote of thanks by disagreement with this single point.[78] Nevertheless, small though the membership was, there was an Ashton branch of the Union and Emancipation Society which in 1863 sent a letter of support to President Lincoln.[79]

When Richard Cobden delivered a pro-Northern speech at Rochdale on 23 November 1864, his welcome far outstripped in receptive warmth that given in Ashton to Milner Gibson. The audience of over 6,000 people showed their complete approval of his views by passing unanimously a vote of confidence in both Bright and Cobden. Cobden himself was cheered when he claimed that the recent victory of Lincoln over McClellan was won through the appeal of abolition to the Northerners.[80]

There was far more strength and continuity in this area amongst those who mistrusted the Northern attitude to Negroes. Most articulate members of the community refused to believe that the North had gone to war primarily in order to free the slaves. The Emancipation Proclamation in no way altered this verdict but rather set off a series of attacks on the

76. Ibid., 28 February 1863.
77. *Oldham Standard,* 21 February 1863.
78. *Ashton Standard,* 23 January 1864; *Ashton and Stalybridge Reporter,* 23 January 1864.
79. *Ashton and Stalybridge Reporter,* 2 January 1864.
80. *Rochadale Spectator,* 26 November 1864.

insincerity and wrongheadedness of the Northern gestures towards aboli-tion.

Condemnation of the proclamation was anticipated by early *Bury Guardian* and *Bury Free Press* editorials which considered that any scheme for sudden emancipation would certainly not be in the best interests of the uneducated slave, who could hardly be helped by a North more embar-rassed by color than the South.[81] A Boltonian living in New York effec-tively advised his extownsmen to urge Northern abolitionists to eschew sudden abolition so that it would be possible to have an educated as well as a free body of black citizens.[82]

The cry of hypocrisy was raised as soon as the proclamation was first aired in March 1862 by the *Bolton Chronicle* and the *Oldham Chronicle.* Both papers saw the proclamation as a devious act of diplomacy intended to conciliate public opinion in Europe and so lessen the danger of inter-ference.[83] While reserving judgment on the embryonic proclamation, the *Wigan Examiner,* on 15 August 1862, expressed total disgust with the dupli-city of Northern intentions about slavery. Anger was in particular stirred by a dispatch from Seward stating that any interference from a European country would "render inevitable and even hurry on, that servile war so completely destructive of all European interests in this country." The *Ex-aminer*'s reaction was both succinct and damning: "We have read some-thing of history both ancient and modern, of both savage tribes and civ-ilised nations, but we remember no parallel to this diabolical wickedness." [84]

When the preliminary proclamation was issued in September 1862, the *Wigan Examiner* contended that as it would further disrupt the cotton trade, it was actually an attack on the industry of south Lancashire.[85] The *Oldham Chronicle* and *Standard,* the *Bolton Chronicle,* and the *Wigan Observer* saw it as an instance of the strategic maneuvering the North was prepared to engage in to extend its tyranny and oppression over "a separate and in-dependent nation." [86] The *Observer,* which sarcastically renamed the pro-

81. *Bury Guardian,* 11 January 1862; *Bury Free Press,* 12 December 1861.

82. *Bolton Chronicle,* 10 May 1862.

83. Ibid., 29 March 1862; *Oldham Chronicle,* 22 March 1862.

84. "Further Correspondence Relating to the Civil War in the United States of North America," *P.P.* vol. (1862), p. 892; *Wigan Examiner,* 15 August 1862.

85. *Wigan Examiner,* 10 October 1862.

86. *Oldham Chronicle* and *Oldham Standard,* 11 October 1862; *Bolton Chronicle,* 11 Octo-ber 1862, 24 January 1863; *Wigan Observer,* 18 October 1862.

Lincoln *New York Herald* the "Jem Crow Journal of Yankeeland," noted that,

> the vice of the rebellious became a virtue in the loyal. If the rebel States will only return to their allegiance before the 1st of January next they may hold all their slaves and enjoy their "peculiar institution." Personal liberty will then be a right limited to white men. What principle is there in this? Obviously none.[87]

The *Bury Chronicle* and the *Rochdale Pilot* told their readers that, far from aiding blacks, this coercive, "execrable and useless" measure would harm and set back their cause.[88]

The passing of time in no way mitigated editorial condemnation of the proclamation and the whole Northern attitude that saw Negroes as "catspaws and cannon-fodder." [89] The strong criticism of Northern duplicity over slavery flowed on through 1863.[90] In September 1864 the *Bolton Chronicle* analyzed and quoted some of a speech made by Seward at Auburn a short while before to prove that any mistrust of Northern motives was fully justified:

> He then confessed, what we have all along believed, that the emancipation proclamations of President LINCOLN were not declarations of a conviction to be maintained at all hazards, but were simply devices to hasten the war to a successful termination. . . . So that it is just as we thought. If the South will give up its independence, the North will not say a word about slavery.[91]

The *Bury Free Press* and the *Ashton Standard* noted Seward's speech with equally complacent antipathy.[92]

In Lincoln's Christmas message in December 1864, the *Ashton Standard* saw no love of freedom but simply a desire to cripple his adversaries—an intention which would, it was felt, surprise or disillusion only members of the Union and Emancipation Society.[93] Even at the close of the war, the *Oldham Standard* was typical in being able to say that emancipation

---

87. *Wigan Observer,* 18 October 1862.

88. *Rochdale Pilot,* 11 October 1862; *Bury Guardian,* 1 November, 20 December 1862, 24 January 1863.

89. *Oldham Chronicle,* 16 May 1863; *Oldham Standard,* 21 February 1863; *Wigan Observer,* 7 August 1863.

90. *Bury Guardian,* 14 November, 5 December 1863; *Wigan Examiner,* 20 June 1863.

91. *Bolton Chronicle,* 24 September 1864.

92. *Bury Free Press,* 20 October 1864; *Ashton Standard,* 24 September 1864.

93. *Ashton Standard,* 24 December 1864.

had never been elevated to a principle held dear in the North.[94] Such editorials were reinforced by letters, such as those by Oldham's William Steeple, that considered Lincoln's aim in issuing the proclamation was to force back the South and not to proclaim liberty to the slave, and that the North must free its own slaves before England would believe it sincere.[95]

Far more of the meetings that opposed the North were centered around local speakers than was the case with those that supported Northern emancipation measures. The virulence of these indigenous speakers in denouncing the Northern policies was no less remarkable than the spontaneity of content and presentation and the enthusiasm with which they were received. The number of lecturers who travelled from other parts of Lancashire in order to voice their mistrust of the North was small, and these were supplemented only by one personality from outside the county borders.

The alien was the Reverend G. Victor Macdona of Richmond, Virginia, a chaplain to the Southern army who in January 1863 addressed large crowds of working men at Mossley and Ashton. He insisted that this was not a war between slavery and freedom and said that he himself was in favor of a scheme for gradual emancipation such as that carried out by the English government. The Ashton meeting was chaired by a local Church of England minister, F. H. Williams,[96] who made very clear his sympathy for Negroes and his rejection of the Northern proclamation:

> It was anything for the Union and nothing for the slaves with President Lincoln, as shown by the desire to restore the Union even with the slaves of the South—(hear, hear). If they loved the Negro so strongly in the Northern States, why not allow them to travel, eat or worship with them? [97]

Joseph Barker strayed from Burnley on several occasions during 1863 to speak with great success at meetings in the southeast. A typical meeting was a large one held early in May at Mossley when he maintained that to save the Union the Northerners "would rivet the chains of

94. *Oldham Standard,* 29 April 1865.

95. *Oldham Chronicle,* 26 December 1863; *Bury Guardian,* 1, 14, 28 February, 26 June 1863; see also *Bolton Chronicle,* 21, 28 February, 14, 28 March, 20 June 1863.

96. F. H. Williams was educated at Trinity College Dublin. He ministered in Edgbaston, Birmingham, between 1852 and 1857 and in Manchester between 1857 and 1858, after which he came to Ashton and stayed until 1865 as the incumbent of Christ Church.

97. *Ashton and Stalybridge Reporter,* 21 January 1863.

the negro still faster, and bind the slaves in chains of eternal bondage to gain their purpose." Barker put a resolution condemning slavery but refusing to endorse a war to exterminate the South, which "was carried by a large majority amidst thunders of applause." [98]

The Reverend A. E. Verity occasionally left his flock at Habergam to address meetings in this area. In Bolton in 1864 he mocked Northern emancipation, and a pro-South motion resoundingly defeated a pro-North amendment.[99] In Bury during February 1864 Verity twice successfully confronted David Thomas of the *Bury Times* as the result of a challenge thrown out by Thomas to Verity. Thomas's accusation that the South wanted to enslave all workingmen was not taken seriously by the operatives in the audience. They were far more disposed to believe Verity when he said that the South was fighting for freedom in every way and the North for repression, which included ill-treatment of blacks. The arguments were summed up by the Reverend F. Wilson, a local minister, who agreed with Verity. At both meetings the reaction of the audience was overwhelmingly in favor of Verity, and at the first an anti-North and pro-South resolution was passed.[100]

T. B. Kershaw of the Manchester Southern Club, at Heywood in June, Lees in September, and Bury in November 1863, plied the familiar argument that the North and Lincoln were not genuinely emancipationist while they allowed blacks to be massacred and enslaved in the North and preferred deportation to co-existence.[101] The Reverend John Page Hopps still could not believe at Ashton, even in September 1864, that the North would extinguish slavery, an institution he utterly reviled and wanted banished.[102]

Oldham was the home of an extremely active Southern Independence Association which sponsored meetings not only in Oldham itself but also in the neighboring districts. On 20 April 1863 J. L. Quarmby, secretary of the association, lectured at Mossley in the Mechanics Institute on

98. *Oldham Standard,* 9 May 1863; *Bolton Chronicle,* 20 June 1863.
99. *Bolton Chronicle,* 23 January 1863.
100. *Bury Guardian,* 6, 13 February 1864.
101. Ibid., 27 June, 12 September, 7 November 1863.
102. *Ashton Standard,* 24 September 1864. Page Hopps had sent a letter similarly denying the sincerity of Lincoln's schemes to a pro-Southern meeting held in Ashton in June 1864, at which F. H. Williams alluded to emancipation as "dust thrown into people's eyes" (see *Ashton Standard,* 25 June 1864; see also *Bolton Chronicle,* 4 July 1863).

the "Emancipation of the Negro." An ardent abolitionist himself, he was cheered after he discredited the Northern emancipation policy and the futile attempts of its supporters to "dupe" and "deceive" the "intelligent" public.[103]

Neighboring Mossley emphasized its lack of faith in Northern abolition at a meeting in June 1863. Since the meeting was organized by the Mossley Southern Independence Association, denunciation of Northern insincerity was to be expected.[104] Less foreseeable and more impressive was the passage of a resolution refusing to support Northern emancipation and placing faith in Southern abolition at a meeting organized by Northern supporters at nearby Lees.[105] Two most successful meetings were held at Oldham in June when John Chadwick and Mr. Steeple, both of the Southern Independence Association of Oldham, attacked, equally, slavery and the North. At the end of the first evening "upwards of fifty persons were enrolled as members of the Association." [106]

As late as January 1865 the Reverend Richard King, chaplain of Prestwich Asylum, denounced the military motivation and failure of Northern emancipation at the Working Men's Institute at Whitfield, near Bury, and an unnamed workingman told the sympathetic meeting that on a visit to the North he had been disturbed by the discrimination that was meted out against the Negro.[107] Evidently mistrust of the North had weathered the years in this region.

The large body of Southern supporters in this region were unanimously opposed to slavery. Most of these preferred a gradual rather than a sudden form of emancipation, and a very large number believed absolutely in the South's intention to emancipate the slave once independence had been gained. Freedom was generally felt to be effervescent enough to bubble over and release slaves from their trammels.

The repudiation of slavery in any form by all Southern supporters in Lancashire was emphasized in a letter from William Romaine Callender, Jr., chairman of the Manchester Southern Independence Association, published in the *Ashton Standard.*[108] Much of the press believed Southern-

103. *Oldham Standard,* 25 April 1863.
104. Ibid., 20 June 1863.
105. *Oldham Chronicle,* 27 June 1863.
106. *Oldham Standard,* 13, 20 June 1863.
107. *Bury Guardian,* 21 January 1865.
108. *Ashton Standard,* 2 January 1864.

organized, gradual abolition to be the answer to the problem of emancipation.[109] There was a blatant mingling of altruism and self-interest by those who cast their sympathy with the Southern emancipation, assuming this would speed Negro freedom and a resumption of cotton supplies.[110]

In passionate agreement with this view were the lectures of J. L. Quarmby at Delph and Waterhead, near Oldham, in the Wesleyan and Primitive Methodist schoolrooms. He judged that abolition could only be brought about "by the influence of love, not malice; by gentle persuasion, not at the point of a sword." [111] Joseph Barker was acclaimed when at a number of meetings he revealed that he had talked to Southern slave-owners and that he thought they would be responsive to moral persuasion.[112] At Bolton a resolution seeking for the abolition of slavery by the moral conversion of the Confederates was given an overwhelming majority by a large meeting.[113]

Lincoln's Emancipation Proclamation stirred the population of Oldham and Ashton to gather together for a public meeting in support of Southern emancipation. Mr. John Shaw, a respected member of the Oldham Relief Committee, confessed at a large meeting that his allegiance had veered from the North to the South because of slavery. He believed that only an independent South would carry through a sincere and "glorious emancipation." The passing of a resolution to recognize the Southern states must be taken as an indication that the majority of the vast crowd was impressed by Mr. Shaw's prophecy. William Aitken, in 1862, and Alfred Reyner, in January 1865, insisted at Ashton that "it was quite evident that separation was the safest guarantee for the gradual and total extinction of slavery." The large meetings seemed in sympathy with this as well as with other pro-Southern sentiments expressed.[114] At Bury, the local minister, the Reverend F. Wilson, M.A., was applauded by large

109. Ibid., 18 October 1862; *Wigan Observer*, 7 August 1863; *Bury Guardian*, 14 November, 5 December 1864; *Ashton Standard*, 5 March 1864; *Bolton Chronicle*, 1 June 1861; *Ashton and Stalybridge Reporter*, 12 July 1862; *Bury Times*, 9 July 1864.

110. *Oldham Chronicle*, 17 May 1862; *Ashton Standard*, 9 August 1862; *Bury Guardian*, 11 April 1863.

111. *Oldham Chronicle*, 22 August 1863; *Oldham Standard*, 13 June 1863.

112. *Wigan Observer*, 14 August 1863; *Bury Guardian*, 13, 20 June 1863.

113. *Bolton Chronicle*, 20 June 1863.

114. *Oldham Chronicle*, 25 October 1862; *Ashton and Stalybridge Reporter* and *Ashton Standard*, 22 November 1862; *Ashton and Stalybridge Reporter*, 2 December 1862; *Ashton Standard*, 23 January 1865.

audiences when he asserted at two meetings that the Southern clergy generally were in favor of gradual emancipation. He said that, in particular,

> the Episcopalians in the South had already begun the great work of the regeneration of the slave, and he had no doubt that some then present would live to see the day, when, by the Southerners themselves, the shackles would be broken from their wrists forever, and black and white would be one in Him, who had died for both alike.—(Loud and prolonged cheering.) [115]

This faith that the South would emancipate the Negro once the war had been won was felt to be more than justified when it became known that there was a possibility that the abolition of slavery might precede victory if the Confederate government decided to enroll the Negro in the ranks of the army. Such a measure would, it was widely felt, prove to the world that the slaves would be only too willing to fight to defend their homeland, the South, rather than the alien North, especially when the prize of freedom lay alongside that of victory.[116]

Belief in the South as the savior of the slave was common to both cotton districts. But in the southeast it was subject to far more attacks than in the weaving area. Here, too, there was more local willingness to credit the North with altruistic motives in its treatment of black Americans—a willingness markedly absent in the northeast. In both regions, however, the atmosphere was that of a battle in which the ultimate victors were the supporters of the South. The victory is the more significant when it is realized that the subject of emancipation was one of the very few on which Northern supporters would take a positive, rather than negative, stand. Whereas they could only oppose mediation or intervention of any kind, they could promote positive approval of the emancipation policy of the North. That overall approval was refused by Lancashire's cotton towns is a signal indication of general rejection of the North.

MANCHESTER

The dedication that was channelled into the Union and Emancipation Society and the Southern Independence Association found expression in a unique Mancunian pamphlet war. This was mirrored darkly in spasmodic meetings organized by the rival factions. The merchants who

---

115. *Bury Guardian,* 5, 12 March 1864.
116. *Bolton Chronicle,* 4 February 1865; *Oldham Standard,* 21 January 1865.

made or lost their fortunes through the American Civil War and the operatives who tottered on the brink of starvation may have provided the background for such intensity, but the large number who were less dramatically affected found more sympathetic representatives in the thoughtful local press.

The Manchester press showed a rare ability to see all sides of the emancipation question. The difficulties surrounding it were authoritatively analyzed and approval of the position adopted by either section was not lightly given. The only major newspaper to provide any substantive support for the North was the *Manchester Examiner and Times.* The Emancipation Proclamation was welcomed despite its military motivation, and the retention of slavery in the Northern states was felt to be constitutionally justifiable.[117]

The lack of any more widespread support for the North in the local press spurred on the Union and Emancipation Society to find other outlets in print for popularizing Federal emancipation. The Society, formed in 1861 by John H. Estcourt and Thomas Bayley Potter, a wealthy Manchester merchant and former chairman of the Manchester branch of the Complete Suffrage Society,[118] in 1863 intensified its efforts to undermine sympathy for the South and substitute respect for Lincoln's emancipatory edicts. Pamphlets were a most powerful weapon in this campaign. Their importance as persuaders rather than as reflectors of public opinion was emphasized by the lack of Manchester or even Lancashire authors. Just as the majority of the members of the society itself was from outside the county,[119] so the authors it sponsored were from outside the locality.

The only pamphlets indisputably originating in Manchester were from the executive committee of the Union and Emancipation Society and attacked Southern dedication to slavery and the myopia of supporters of the South.[120] A number of anonymous pamphlets attacking the Southern slaveowner as cruel and barbarous may have been written by

117. *Manchester Examiner and Times,* 23 October 1861; *Manchester Weekly Times,* 11 October 1862, 10 January, 17 January, 26 December, 7 February, 12 March 1863; *Manchester Examiner and Times,* 3 August 1864.

118. Potter became Liberal M.P. for Rochdale on Cobden's death in 1865 and founded the Cobden Club in 1866.

119. Only 55 of the 156 vice-presidents of the society were from Lancashire.

120. J. H. Estcourt, *Rebellion and Recognition;* Executive Committee of the Union and Emancipation Society, *Earl Russell and the Slave Power* (Manchester, 1863) p. 7.

Manchester authors but were just as likely to have been formulated elsewhere and then published in Manchester.[121] Other pamphlets denouncing Southern adherence to racialism were published in Manchester but written by authors with no connection with Lancashire.[122]

Most of the Manchester pamphlets were reprints of lectures delivered in Manchester and elsewhere but rarely by Manchester men. Speeches defending Northern abolition delivered in Manchester by the London-based Reverend Marmaduke Miller were printed by the society.[123] Those of the Connecticut-born, American Presbyterian minister and abolitionist, Henry Ward Beecher, given not only in Manchester but also in Liverpool, Edinburgh, and Glasgow, defended Lincoln's sincerity on emancipation and were also published by the society in 1863.[124] One of the few lectures delivered by a Manchester man to be published as a Union and Emancipation Society pamphlet was by the Reverend Joseph Parker, D.D., who asserted that "Slavery is written on the very heart of the South," but its demise through the Northern sword was witnessed by Dr. Massie.[125] The last meeting of the society was addressed by Goldwin Smith, who admitted that many in the South were not concerned with retaining slavery. Smith displayed surprising honesty in reporting that the society had been founded to stem the tide of sympathy for the South.[126] Lectures delivered outside Lancashire by Samuel Pope, Handel Cosham, Dan Gow, and W. E. Forster all supported Northern emancipation and all were published by the society in 1863.[127]

The few much-publicized pro-Northern meetings that were held in Manchester were contrived to create a specific impression, instead of

121. *Fallacies of Freedom and Foes of Liberty* (Manchester, 1863), pp. 30, 35; *The Negro, or the Crimes and the Recompence of the North and the South* (Manchester, 1863), p. 12.

122. F. W. Newman, *Character of the Southern States of America* (Manchester, 1863), p. 11; J. M. Ludlow, *The Southern Minister and His Slave Convert* (Manchester, 1863).

123. Miller, *Slavery and the War*, p. 32.

124. Henry Ward Beecher, *American Rebellion. Report of Speeches of the Rev. Henry Ward Beecher* (March, 1864), pp. 12–14.

125. Rev. Joseph Parker, *American War and American Slavery* (Manchester, 1863), pp. 5–6; *Union and Emancipation Society, Report of the Proceedings of a Conversazione* (Manchester, 1864), pp. 14–15.

126. Goldwin Smith, *The Civil War in America* (Manchester, 1866), p. 74.

127. Samuel Pope, *The American War: Secession and Slavery* (Manchester, 1863), p. 4. Handel Cosham, *The American War; Facts and Fallacies* (Manchester, 1864), pp. 98, 101–2, 114; Dan Gow, *Civil War in America* (Manchester, 1862), pp. 7, 32; W. E. Forster, M.P., *Speech on the Slaveholders' Rebellion;* Professor Goldwin Smith, *Letter on the Emancipation Proclamation* (Manchester, 1863), pp. 7, 13.

springing from spontaneous conviction. The most famous and most misleading meeting of the war years was held in the Free Trade Hall on 31 December 1862. This carefully arranged demonstration created an artificial but lasting impression of sincere working-class support for the North. It was supposedly composed mainly of workingmen and called together quickly by two operatives, Edward Hooson and J. C. Edwards, but the Union and Emancipation Society was strongly and vocally represented by Thomas Bayley Potter, John Watts, Samuel Pope, and W. A. Jackson. Even more ironically, the formally attired mayor of Manchester led a middle-class deputation which probably dominated the meeting and was largely responsible for resolutions that were passed denouncing Southern slavery and supporting the North's emancipation policy. Edward Hooson then successfully moved a resolution:

> That this meeting, composed mainly of the industrial classes of Manchester, desires to record its profound sympathy with the efforts of President Lincoln and his colleagues to maintain the American Union in its integrity; and, also, its high sense of the justice of his proclamation of emancipation, and other measures tending at once to give freedom to the slave, and restore peace to the American nation.

He also praised Lincoln's ability as a leader, and the meeting closed with the adoption of an address of sympathy with President Lincoln and a speech by W. A. Jackson. Aspersions were immediately cast on the character of this meeting by a number of Manchester editors who noted with sarcasm that this supposedly spontaneous, working-class meeting was chaired by the very middle-class mayor of Manchester attired in his full regalia. It was suggested by more than one editor that this was a carefully selected meeting of handpicked men who in no way represented the feelings of the town and should not be falsely depicted as doing so. The *Manchester Courier* condemned the meeting as

> . . . a very artfully contrived enterprise on the part of the friends of Messrs. Cobden and Bright and the peace-at-any-price party; but there was sadly too much contrivance for the trick to be successful. For instance, it was a curious coincidence that the Mayor of Manchester, Mr. Bazley, Mr. T. B. Potter, and others of that party, should happen to be present at (sic) a "meeting of working men" quite by accident.[128]

128. *Manchester Weekly Express*, 3 January 1863; *Manchester Guardian*, 2 January 1863; *Manchester Courier*, 3 January 1863; *Salford Weekly News*, 3 January 1863.

In the light of this local disassociation from the meeting it is strange, but oddly significant, that the sentiments voiced there were for many years and in many places taken to typify the feelings of operatives not only in Manchester but throughout Lancashire; myths are easily born but are often an unconscionable time dying.

The arrival of the *George Griswold,* with her bountiful supplies, was the occasion for a further expression of Northern sympathy. A meeting was held in the Free Trade Hall on 24 February 1863 with a small number of operatives and a very high proportion of representatives of the Union and Emancipation Society among the assembled crowd. The chairman, T. B. Potter, made it clear that he believed that this was the "dawn of freedom for the negro slave. (Applause)." The need to yet convert Manchester to belief in the abolitionism behind Northern policy was made obvious when he commented favorably on the good work of informing and converting being embarked upon by the society.[129] An antislavery conference of religious ministers battled unsuccessfully to rouse support for Northern emancipation and the meeting ended in utter confusion.[130] The *Manchester Courier* commented that

> Federal sympathy has not received much encouragement in this city, and we dare say that the Anti-Slavery Society now feel very sorry that they tried the experiment of Wednesday evening. Ninety-nine out of every hundred of the population are as averse to slavery and the slave trade as the Society itself, and most of us regret that such a cause should be compromised by being mixed up with that lust of mingled conquest and vengeance which fills the Federal Government, and causes it to be so generally unpopular. Some months ago, we contended that any attempt to get up sympathy for the North would be sure to be met by a counter movement on the part of the South, and that the intrusion of the antislavery element into the contest would only embitter it, and have a tendency to damage the anti-slavery cause, and bring it into contempt for lending its cloak to those who would only use it while the war lasted and fling it away afterwards. The North did succeed in borrowing the cloak of the Anti-Slavery Society, and for some time they managed to hoodwink the people, and get a few public meetings to declare in their favor. But the humbug was soon discovered. When the friends of the South began to bestir themselves the tables were turned; and now it has become one of the most difficult things in the world to induce a

129. *Manchester Courier,* 28 February 1863.
130. Ibid., 6 June 1863.

public meeting to express sympathy with President LINCOLN and the North.[131]

The visit of Henry Ward Beecher in October gave rise to a further meeting held under the auspices of the Union and Emancipation Society, but, even this handpicked audience greeted Beecher's assertions with disbelieving contradictions that tumbled the meeting into a state of uproar.[132] Confined to a select group of members of the Union and Emancipation Society was a soiree to bid farewell to George Thompson in January 1864. Stalwarts of the society such as J. H. Estcourt and John Watts voiced their total agreement with George Thompson when he claimed that Northern America would not just free the Negro but would give him real social equality.[133] This optimistic view may have been held by other, more representative Manchester citizens, but if so it was harbored in unusual silence.

It is a telling fact that some of the best and most impartial testimonies to the strength of support for the South as far as emancipation was concerned came from speakers and writers dedicated to furthering the cause of the North. Goldwin Smith admitted in 1866 that all classes, including the lowest, had misguidedly sided with the South, and that it had been "to stem this tide of sympathy with the slave-owner" that the Manchester Union and Emancipation Society had been formed.[134] J. M. Sturtevant, who had come from the Northern states, where he was president of Illinois College, to assess and establish sympathy with the North, was most disturbed by the general prevalence of antislavery but proSouthern feeling among all classes.[135]

The Manchester press fitted this image and uniformly condemned the Emancipation Proclamation as an arrogant act of necessity that would not benefit the slaves and was a "Demon of FOLLY and DESTRUCTION." [136] The *Guardian* denied that Manchester had been duped

131. Ibid.
132. Ibid., 10 October, 24 October 1863.
133. Ibid., 22 January 1864.
134. Smith, *The Civil War* (1866), p. 73.
135. J. M. Sturvetant, *English Institutions and the American Rebellion* (Manchester, 1864); idem, *Three Months in Great Britain* (Chicago, 1864), pp. 3–6.
136. *Manchester Guardian,* 2, 7, 9 January 1863, 22 August 1864; *Manchester Weekly Express and Review,* 8 February, 19 April, 11 October, 20 December1862; *Manchester Weekly Times,* 11 October 1862; *Manchester Courier,* 22 March 1862, 10, 17 January, 1 August 1863; *Cotton Supply Reporter,* 15 October 1862.

by Lincoln's proclamation, or by the inadequate arguments of the Union
and Emancipation Society and itinerant lecturers from the Northern
states. Harriet Beecher Stowe, of *Uncle Tom's Cabin* fame, was indeed applauded only for having the acumen to realize that the North had almost
no supporters among any branch of the Manchester population.[137] The
Guardian also insisted that the Union and Emancipation Society was qual-
ified to speak for itself alone, but instead made continual attempts to mis-
interpret as well as alter the feelings of the masses.

> Our people are not so easily deluded. They have a few old-fashioned
> moral maxims for these matters which they revert to after the fuss
> about questions which they little understand is exhausted. Much
> more than about the difference between the systems of free labour
> and slave labour, they think of the difference between the weaker
> combatant and the stronger, between the one who is defending his
> independence and the one who is bent upon imposing an alien yoke.
> Mr. LINCOLN, even if he had abler representatives than he has
> found in this country, could not lead the working classes so far away
> as he requires from the landmarks which have served their purpose
> for many generations. . . . The few surviving chiefs of the great anti-
> slavery struggle in England, and the representatives of those who are
> gone, will have nothing to do with the hypocritical adoption of their
> cherished principles as a pretext in the last resort for the further
> shedding of human blood.[138]

The Manchester press considered Southern enlistment and emancipation to be the true end of slavery, denouncing the disapproval of Northern abolitionists as proof that they were both insincere and partisan.[139]
Trust was too complacently placed in an extract from the *Richmond Inquirer* of 16 December—"We prefer liberty with free society to re-union
upon the securest basis of slavery." [140]

The Southern Independence Association of Manchester did not, it
would seem, need to make very strenuous efforts to appeal to a city that
was apparently already convinced of the validity of its arguments. This
does much to explain the lack of organized pro-Southern meetings and
the confident note of the publications of the association.

137. *Manchester Guardian,* 9 February 1863.
138. Ibid., 20 February, 1863.
139. *Manchester Courier,* 12 September 1863, 4 January 1865; *Manchester Examiner and
Times,* 5 November 1864.
140. *Manchester Guardian,* 25 April 1865.

A sheet was circulated by the association to make absolutely clear to friends and enemies alike that there was no room for doubts about emancipation. Headed "STOP THE WAR," it made two precise statements: "STOP THE WAR DOES *NOT* MEAN BONDAGE TO THE BLACK" and "STOP THE WAR DOES MEAN JUSTICE TO THE SLAVE." The concluding section declared:

> STOP THIS WAR.
> GIVE PEACE TO AMERICA.
> GIVE FREEDOM TO THE SLAVE.
> GIVE PROSPERITY TO LANCASHIRE.[141]

An official association pamphlet condemned Lincoln's Emancipation Proclamation as an insincere and murderous "war measure," agreeing with Lincoln's confidence to Wendell Phillips "that the greatest folly of his life was the issuing of the Emancipation Proclamation." [142] Another was designed to quell any uneasiness that might exist about the organization's attitude to slavery:

> We regard slavery as repugnant alike to the reason and the sentiments of the present age; we believe it to be highly prejudicial to the real interests of the South; we deprecate the system and desire its removal not in passion or vindictiveness, but by calm and direct provisions, so that the momentous change in the condition of four millions of people may not lead to anarchy and ruin, but result in benefit to all classes of the community. We have no faith in the slaughtering of white men as means of benefiting those of another colour. We hold that the independence of the South is the true and sure means of extinguishing slavery.[143]

The North was denounced for its inhuman and inegalitarian treatment of Negroes. The failure of the Republican party to act against discriminatory state laws was here interpreted as symbolic of a lack of any real determination to abolish slavery in a North which at present massacred those it claimed to save.[144]

Pamphlets by individual Mancunians reflected the official view. Thomas Bently Kershaw, James Paul Cobbett, and C. A. Duval de-

141. Loose sheet in American Pamphlet Collection in Manchester Central Library.

142. *The Principles and Policy of President Lincoln,* Papers for the People, no. 5 (Manchester, 186?), pp. 1–4.

143. *Notes on Slavery, Especially in Relation to the American Question,* Papers for the People, no. 6 (Manchester, 186?), pp. 1, 4.

144. *The Negro in the North,* Papers for the People, no. 8 (January 1864), pp. 2–4.

nounced Lincoln's proclamation as an ineffectual war measure, condemning with abhorrence mistreatment of the Negro in the North, and placed their faith in gradual emancipation by an independent South.[145]

Meetings to propound the pro-Southern viewpoint were not numerous and possibly not necessary in the light of the Union and Emancipation Society's avowed aim of converting the mass of Manchester men from agreement with what they supposed to be the Southern attitude to emancipation. Of those that were held, one of the most successful, and certainly the most exuberant, took place in the Corn Exchange on 5 June 1863. Joseph Barker delivered the second of two well-applauded lectures on the mistreatment of Negroes by the North and a great majority of the large audience gave a vote of confidence in the South and cheered Jefferson Davis.[146] It is interesting to note that, in July, George Thompson and the Union and Emancipation Society as a whole refused to face Joseph Barker in an open debate.[147] This certainly seems to indicate that the Southern partisans felt more confident of their reception in the city than those of the North.

A meeting was held in October 1863 which marked the beginning of the Manchester Southern Independence Association. Before this there had been two separate bodies known as the Manchester Southern Club and the Association for the Recognition of the Southern States. The amalgamation provided an occasion for the airing of the antislavery convictions of those dedicated to the Southern cause. The comparative lack of propaganda on the Southern side was referred to with some pride, but anxiety was felt about the possibility of acceptance of erroneous Northern claims that Southern supporters were pro-slavery. The real supporters of slavery were thought to be based in the Northern states themselves, not in the Southern Clubs of Manchester or even within the boundaries of the South. A "well-digested scheme of emancipation" was anticipated from an independent Confederacy.[148]

145. Kershaw, *The American Question*, pp. 15, 17, 25, 28, 32. J. P. Cobbett, *The Civil War*, pp. 4–5; C. A. Duval, *Is Slavery Conducive to the Civilization of Races?* (Manchester 186?), pp. 6–7. C. A. Duval was born in Beaumaris, Anglesey, in 1808, but he had long been resident in Manchester.
146. *Manchester Courier*, 6 June 1863.
147. *Bury Guardian*, 18 July 1863.
148. *Manchester Courier*, 10 October 1863; *Manchester Guardian*, 9 January 1864.

The predominant note in Manchester was not, as so often has been imagined, one of faithful approval of Northern policy. This was a myth propagated by a few carefully arranged and well publicized meetings and furthered by a select number of prominent men, who formed the hard core of the Manchester Union and Emancipation Society. No such publicity greeted the birth of the Manchester Southern Club and other similar organizations. Their efforts were less strenuous but more genuinely successful. They shared an asset common to most successful public movements—a populace already predisposed to accept the validity of their arguments.

LIVERPOOL

Liverpool did conform a little more closely to its conventional image as a "Southern" city. There was an undoubted solid amount of support for the South which, as in Manchester, was based on the supposition that secession would benefit Negroes far more than victory by the North. In some cases this must have been the result of conscious or subconscious rationalization of instincts created by the basic material need for cotton, but in many instances conviction overrode material considerations and the South was supported in the face of financial loss. Merchants such as James Spence had multiple business interests in the North, and these were deliberately sabotaged when the arguments for the Southern case seemed too strong to allow in conscience any course other than that of sympathy with the South. This "image" of Liverpool is not, however, totally accurate. There was a greater degree of backing for the North there than perhaps has been realized. The motives behind this backing were also often materialistic in origin in that more than a few merchants made their fortunes out of the high prices artificially created by the war, and many sold cotton to the New York merchants who could afford to pay these exorbitant sums. It was commonly believed in Liverpool that the South would ultimately win the war, so that any move that might encourage the North was partly intended to prolong the war and the era of swift fortunes. Expressions of sympathy with the emancipation policy of the North were intended to give the Northern side essential moral stimulus and support.

Such support was only very rarely expressed through the editorial columns of the city's newspapers. The *Liverpool Daily Post,* considered the

most pro-Northern local newspaper, made no more than a few inter-
mittent gestures of approval for the North's emancipation policy during
the course of the war; the fierce individuality of J. M. Whitty seemed to
preclude any blind loyalty to either side.[149] No other major Liverpool
newspaper gave the North any substantial backing after the first doubtful
months when sides were being taken and prejudices hardened. Only the
Liverpool Mercury could also, on two lone occasions, grudgingly recognize
the humanity behind Lincoln's commitment to abolition.[150]

Far more backing for Northern policy over emancipation was provided by lecturers than by the press. The Union and Emancipation
Society was determined to demonstrate its power in Liverpool as well as
in the rest of Lancashire, and convinced Northern adherents travelled to
the Southern stronghold in an attempt to convert the heretics. Clergymen
in particular were eager to show their faith in Lincoln. Several meetings
were planned only as demonstrations of strength and were actually
warned that attenders were expected to be unquestioning supporters of
Lincoln. The *Albion* was most scathing about such meetings and dismissed
them as less than worthless as indications of public opinion. Any meeting
where dissent was inadmissible and would result in bodily removal from
the room was seen as nothing but a hollow sham.[151]

The Northern campaign began on 17 January 1863 with a small
conference that passed a resolution to inform Lincoln of the gathering's
approval of his policy and that established a committee to instruct the
public, through lectures and discussions, in the virtues of Northern emancipation.[152] The *Mail* was amused by this attempt to educate a public
which would most surely remain unconverted, adding that a cause which
found it necessary to hire its advocates had little genuine appeal.[153]

W. G. Langdon, a former calico printer from Glasgow, was one of
the most determined and constant speakers for the North in Liverpool.
On several occasions in January 1863, he praised Lincoln's courage in

149. *Liverpool Daily Post,* 28 January 1863; 9 October 1862, 11 February 1863, 20 January 1864.
150. *Liverpool Weekly Mercury,* 11 October 1862, 7 February 1863.
151. *Albion,* 2 February 1863.
152. *Liverpool Daily Post,* 19 January 1863; *Albion,* 19 January 1863; *Weekly Express,* 24
January 1863; *Liverpool Weekly Mercury,* 17 January 1863.
153. *Liverpool Mail,* 24 January 1863.

proclaiming emancipation. Langdon's meetings were among the few "open" gatherings. A more cynical view of the American leader was put forward on 17 January by a Liverpool man, William Lendrum, who accused Lincoln of using slavery and emancipation as tools for power, and a workingman, Mr. Dicks, was outraged by the notion that the opinions of the operatives could ever favor Lincoln's unfair scheme.[154]

John Patterson, who had been a constant supporter at Langdon's lectures, displayed in his own lectures an admiration for the North and its abolition plans that may have been influenced by the fact that he was a corn dealer dependent on trade with the North. At one lecture his suggestion that Liverpool be educated in the merits of the North was greeted with derisive hooting. Nevertheless a motion supporting Federal abolition narrowly and, it was said, doubtfully, defeated an amendment denouncing Northern emancipation and forecasting emancipation in the South.[155]

Only at these few meetings was disagreement with the Northern view of emancipation tolerated. Dissentients were usually excluded or, once in a meeting, were speedily silenced. At a meeting of three to four thousand persons the Reverend Hugh Stowell Brown, an evangelical minister, attempted to crush pro-Southern heckling by reading the advertisement covering the meeting.

> . . . of persons in favour of adopting an address to President Lincoln. . . . Every man Jack of them had come there either to approve of that address or to make an ass of himself (loud laughter and much confusion).

It was at this precise point that a motion to approve an address of support for Lincoln and his emancipation policy was put amidst total chaos, and was said to be carried. The ludicrous nature of the proceedings was attacked by the *Albion,* the *Mail* and the *Manchester Courier.* Invitations to the meeting had been extended only to known Lincoln sympathizers, and most Liverpudlians would in any case be disinclined to attend. Those Southerners that did go were certainly not allowed a fair hearing and had to content themselves with their protests and cries of "Cut it short—the

154. *Liverpool Daily Post,* 22, 24, 29 January 1863; see also *Liverpool Weekly Mercury,* 24, 31 January 1863.

155. *Liverpool Daily Post,* 12 February 1863; *Liverpool Weekly Mercury,* 14 February 1863.

Alabama is coming!" The *Albion* claimed that no Northern supporter would dare ask a Liverpool crowd to vote fairly on emancipation.[156]

When, during the same week, the Reverend Brown introduced C. W. Denison to a Liverpool audience, he acknowledged that there were great differences of opinion over emancipation but recommended that the gifts brought by the *George Griswold* be kept in mind.[157] A more blatant appeal to pocket or stomach was rarely made throughout the war.

In the autumn of 1863 the Reverend William Channing gave two lectures on the Northern desire for a free as well as united America and was attacked by the Liverpool Baptist, Joseph Stoner.[158] In October, Henry Ward Beecher trod gently over the acknowledged Southern predilections of his audience but insisted, over vociferous opposition, that the North fought for abolition. When Beecher had returned to the North, the *Albion* cited approvingly his admission that the sympathy of all classes was with the South.[159]

At a complimentary breakfast given in the Adelphi Hotel on 22 January 1864 for George Thompson before his departure for America, Thompson himself declared that slavery had been mortally wounded, and a pro-North resolution was successfully proposed.[160] No doubt the fact that a farewell breakfast was held in Liverpool for Thompson had more to do with the circumstance that he sailed from that port than with the strength of Northern sympathy there. Nevertheless the occasion still helped to demonstrate that there was in Liverpool a tiny core of people dedicated to the cause of the North.

The paucity of the numbers of such supporters was borne out by one of Liverpool's most ardent Northern enthusiasts, John Cropper. Cropper was present at almost all the meetings held to gather sympathy for the North, and he was part of a deputation formed by the committee of the English and Foreign Anti-Slavery Society which had an interview with Charles Adams in London on 3 February 1863. On this occasion Cropper

156. *Liverpool Daily Post,* 20 February 1863; *Liverpool Weekly Mercury,* 21 February 1863; *Albion,* 23 February 1863; *Liverpool Mail,* 21 February 1863; *Manchester Courier,* 21 February 1863.

157. *Liverpool Daily Post,* 17 February 1863.

158. Ibid., 16, 18 September 1863.

159. Ibid., 17 October 1863; *Albion,* 19 October, 14 December 1863; *Liverpool Weekly Mercury,* 17 October 1863.

160. *Liverpool Daily Post,* 23 January 1864.

wryly commented that "Liverpool had stood rather prominently forward—he might almost say in secession"—he could only bear witness to
the accepted verdict that Liverpool was basically a Southern city.[161]

The Liverpool press was certainly loud in its criticism of Northern
policy. The Northern view of Southern blacks was consistently painted by
the *Post* in a cynically unflattering light that well reflected the views of the
Albion and *Liverpool Mail:*

> The Yankees have always regarded with something more than dis-
> like the negroes of the Southern States. To some extent they encour-
> aged fugitive slaves, not because of sympathy with them, but be-
> cause of abhorrence of the slave-owner. The black was endured
> rather than welcomed, while any approach in thought to equality
> was regarded as a kind of moral and social blasphemy. Now, how-
> ever, the abhorrence of colour has greatly subsided. The slave pre-
> sents himself as an instrument for the subjugation of the enemy.

Gore's General Advertiser, the *Post, Albion,* and *Mail* were continually disgusted that Negroes were not even held by the Northerners to be men at
all, and were "horribly" mistreated by them in the face of illusory freedom.[162]

Far more faith was deposited in hopes of indigenous Southern
emancipation. Early in the war the *Daily Post* was convinced that slavery,
partly because it was so uneconomic, would soon die a natural death.[163]
Gradual emancipation by a free South was forecast by the *Albion* in 1863,
and the *Mail* believed that the main hope of freedom for the Southern Negro lay in his willingness to fight for the Confederacy. The enrollment of
the Negro was predicted by the *Mail* in 1863 and by the *Albion* in 1864,
when it was anticipated he would fight with more heart than his 200,000
brothers in the Northern army; they also noted with pleasure abolitionist
sentiments in the Richmond press.[164] The actual enlistment in March

161. *Liverpool Mercury,* 5 February 1863; *Liverpool Weekly Mercury,* 7 February, 3 January 1863; *Albion,* 23 February, 14 December 1863.

162. *Liverpool Daily Post,* 25 June 1861, 28 July 1862, 2 January, 21 January 1862, 11
August 1862, 6 October 1863; *Gore's General Advertiser,* 7 August 1862; *Liverpool Mail,* 19
April, 13 September, 6 December 1862, 10, 17 January 1863, 1 April 1865; *Albion,* 2, 23 Feb-
ruary, 10 August 1863, 1 February 1864.

163. *Liverpool Daily Post,* 12 June 1861; 8, 21 March 1862.

164. *Albion,* 2 February 1863, 17 October 1864, 16 January 1865; *Liverpool Mail,* 12
September 1863, 18, 25 March 1865.

1865 was rapturously greeted, as was Jefferson Davis's regret that the Negro had not been armed sooner.[165]

James Spence was equally convinced that the way to true integrated emancipation was by giving the South its independence. A free South would be exposed to the force of European influence and would instigate its own system of gradual abolition. He was quite clear that "emancipation is impossible, except with consent of the people of the South." Neither he nor Thomas Ellison thought that Lincoln's proclamation in any way benefited the Negro or that Lincoln sincerely was trying to solve the problem of slavery. Thomas Ellison also believed that a system of gradual emancipation that would free all existing slaves, incorporating education and Christianization and total integration, was the only answer to the slavery question. He predicted that the race problem itself would disappear with the mingling of bloods.[166]

A Southern Baptist clergyman, Joshua R. Balme, who had settled in Liverpool, was violently against slavery. During the war he wrote a series of letters to the *Liverpool Mercury* and other journals and later published the letters as a pamphlet. He condemned the North for regarding the black as inferior to the white race; the plan for Liberia sprang from fear of close contact with blacks, and in the Northern states themselves "black laws" denied the freed slave elementary rights. The idea that the North was concerned with freedom he dismissed as a strange illusion, harbored only by Bright and his sympathizers.[167]

The successful Liverpool merchant and Conservative M. P., Thomas Horsfall, would seem to have accurately reflected the prevalent feeling in Liverpool when he told the local Chamber of Commerce that emancipation was irrelevant to the war and consequently no barrier to Southern recognition.[168] The Emancipation Proclamation was denounced as "odious" and "abominable" by Sir Robert Peel to a wildly cheering Liverpool audience at Fazely in January 1863.[169] The two meetings repre-

165. Ibid., 1 April 1865.

166. J. Spence, *American Union*, 4th ed., pp. 152, 159–65; idem, *Recognition*, p. 22; idem, *Southern Independence*, pp. 23–25, 28–29. T. Ellison, *Slavery and Secession*, 2d ed., pp. 254–5, 258, 265–9, 270.

167. J. R. Balme, *Letters*, pp. 4–6, 9–10, 13, 15, 17–18, 102.

168. *Albion*, 2 February 1863.

169. *Manchester Courier*, 31 January 1863.

sented very different sections of the city but were bound together by the stubborn mistrust of the North's attitude to abolition that seemed rampant in the city.

That the most common view in Liverpool held the Emancipation Proclamation to be of no real value to Negroes was borne out by T. H. Dudley. As U.S. consul to Liverpool he spoke mainly of that city when he made general judgments, and he reluctantly admitted that, while Bright recognized the sincerity of Northern abolitionism, "among his countrymen at that time he stood almost alone." [170] Faith was instead pinned on emancipation by the South which would free the Negro and integrate him into a white society. The contrast with the powerful efforts of the Northern sympathizers to gain support through carefully organized meetings provided a telling instance of the assurance of Southerners that Liverpool needed no conversion to the cause of the South. That the accent of the Liverpool Northerners was, to the end, so much on conversion was in itself a symptom of failure.

THE WEST

Only a few editors in the west of Lancashire rejected Northern emancipation as a fraud. A far higher proportion there than in any other region of the county believed in the value and integrity of Lincoln's abolition measures. Their interest was spasmodic and often lethargic but epitomized the extent and nature of the involvement of the area in the problem. The general detachment was such that there were no spontaneous meetings—only carefully arranged lectures by members of the Manchester Union and Emancipation Society.

The *Warrington Guardian* was among the many newspapers of this area that poured unstinted praise on the Emancipation Proclamation;[171] doubt about Lincoln's motives and the effectiveness of his edict was expressed in the press to a far lesser extent.[172] Although a couple of news-

170. T. H. Dudley, *Diplomatic Relations,* p. 7.

171. *Warrington Guardian,* 17 January 1863, 29 April 1865; *Lancaster Guardian,* 18 October 1862, 17 January 1863, 4 March, 22 April 1865; *Southport Independent,* 24 December 1862; *Fleetwood Chronicle,* 16 January 1863; *Leigh Chronicle,* 17 January 1863, 24 December 1864.

172. *Southport Independent,* 7 May 1863; *Lancaster Guardian,* 22 March 1862; *Soulby's Ulverston Advertiser,* 22, 29 January 1863; *Warrington Advertiser,* 17 January 1863; *Lancaster Gazette,* 7 February 1863; *Barrow Herald,* 26 December 1863.

papers wondered whether the Negro was not better off in the South than in the North, only one, the *Lancaster Guardian*, predicted Southern emancipation.[173]

The long arm of the Manchester Union and Emancipation Society stretched out frequently to these western towns. The effort seemed worthwhile, as the society's lectures met with a warm response. In the summer of 1863 Peter Sinclair and W. A. Jackson stimulated the unanimous passage of an anti-Southern motion at Southport, and at Leigh made it clear that support of the South meant support of slavery, while Lincoln was the savior of Negroes.[174] Warrington in 1864 gave E. O. Greening and Mason Jones the impression that the town was favorably predisposed to their defense of Lincoln's proclamation on moral and legal grounds.[175] In the west the meetings were coolly on the side of the North as the side of right. There was no need there to find arguments that would justify support of the South and emancipation simultaneously. There was no need there of rationalization.

Unlike the cotton manufacturing districts, Manchester, Liverpool, and the west presented no clear-cut view of emancipation. The west stood alone in all Lancashire in its basic faith in Northern abolition. Manchester and Liverpool divided their allegiance but in the last analysis would seem to have condemned Lincoln's Emancipation Proclamation as a useless act of war and pinned their faith on emancipation by a free South. It was rough but fitting justice that James Spence, who did most to convince others in both cities that this was a valid view, should lose his appointment as financial agent to the Confederacy because the South was not then ready for his proselytizing enthusiasm for emancipation. The Southerners may have pragmatically reconciled themselves to emancipation before the war drew to a close, but not as soon or as fully as their followers in the Lancashire cotton cities and towns would have liked.

173. *Soulby's Ulverston Advertiser*, 21 May, 19 November 1863; *Warrington Advertiser*, 30 January 1864; *Lancaster Guardian*, 14 March 1863.
174. *Southport Independent*, 23, 30 April 1863; *Leigh Chronicle*, 9 May 1863.
175. *Warrington Advertiser*, 13, 20, 27 February 1864.

4

THE NEGATIVE APPEAL OF NEUTRALITY

CHEER up a bit longer, mi brothers i' want,
There's breeter days for us i' store;
There'll be plenty o' tommy an' wark for us o,
When this 'Merica bother gets o'er.
Y'on struggled reet nobly, an' battled reet hard,
While things har bin lookin' so feaw; [1]
Y'on borne wi' yow troubles an trials so long,
It's no use o' givin up neaw.

SAMUEL LAYCOCK[2]

A mood of resignation, of pacific acquiescence in the suffering and hardship prompted by the American war is often assumed to have prevailed in
Lancashire throughout the course of the fratricidal struggle. The official
position of neutrality adopted by the British government at the start of
the war and maintained to its termination has generally been presumed
to have reflected the views of the mass of Lancastrians. But despite the tes-
timony of Bright and Cobden, the weight of the evidence can be seen to
swing heavily in favor of there being a far more general desire for some
form of partisan action on behalf of the South. A feeling for mediation or
arbitration by Britain, preferably as part of a joint Anglo-French effort,
was frequently overshadowed by a clear-cut demand for the recognition
of the South as an independent nation. The numbers of those who wished
Britain actually to get involved in the fighting were fewer but constituted
at times a force to be reckoned with. Those who wanted to break the
blockade were often aware that this course might well lead to open warfare, but considered the risk worth taking. Many in Lancashire advocated
all of these alternatives at different points of the war; the fact that none of
them were adopted as official British policy was far more the result of the
inability of most of the people in Lancashire to bring effective pressure to
bear upon the government than the existence of any massive backing for
neutrality. Support for noninterference there certainly was, but it was
small and insignificant when compared with the demand for a move to
aid the South. Bright was actually so worried about the lack of support
for the North and enthusiasm for neutrality that, with a flash of brilliance, he suggested to Sumner that the North should send cargoes of food

1. Foul, bad.
2. "Cheer up a Bit Longer," in Harland, *Ballads and Songs,* p. 500.

to Lancashire. This, He was convinced, "would cover with confusion all who talk against you."[3] It was no accident that almost all these resolutions demanding continued official neutrality were passed either in the presence of the Reverend Charles Wheeler Denison, chaplain of the provision ship *George Griswold,* or around the time when he was touring Lancashire acting as a catalyst for feelings of indebtedness to the North.

Expressions of neutrality in Lancashire were themselves often ambivalent in intention and implication. It was perhaps most frequently assumed that adherence to nonintervention demonstrated an intrinsic bias towards the North. This seemed a logical enough conclusion because the North was in no need of foreign interference on its behalf; it did not, like the South, need "recognizing" or to have a blockade of its coasts broken. The most notable supporters of the North such as Bright, Cobden, and Milner Gibson did in fact constantly urge neutrality, while such detachment was on the whole denounced by Southern sympathizers because it gave a negative kind of aid to the North. There were occasions, however, when supporters of the South themselves urged neutrality. These occasions were mainly meetings organized by Northern agents to enlist sympathy for the Northern cause. The Southern element frequently managed to obtain the passage of an amendment in favor of nonintervention over a motion praising the North. Detachment was also favored by Southern sympathizers who were deluded in imagining that the South was in no need of foreign aid but could win alone.[4] Nonalignment was more obviously sought by those who were basically isolationist and wished to remain firmly aloof from the turmoil across the Atlantic. Apathetic Southern sympathizers provided many of the rank and file of this group, and the government might well have been termed its unofficial leader.

THE NORTHEAST

The northeast cotton region showed an almost negligible interest in a neutrality which seemed only to delay the desperately needed renewal of the supply of Southern cotton. The only strong (though certainly not large) demonstration of a pro-Northern, anti-Southern feeling for neutrality came from the little town of Brierfield, near Burnley, in June 1863. A

3. John Bright, *Diaries,* p. 264.
4. James Williams, former U.S. ambassador to Turkey, claimed that to earn self-respect the South needed to be self-reliant and win unaided; see James Williams, *The South Vindicated* (London, 1862), p. 432.

small meeting there passed a resolution condemning attempts at Southern recognition, and a petition incorporating this decision was sent to the Marquis of Hartington for presentation to the Commons.[5] Burnley itself sent three petitions against the recognition of the Confederacy to the Commons in the summer of 1863.[6]

More deviously in favor of nonintervention was a meeting summoned in Blackburn to pay homage to the crew of the *George Griswold,* on 18 March 1863. One of the several resolutions there, stimulated by the Northern gifts, deprecated aid given to the South and recommended approval of nonintervention.[7] The *Preston Chronicle* was angered by such manipulation of the gratitude of starving operatives and attacked the Blackburn meeting for fostering hypocrisy.[8]

At least two meetings in April, at Burnley and Rawtenstall, reflected the efforts of tried Northern campaigners, such as Peter Sinclair, to secure a vote of confidence in the North. Instead the meetings voted for neutrality amendments, with a Southern bias, proposed by William Cunliffe, a local cotton operative. Burnley declared:

> That this meeting, while it deplores the civil war now raging in America, and its attendant evils, does consider as unwarrantable and unjust, and as a breach of strict neutrality, any public demonstration of sympathy with either of the contending factions in this war, and that this meeting especially views with indignation, the attempt of Northern agencies to interfere with the very sentiments and judgement of the people of England.[9]

Equally abysmal failure to rally support was met by the Northern agents in Bacup a few weeks later. Protest votes for neutrality were again registered.[10] This was not a surprising outcome for a meeting held in a town which was in the same month denounced bitterly by the *Bury Times* as dangerous for any but a Southern supporter![11]

A keen desire to remain utterly detached from the conflict was rare in this area. Its strongest expression came from W. Singleton, a Preston

5. *Burnley Advertiser,* 27 June 1863.
6. "Report of the Select Committee on Public Petitions," Session 1863, p. 893.
7. *Blackburn Standard,* 25 March 1863.
8. *Preston Chronicle,* 28 March 1863.
9. *Burnley Free Press,* 11 April 1863; *Manchester Courier,* 18 April 1863.
10. *Preston Guardian,* 2 May 1863.
11. *Bury Times,* 16 May 1863.

wheelwright and provision dealer, who protested to the *Preston Guardian* in July 1862 against the prevailing feeling for mediation and recognition. He claimed that nothing, certainly not cotton, would be gained and much would be lost, including grain and Northern friendship, by abandoning neutrality.[12]

The press warily began by approving the official policy of neutrality; when 1862 heralded the rapid increase in distress, more actively pro-Southern policies were preferred.[13] Only the *Burnley Free Press* had a word of approval for nonintervention as late as January 1863 but muffled its effect by simultaneously predicting that recognition might well soon become necessary.[14] Support for neutrality was tepid and certainly never the preferred course of any but the most tiny minority.

THE SOUTHEAST

The spinning towns were more seriously interested in neutrality. The slow growth of distress in many towns made any more dramatic stand seem initially unnecessary. Even when the need for cotton grew urgent, nonintervention was for some still impregnated with a lingering appeal. This appeal was largely confined to the towns least impoverished by the cotton famine. Ashton and Oldham, with their high consumption of cotton for their coarse thread, and their consequent destitution, had a marked lack of rapport with neutrality or the North. Bolton and Bury, which spun fine counts of cotton needing less raw material, were less distressed and at times opted for noninterference. Rochdale, with its unique combination of numerous woolen mills and the persuasive oratory and leadership of Cobden and Bright, was alone in having more apparent adherents of neutrality than of pro-Southern action.

Cobden and Bright set the mood for neutrality in Rochdale when they addressed a large meeting there in June 1861. Cobden alluded to his and Bright's reputation as "the two members for the United States" and, admitting their admiration for the American system, pleaded for nonintervention during "the lamentable strife." [15] An October editorial of the

12. *Preston Guardian*, 26 July 1862.
13. *Blackburn Standard*, 28 August 1861, *Preston Pilot*, 17 August 1861; *Preston Mercury*, 2 November, 14 September 1861; *Preston Guardian*, 28 October 1861, 5 January 1862.
14. *Burnley Free Press*, 31 January 1863. Recognition was later approved.
15. *Rochdale Spectator*, 29 June 1861.

Rochdale Observer echoed the advice not to intervene or break the blockade, however exhausted cotton supplies might become.[16]

All neutral feelings were severely tested by the seizure of the Confederate agents Mason and Slidell off the British ship *Trent,* but Richard Cobden warned a meeting in Rochdale, through a letter read in his absence, that "any act of intervention on the part of a European power, whether by breaking the blockade, or a premature acknowledgement of the independence of the South, or in any other way, can have no other effect but to aggravate and protract the quarrel." John Bright, in his turn, strongly cautioned his listeners: "Don't let your newspapers or your public speakers, or any man, take you off your guard, and bring you into that frame of mind under which your Government, if it desires war, can have it with the public assent, or if it does not desire war, may be driven to engage in it; for one may be as fatal and as evil as the other." [17] Bright made a well-tuned appeal for neutrality at a relief meeting in Rochdale in January 1862 when he optimistically forecast that, if no foreign interference took place, the war in America would be settled in six months.[18] The *Rochdale Observer* loyally used the same reasoning to show that interference would not be likely to keep Southern cotton out of the market indefinitely.[19]

Late in 1861 George Thompson had emphasized the importance of continued neutrality to a receptive audience.[20] A crowded meeting in February 1863, convened to thank the North for the provisions shipped in the *George Griswold,* was again advised by John Bright on the merits of nonintervention.[21] Such continuous persuasion was not totally superfluous even in Rochdale. When Cobden and Bright, in November 1863, reiterated that neutrality must be adhered to, a few among the assembled crowd were in vocal disagreement.[22] The *Rochdale Pilot* had as early as June 1861 doubted the value of neutrality.[23] However, there seems little doubt that a

16. *Rochdale Observer,* 26 October 1861.
17. *Rochdale Spectator,* 7 December 1861.
18. *Blackburn Standard,* 15 January 1862.
19. *Rochdale Observer,* 3 May 1862.
20. *Rochdale Spectator,* 2 November 1861.
21. Ibid, 7 February 1863.
22. Ibid, 28 November 1863.
23. *Rochdale Pilot,* 8 June 1861.

majority in Rochdale was persistent in its faith in nonintervention, and Bright could fairly be said to still speak for his home town as well as his constituents when he pleaded for unflagging neutrality in Parliament in 1864.[24] Ernest Jones was in equal accord with his cheering Rochdale audience when, on 7 March 1864, he preached against Southern recognition.[25] Certainly no doubt remained when, in November 1864, an open-air meeting of operatives passed a resolution giving complete support to absolute noninterference.[26] This was far more decisive than the petition presented by Cobden in mid-1863 against recognition, which was signed by only sixty inhabitants.[27]

Early in the war, the press in other towns commended the British proclamation of May 1861 for taking a reasonably neutral position.[28] But only the *Bury Times,* with hesitant and occasional agreement from the *Ashton and Stalybridge Reporter,* maintained until 1863 that neutrality was the best means of passively aiding the North and thwarting the South.[29]

Bolton generally was mildly responsive to the idea of neutrality. A sizeable meeting narrowly voted for neutrality and against mediation after an address by W. A. Jackson in June 1863, despite the protests of several workingmen. Peter Sinclair, during the same month, tautly linked the cause of the North with that of nonintervention but did not hazard a vote.[30] Hardly indicative of real feelings, but not to be ignored, was the approval for neutrality elicited by the Reverend Denison as he passed through Bolton on his gratitude-evoking tour of the county. Local scorn was afterwards, however, poured on the chaplain of the *George Griswold* and his admirers for the essentially prejudiced neutrality they sought to stimulate.[31]

A similar speech drew a parallel response at Bury, which was an unfruitful haunt of the most biased pro-Northern advocates of neutrality, in-

24. *Hansard Parliamentary Debates,* 3d ser., vol. 113,1 (1864), p. 1924.

25. Ernest Jones, *Oration on the American Rebellion* (Rochdale, 1864) p. 15.

26. *Rochdale Spectator,* 19 November 1864.

27. "Report of the Select Committee on Public Petitions," 1863, p. 893.

28. *Wigan Observer,* 18 May 1861; *Bolton Chronicle,* 22 June 1861; *Ashton and Stalybridge Reporter,* 6 July 1861.

29. *Bury Times,* 16 May, 19 August, 24 October 1863, 2 July 1864; *Ashton and Stalybridge Reporter,* 19 July, 16 August, 27 December 1862.

30. *Bolton Chronicle,* 20 June 1863.

31. Ibid., 4 April, 16 May 1863.

cluding paid Northern agents such as Peter Sinclair, Henry Vincent, and Mason Jones.[32] These were preceded by a far less partisan supporter of nonintervention in the shape of the celebrated Baptist preacher from Southwark, the Reverend C. H. Spurgeon. In December 1861 Spurgeon, preaching at the Bury Tabernacle Chapel, stressed the undesirability of war with America.[33] The only other approving mention of neutrality in Bury came from the local M.P., Frederick Peel, who affirmed late in the war that the best policy was the official one of neutrality, while making no secret of his own Southern predilections.[34]

Even Ashton was not spared the efforts of pro-Northern noninterventionists. But George Thompson, Ernest Jones, and Dr. Massie were all frigidly received and Milner Gibson's annual speeches championing the North and neutrality provoked increasingly intense opposition.[35]

Elsewhere neutrality was dismissed as too obviously favoring the North. The *Wigan Observer* made a typical appeal for an attitude less slanted than the existing "craven and false doctrine of neutrality," which did not even satisfy the Northern states and was abhorrent to those whose livelihoods were entwined with cotton spinning.[36]

MANCHESTER

In the cotton center, neutrality was the course automatically espoused by the influential group of merchants and philanthropists who sought to encourage the North and to help destroy the South. One of the most vital aims of the Manchester Union and Emancipation Society was to convince all levels of society of the desirability of nonintervention. As J. Estcourt pointed out in a letter to H. J. Wilson:

Our agitating time was from 1862 to the Spring of 1864, by which date Parliament and people had felt the power of its organisation and the tide and the stream had flowed in favour of non-intervention and non-recognition of the proposed slave empire. There is

32. *Bury Times,* 4 April 1863; *Bury Guardian,* 21 November 1863, 5 March, 30 April 1864; *Bury Times,* 30 April 1864.

33. *Bury Free Press,* 12 December 1861.

34. *Bury Guardian,* 16 January 1864, 28 January 1865.

35. *Ashton and Stalybridge Reporter,* 15 January, 22 February 1862; Ernest Jones, *The Slaveholder's War* (Ashton, 1863); *Ashton Standard,* 23 January, 1 October 1864, 21 January 1865.

36. *Wigan Observer,* 31 July 1863.

now no danger of any changes and we rest—watching and waiting.—
Keeping up by circulation of sound literature and through the press,
the main facts and issues of the struggle.[37]

Certainly by this time the society had created the illusion that at least
Manchester was solidly behind the North and in favor of neutrality. Vast
numbers of pamphlets and carefully arranged and organized meetings
bore witness to this apparent fact. It is difficult to determine how much
truth there was behind the facade, but the existence of a far more substantial, if less publicized, campaign for a move to help the South would
seem to give it the lie.

R. A. Arnold was one of those who through personal conviction
helped perpetuate the myth of a Manchester and indeed a Lancashire almost solidly against any form of intervention. When he said that "few
were the voices raised for an armed interference in America, which
though it might have curtailed the profits of many of the rich, would certainly have given work and food to many of the poor," [38] he was fairly accurate. But he ignored the vast numbers who wanted milder forms of intervention such as mediation or recognition of the South.

John Watts similarly supported both the North and neutrality and
insisted that many felt as he did.[39] At a public meeting in the Free Trade
Hall in 1863 he claimed that nothing would be gained and much lost financially through intervention. Samuel Pole, a barrister and vice-president of the Union and Emancipation Society, successfully moved a resolution condemning all aid to the Confederates.[40] The visit of the *George
Griswold* occasioned a public meeting in the Free Trade Hall on the 24
February 1863 to thank the captain and his men for bringing needed provisions to the Lancashire operatives. No doubt affected by this generosity,
the meeting passed a resolution pledging its gratitude and asserting its allegiance to the principle of neutrality.[41]

Manchester greeted Henry Ward Beecher with skeptical interest;
6,000 people attended a lecture on 9 October 1863 at which he pleaded

37. Estcourt to Wilson, 31 January 1865, Rawson Collection, English Mss. 741, John
Rylands Library, Manchester.

38. Arnold, *Cotton Famine*, pp. 76, 216, 306.

39. Watts, *Facts*, p. 123.

40. *War Ships For The Southern Confederacy*, Report of Public Meeting in the Free
Trade Hall, Manchester (Manchester 1863).

41. *Manchester Courier*, 25 February 1863.

strongly for neutrality. No vote was taken, but even the presence of such a large and passive audience to hear his well-known views must have reflected some degree of approval.[42] On 1 February 1864, a "Conversazione" was held in the Manchester Atheneum to hear Dr. Massie report on his mission to the American churches. John Watts here again issued his personal warning against any kind of pro-Southern intervention.[43]

In an address read to the final meeting of the Manchester Union and Emancipation Society in 1865, Goldwin Smith threw new light upon the activity of the society when he stated that its constant aim was to ensure the triumph of neutrality and the failure of any form of intervention that might have ridden on the tide of Southern sympathy.[44] The fulfillment of this aim was possibly aided by the picture it presented of a quiescent Lancashire backing the government in the attitudes it wished and intended to maintain.

Almost all the pamphlets supporting neutrality were written and published by the Union and Emancipation Society; any others were the work of confirmed Northern advocates. The chairman, J. Estcourt, in a pamphlet in 1863, produced a clear-cut attack on recognition. Those who wished to aid the South he condemned as mistaken: "NON-RECOGNITION OF THE SLAVE POWER, NON-INTERVENTION IN THE AMERICAN WAR, AND NEUTRALITY ARE AND WILL BE THE SAFEGUARDS OF THE PEACE, COMFORT, AND TRUE DIGNITY OF A FREE, CIVILIZED, AND CHRISTIAN NATION." [45]

Pamphlets by W. E. Forster, F. W. Newman, Samuel Pope, and Goldwin Smith deplored the idea of any kind of pro-Southern intervention, while an attack on Lord Russell for favoring the South and imperilling neutrality was made by the executive of the Union and Emancipation Society itself.[46]

Only the *Manchester Examiner and Times* displayed much predilection for nonintervention to safeguard the time-worn link between England

42. Henry Ward Beecher, *American Rebellion*, p. 11; *Manchester Courier* 24 October 1863.
43. Union and Emancipation Society, *Report of the Proceedings of a Conversazione*, pp. 18–19.
44. Smith, *The Civil War*, p. 74.
45. Estcourt, *Rebellion and Recognition*, p. 28.
46. W. E. Forster, *Rebellion*, pp. 6, 7, 9; F. W. Newman *The Southern States*, pp. 12, 14; Samuel Pope, *The American War*, p. 4; Goldwin Smith, *England And America*, p. iv; *The Negro*, p. 16; Executive of the Union and Emancipation Society, *Russell*, pp. 5, 7, 8, 9, 10, 11.

and the United States.[47] The *Manchester Courier* and the *Manchester Guardian* at times argued for passivity while explicitly retaining their Southern sympathy and often assuming that the Confederacy was in no need of aid.[48]

The press reflected the two kinds of neutrality that ran through Manchester, with the stronger, pro-Northern element overshadowing that which passively favored the South. Much of the strength of the neutral school lay in the backing of the professional families with strong Liberal traditions, such as the Hopkinsons.[49] These families followed the lead of the allies of Cobden and Bright who formed the core of the Union and Emancipation Society. But such support of neutrality found it hard to match the appeal of the various forms of active Southern agitation.

LIVERPOOL

Pockets of sympathy for neutrality did exist in Liverpool but they were mainly built around the belief that the South was inviolable. This was particularly marked in the reaction of the local press, especially the *Mail* and the *Mercury,* which tended to favor nonintervention only when the future of the South seemed secure—aid was then judged unnecessary and impolitic.[50] The *Liverpool Daily Post* never suffered under delusions of Southern invincibility and followed the military progress of the war with a keen eye. Whenever the North seemed likely to win and so bring hostilities to an end, neutrality was urged.[51] The *Albion* was less pragmatic, abandoning an early liaison with the idea of neutrality for a singular loyalty to active aid for the South.[52]

Few individuals in Liverpool expressed any faith in neutrality. One of those few was the wealthy shipowner George Melly, who was appalled at the breach of neutrality he saw in English ship-building for the Con-

47. *Manchester Examiner And Times,* 7 January, 10 March, 21 April 1863; *Manchester Weekly Times,* 29 August 1863.

48. *Manchester Courier,* 5 July 1862, 3 January, 6 June 1863; 1 January 1864; *Manchester Guardian,* 20 February, 4, 15 July 1863.

49. Katherine Chorley, *Manchester Made Them* (London, 1951) p. 235.

50. *Liverpool Mail,* 26 April, 3 May 1862; 9 May, 10 October 1863; 18 March 1865; *Liverpool Weekly Mercury,* 29 June 1861, 11 January, 25 January, 8 February 1862, 5 February, 21 June, 2 July 1863.

51. *Liverpool Daily Post,* 25 April 1862; 16 June, 24 July, 15 November 1861; 26 March, 25 June 1862; 24 April, 28 May 1863; 19 May 1864.

52. *Albion,* 13 May 1861.

federacy. In a letter of 14 April 1863 to H. Romilly, Melly said he was pleased that

> the Minister seems to be waking up from this long and rather stupid sleep on the subject of Confederate Ships of War, manned with British sailors, armed with British guns and decoying their victims with the British flag.[53]

The Rathbones, who traded almost exclusively with the Union, were also firmly behind the neutrality that passively aided the Federal cause.[54]

The Liverpool Chamber of Commerce tended to support the South in its public pronouncements but was always circumspect. The nearest any of its members came to public approval of neutrality was when the senior M. P. for the city, J. C. Ewart, advised against intervention at the annual meetings in early 1862 and 1863; in typical Liverpool fashion he accompanied this advice with the hope that the North would allow the South its independence.[55]

There was a marked absence of lectures or meetings in Liverpool specifically in support of neutrality, although there were several held to demonstrate solidarity for the Northern attitude to emancipation. At one such lecture, given by W. G. Langdon, a member of the audience, William Lendrum, argued that such partisan backing for Lincoln and the North was in itself a breach of the perfect neutrality that was "England's true and proper position."[56] T. M. Mackay similarly urged neutrality even if it should alienate and anger the North.[57]

Only the American preacher William Channing made a plea for neutrality that emphasized an approval of the Northern cause. His speech in 1861 wanted both noninterference and moral backing for the North.[58] He set a precedent that was to be ignored.

53. George Melly, private correspondence, 1863, vol. 6, 1470, Liverpool Public library.

54. Rathbone papers, University of Liverpool Library; Sheila Marriner, "Rathbone's Trading Activities in the Middle of the Nineteenth Century," *Transactions of the Historic Society of Lancashire and Cheshire* 108 (1956): 105–27.

55. *Liverpool Weekly Mercury,* 8 February 1862; *Liverpool Mercury,* 27 January 1863; *Albion,* 2 February 1863.

56. *Liverpool Weekly Mercury,* 24 January 1863; see also *Liverpool Daily Post,* 22 January 1863.

57. *Liverpool Daily Post,* 22 November 1861.

58. William H. Channing, *The Civil War In America* (Manchester, 1861?), pp. 97–99.

Despite the lack of open preference for neutrality in Liverpool, the fluctuations of the cotton market and the fortunes made because of the short supply occasioned by the war, must surely have influenced some of the cotton traders to hope for continued nonintervention. Any move which might have foreshortened the war would have speedily curtailed the enormous profits. The cotton circulars of George Holt, of Hall and Mellor, and of R. C. Hall show clearly how the slightest change of fortune in the war or rumor of intervention caused rapid alterations in the price of cotton on the market.[59] On July 19 1861 George Holt's circular noted that: "The most striking feature in the business of the week, and we think we may say without precedent in our market on anything approaching a large scale, is an export demand for Cotton to America." [60] Those who exported cotton to the North could hardly wish for intervention on behalf of the South. R. Charlton Hall was only one of those who made vast profits exporting to the North and who supported Lincoln and his emancipation schemes. The possibility of war between Britain and America over the *Trent* affair caused an immediate depression on the market! [61] "X.Y.X." used tables and statistics in a letter to the *Daily Post* on 2 December to prove that the interests of the cotton traders would be best served by peace and neutrality, and he was happy to predict that these would prevail.[62] However, the large stocks of cotton were inevitably reduced as the years went on, and the numbers who could successfully play the speculative game grew less. Neutrality, which always had a limited appeal in Liverpool, must have lost even that. The little preference there was for noninterference sprang mainly from the belief that the South could win by herself and indeed, as ex-governor Ross of Delaware made clear on his visit to Liverpool during the war, needed to win by her own efforts.[63]

59. *George Holt & Co's Cotton Circular,* 26 April, 10, 24 May, 5, 19 July, 9 August, 6 September, 25 October, 22, 29 November, 27 December 1861; 7 March, 17 April, 2, 23, 30 May, 13 June, 4 July, 19 September, 3, 10 October, 19 December 1862; *Cotton Circulars 1860–64 R. C. Hall and Mellor,* 31 December 1860, 25 January 1861, 25 April, 3 May, 1 August 1862, 16 January, 22 May, 12, 24 June, 31 July, 2 October 1863; *The Liverpool Cotton Brokers' Association Weekly Circular,* ed. R. C. Hall, 9 September, 25 November, 2 December 1864.
60. *George Holt & Co's Cotton Circular,* 19 July 1861.
61. Ibid., 29 November 1861.
62. *Liverpool Daily Post,* 2 December 1861, 22 May 1862; see also all cotton circulars quoted for 1860–64.
63. Dudley, *Diplomatic Relations,* p. 15.

THE WEST

The uninvolved west saw more clearly than any region in Lancashire, except Rochdale, that the only sane course for Britain to take was one of detachment. This was to be expected from an area where cotton was not a prerequisite for survival—an area which stood to lose men and money in a war which could only provide cotton in return. Neutrality provided an almost magnetic attraction for the local press. Newspapers which favored the South joined Northern supporters in recommending noninterference.[64] At the end of 1861 the deepest concern with neutrality, or indeed with the war, was displayed by the pro-Southern *Lancaster Guardian.* Its determined detachment harbored no illusions about the broad motives behind nonintervention, in which the interests of Lancashire played no part.[65] Roebuck's attempt to gain approval for recognition was condemned as impolitic and ill-timed, but Bright's contention that the mass of English people would welcome a Federal victory was fiercely denied.[66] Other newspapers with Southern sympathies were only slightly ess tenacious in their approval of neutrality. *Soulby's Ulverston Advertiser,* he *Ulverston Mirror,* and the *Warrington Advertiser* agreed that it was in Britain's best interests to stand aloof from the war, neither mediating nor recognizing the South.[67]

Seasoned speakers for the North found the west fertile ground for sowing seeds of neutrality. Meetings were never addressed by local lecturers, but travellers from the Manchester Union and Emancipation Society met with audiences that varied from quiescent to enthusiastic without ever cooling off into the hostility found in the east.

George Thompson spoke first for nonintervention in Warrington in November 1861.[68] He was followed by Peter Sinclair and W. A. Jackson,

64. *Fleetwood Chronicle,* 17 May 1861, 16 January 1863; *Southport Independent,* 24 December, 2 January 1862; *Warrington Standard,* 7, 28, December 1861; *Ormskirk Advertiser,* 5 December 1861.
65. *Lancaster Guardian,* 17 August, 30 November 1861; 1 January, 3 May, 7, 14 June 1862; 14 February, 28 February 1863.
66. Ibid., 2 May 1863, 27 June, 10 May 1863.
67. *Soulby's Ulverston Advertiser,* 22, 29 January, 30 April, 21, 28 May, 16 July 1863; *Warrington Advertiser,* 27 June 1863, 30 January, 3 December 1864; *Ulverston Mirror,* 29 April 1865.
68. *Warrington Guardian,* 30 November 1861.

who toured the area in the spring of 1863. In separate meetings, both urged neutrality in Southport in April; at Jackson's meeting a resolution was passed unanimously, condemning recognition of the South or any interference in the war.[69] They then joined forces at the crowded Town Hall in Leigh at the beginning of May to disperse any latent Southern sympathy and paint glowing pictures of the estimable qualities of the North and neutrality to an assenting audience.[70]

Lecturers for the South travelled to this area on few occasions. Joseph Barker did make the effort in July 1863 to prove to Southport that the Southerners also had their virtues but was moved by the hostility of the meeting to propose only a vote for neutrality, which met with unanimous approval.[71] T. B. Kershaw, lecturing on Southern recognition, however, received sufficient encouragement from Warrington in February 1864 to spur E. O. Greening to give a lecture in reply, denouncing any such breach of neutrality. Greening was listened to with interest, and Mason Jones consolidated the Northern position in Warrington with a lecture at the end of the month.[72]

Any spark of Southern sympathy was in the west quite easily put out. Neutrality kept Lancashire out of a war that would in this area have exchanged heavy losses for small gains.

In Lancashire during the American Civil War neutrality had its protagonists, many of whom were firm and faithful. Their weakness was that they never amounted to more than a minority anywhere except Rochdale and the west. Their overriding strength was the knowledge that theirs were the voices that the government wanted to hear. Theirs were the pleas that were answered, because it was politic to do so, while the petitions of their more recalcitrant neighbors fell on deaf ears.

69. *Southport Independent,* 25, 30 April 1863.
70. *Leigh Chronicle,* 9 May 1863; *Bolton Chronicle,* 9 May 1863.
71. *Southport Independent,* 13 August 1863.
72. *Warrington Advertiser,* 13, 20, 27 February 1864.

5

THE QUEST FOR RECOGNITION

The President of the Confederate States believes that he cannot be mistaken in supposing it to be the duty of the nations of the earth, by a prompt recognition, to throw the weight of their moral influence against the unnecessary prolongation of the war.[1]

The time has arrived when it becomes the duty of the governments of Europe to acknowledge that another power is added to the family of nations. For a considerable period the Southern States of America have maintained an established government, which is manifestly in accordance with the free will of their people. The effort made to prevent their independence is obviously a failure, and if continued, can only waste more human life to no purpose.[2]

To the British government the victory of the South in the Civil War often seemed a strong possibility but it was never the foregone conclusion that would have made recognition of Southern independence an automatic gesture. The risk of acknowledging the branch nation while it had only partially splintered off from the tenacious and powerful Union tree was too great. The anger of an opposed North was feared more than that of a frustrated South. Proof that the South was unlikely to succeed without some foreign support was evident in the persistence with which the envoys and friends of the South pleaded for recognition. British arrogance was not such as to imagine that her moral strength would provide failing Southern arms with a shield of invincibility.

Under pressure from the cotton famine, Lancashire would have eagerly thrown such caution to the swiftest of winds. While it was thought obvious that the Confederacy could not indefinitely withstand the superior resources of the Northern army, British recognition was expected to be followed by not only French but also Danish, Spanish, and Belgian acknowledgment. It was reasoned that this would be a strong enough weapon to halt the onslaught of the Union forces. The desperate attempt of the Confederacy to win direct French recognition in 1863 took the form of the suicidal Erlanger loan, the illusory success of which masked a con-

1. In Virginia Mason, *The Public Life and Diplomatic Correspondence of James M. Mason* (New York and Washington, 1906), p. 254.
2. J. Spence, *Recognition*, p. 2

siderable financial loss for the South and its many Lancashire backers—a loss that both could ill afford.[3]

Exasperation was felt in Lancashire that the South was not acknowledged in the same way as any other emergent nation which had won its right to independence by reliance on popular support. It could not be understood why the subtle argument that the Southern slaves would share in Southern freedom, an argument so popular in the county, should escape the cabinet. That slavery had any influence on the government's refusal to recognize the South was dismissed as highly improbable. Confederate offers to initiate emancipation in return for recognition were ignored by England.[4] When the South did enlist Negroes, in a clear step towards abolition, no belated prop of acknowledgment was held out towards the almost defeated South.

Lancashire made unparalleled individual and concerted efforts to induce the government to recognize the Confederacy. The attempts at persuasion took two main forms. The more articulate friends of the South in Liverpool tried to convince the prime minister, Lord Palmerston, and his foreign secretary, Lord Russell, of the diplomatic value of recognition. William Lindsay and James Spence did this through personal interviews with Palmerston and Russell as well as with letters to the *Times* and, in Lindsay's case, speeches and motions in Parliament. Spence also acted as an *eminence gris* behind James Mason's official overtures. The pro-Southern arguments of such men, and of the Liverpudlian chancellor of the exchequer, William Gladstone, have been generally acknowledged as isolated instances of sympathy whereas they were actually fully representative of the cotton interests of the entire county.

Optimum energy was expended by Lancashire on obtaining recognition in the summer of 1863, when meetings, editorials, resolutions, and petitions gave implicit, and sometimes explicit, backing to Roebuck's mo-

3. The Erlanger company organized the sale of $15 million worth of cotton bonds in Europe during the early part of 1863. Only $6.8 million was realized by the Confederacy (see S. B. Thompson, *Confederate Purchasing Operations Abroad* [Durham, N.C., 1935], p. 71) Spence and his brother were among those who lost heavily through buying bonds.

4. Duncan Kenner of Louisiana was in the winter of 1864/65 appointed by the Confederacy as special envoy to England and France specifically to discuss the possibility of emancipating the Negroes if slavery was an obstacle to recognition. In an interview with Mason, Palmerston ignored allusions to slavery in relation to recognition (Mason, *James M. Mason*, pp. 551–60).

tion in the Commons for the official recognition of the Southern states. As the opposition of the cabinet made defeat inevitable, the motion was withdrawn, but the campaign in Lancashire was not abandoned.[5] The enthusiasm that reached its height in mid-1863 had been apparent long before this and remained staunch and only a little daunted throughout 1864. The 285 Lancashire members of the 854 strong Manchester Southern Independence Association, which worked assiduously for recognition in the later stages of the war, were only the tip of the iceberg.[6] Southern clubs and independence associations sprang up in most Lancashire towns and helped organize meetings and petitions; elsewhere entire populations petitioned for recognition though no formal pro-Southern organization existed. Only a few of the vast numbers of meetings that voted for recognition owed anything to the suggestion that James Spence made in reply to the questions with which he was plied by workingmen as to how the feelings of the people could be directed with greatest impact to the attention of the government. Though he did advise that petitions resulting from meetings be sent to the government and even helped with the wording of some resolutions,[7] the most impressive meetings and petitions were totally spontaneous and in no way a result of outside advice. The convictions of a wide variety of Lancastrians were simply and forcibly expressed in an attempt to alter the policy of the government in favor of acknowledging the independence of the Confederacy.

THE NORTHEAST

In Northeast Lancashire there was concentrated agitation for recognition during the crucial summer of 1863. Large meetings voted for recognition, and petitions for it were sent to Parliament from the three major towns. Southern clubs with the express aim of working for recognition were formed in large and small towns alike in the area: clubs in Blackburn, Preston, and Rawtenstall were equally successful. Both before and alongside the formation of the clubs and the great meetings, editors and

---

5. For Roebuck's speech advocating recognition on 29 May and 30 June, see *Hansard*, 3d ser., vol. 171 (1863), pp. 1771–1812. On the advice of Palmerston, Russell, and Spence, the motion was withdrawn before a vote was taken.

6. Membership sheets of the Southern Independence Association of 26, Market Street, Manchester, in local history library, M.C.L.

7. Spence to Mason, 28 April, 3 June 1862, Mason papers, Library of Congress, Washington.

correspondents waged a quiet guerilla war in the press against the attempt to leave the South unacknowledged.

The recognition on 13 May by Britain of the belligerency of the South was initially approved by the *Blackburn Standard*[8] but was soon dismissed as inadequate: "That we must interfere in the quarrel, by recognizing the independence of the South, and that we have good reason to do so, seems now hardly to admit of a doubt, the neutrality we have hitherto observed is a neutrality which gives a great advantage to the North."[9] Clear echoes of this view rang out later in 1862 in *Preston Pilot* editorials and in a letter by J. Sutcliffe to the *Burnley Advertiser*.[10] According to the *Blackburn Standard*, a "universal" feeling in favor of recognition existed.[11] The *Preston Chronicle* and the *Preston Pilot*, in late 1862, urgently pleaded that "this tide in the affairs of the Americans be taken at the flood" by recognizing the South and restoring general "peace," "harmony" and "contentment."[12] As the spring of 1863 passed into summer the press became firmer and more assured in its demands for Southern recognition and gave Roebuck full support in his ill-fated efforts to initiate parliamentary action on this point.[13] The *Preston Chronicle* continued faithfully to urge recognition, not only in October 1863, but as late in the war as December 1864.[14]

June 1863 marked the start of a period of agitation for recognition in the major towns of the area. By the beginning of June over five thousand Burnley inhabitants had signed a petition for the recognition of the Southern states. As the *Burnley Free Press* witnessed, the signatories were fully representative of the town: "The petition has been signed by the Mayor, Magistrates, Aldermen, Town Councillors, clergymen, solicitors, surgeons, cotton spinners, manufacturers, tradesmen and artisans." The document was forwarded to the Marquis of Hartington for presentation to Parliament.[15] An indication of the mood of the town had been given a

8. *Blackburn Standard,* 8 January 1862.

9. Ibid., 22 January 1862.

10. *Preston Pilot,* 21 June, 18 October 1862, *Burnley Advertiser,* 28 June 1862.

11. *Blackburn Standard,* 9 July 1862.

12. *Preston Pilot,* 13 December 1862; *Preston Chronicle,* 29 November 1862.

13. *Preston Pilot,* 24 January, 21 March, 4 July 1863; *Blackburn Standard,* 18 February, 3 June 1863; *Preston Chronicle,* 30 May, 4 July 1863.

14. *Preston Chronicle,* 11 October, 1863, 24 December 1864.

15. *Burnley Free Press,* 6 June 1863.

few months earlier, in April, when after a highly successful lecture by Joseph Barker a very anti-Northern resolution was passed. Barker ended the proceedings by allaying fears aroused by Robert Arnold that Lancashire would be short of "bacon and cheese" if the South was recognized.[16]

In a letter to the *Preston Chronicle*, "H. J." pointed out on June 12 that he was sure the sympathies of Preston were similarly with the independence of the South, and he hoped that a public meeting might soon prove it.[17] Such a meeting was speedily arranged, and the *Preston Pilot* of 20 June had no doubt that the meeting would give overwhelming support to recognition.[18] This was indeed the case when the meeting assembled a few days later. The Reverend William Squier proposed a resolution upholding Southern independence which was passed almost unanimously. Joseph Barker then suggested that to obtain recognition pressure should be brought to bear on the government, as "no step of a definite character would be taken without that." Consequently a further motion was passed to the effect "that a petition be presented to the House of Commons in support of Dr. Roebuck's motion in favour of recognising the Confederates."[19] The tenacious *Preston Pilot* over-optimistically anticipated that the government might take heed of this "pressure from without" and act upon it.[20]

During these same summer months a branch of the Southern Club was started in Preston and was an immediate success, with the Reverend Verity delivering an address under its auspices.[21] Lone protestations from the chairman, Mr. Thomas Dixon, a local corn dealer, in no way impeded passage of a motion that urged England to help bring the war to an end by recognizing the South.[22] A few weeks later Joseph Barker was applauded in Preston when he asserted that recognition by Britain would inspire the South to victory and bring cotton to Lancashire. Questions from "Northern" stalwarts were handled with aplomb—to the delight of the audience.[23] The meetings of the Southern Club and the lectures given by

16. *Burnley Advertiser*, 18 April 1863.
17. *Preston Chronicle*, 13 June 1863.
18. *Preston Pilot*, 20 June 1863.
19. Ibid., 27 June 1863; *Preston Chronicle*, 27 June 1863.
20. *Preston Pilot*, 27 June 1863.
21. Ibid., 1 August 1863; *Preston Chronicle*, 27 June 1863.
22. *Preston Chronicle*, 18 July 1863.
23. Ibid., 25 July 1863.

Barker were contrasted favorably by the *Preston Pilot* with the rigid structure and lack of freedom exhibited at any meeting held by the Union and Emancipation Society in the town. Questions, even attacks, were welcomed and openly met at Barker's lectures and at Southern Club meetings, whereas no such licence was extended by the opposition.[24] This freedom from restrictions was but one indication of the stronghold that Preston had become for supporters of the South and its independence. The *Pilot* claimed that the people of Preston were completely behind the South and in total agreement with the need for recognition as expressed by Barker and other Southern advocates.[25]

Blackburn no less enthusiastically demonstrated its belief that recognition of the South was the best path for Britain to tread. On 29 July an enormous public meeting in the Town Hall passed a motion:

> That in the opinion of this meeting the unity of purpose of the Southern States of America, the heroic and successful perseverance with which they have waged a war of upwards of two years duration for their independence, and their proved possession of the elements necessary for the composition of an independent people, entitle them to recognition as a sovereign and independent nation; and that it is therefore the opinion of this meeting that the government of this country should co-operate with the other European governments in recognising the Southern Confederacy.[26]

An amendment in favor of neutrality proposed by Ernest Jones was defeated. When over a year later no official move had been made by Britain, Blackburn chose a more direct form of action. In October 1864 an Address was sent directly to the American people, through the governor of New York, asking for a cessation of the war and recognition of the South.[27]

Other, smaller towns also affirmed their faith in the South and their conviction that it ought to be recognized. In July Accrington passed a resolution by a large majority to recognize the South.[28] In Rawtenstall the formation of an active Southern Club in September 1863 was evidence of a strong core of Southern support.[29] On 18 November 1863 Darwen was

24. *Preston Pilot*, 1 August 1863.
25. Ibid.
26. *Blackburn Standard*, 5 August 1863, *Preston Guardian*, 1 August 1863.
27. *Blackburn Patriot*, 5 October 1864.
28. *Manchester Courier*, 4 July 1863.
29. *Burnley Free Press*, 5 September 1863.

the scene of a large meeting in favor of the recognition of the South by Britain and the rest of Europe.[30] Hope that this would happen was fading by December 1864 when the Reverend Verity addressed a meeting in Great Harwood. The audience seemed to share his belief that the South should be recognized and his disillusionment with the government—"if they waited until the Government moved, they would have to wait until the end of their lives." [31] They at any rate waited in vain until the end of the war. But they and the other inhabitants of the northeast had not waited in silence.

THE SOUTHEAST

Southeast Lancashire towns outstripped those of the northeast in the vehemence of their determination to win official approval for Southern recognition. Meetings demanding such recognition were not confined to 1863 but, weighted with resolutions and petitions, clamored for attention in 1862 and continued, through the crescendo of 1863, well into 1864. Considering that this was the area that the Manchester Union and Emancipation Society looked upon as its special garden, likely to bear good fruit if tended with care, the number and size of the demonstrations for Southern independence are impressive and surprising. Any help given by Spence or other "professional" Southerners could account for only a tiny surge of the massive wave of support that rose up for acknowledgment of the Confederacy.

The basically indigenous strength of the movement for recognition sprang from the crippling impact of the dearth of cotton. It is through this movement that the link between deprivation and desire to aid the South is most clearly established. The most acutely distressed unions held massive and multiple meetings which urged recognition through resolutions and petitions: Ashton held at least 14 such meetings, passed 11 resolutions, and sent 5 petitions; Oldham held 7 meetings, passed 4 resolutions, and sent 3 petitions. Less disturbed unions, such as Bury, could summon only one or two meetings unemphasized by resolutions or a petition. To towns experiencing destitution, recognition of the South seemed the most obvious and direct way of securing both peace and cotton.

The press of the area passed through shades of enthusiasm for recog-

---

30. *Blackburn Standard,* 5 August 1863.
31. *Blackburn Times,* 17 December 1863.

nition that varied in intensity as the degrees of distress deepened or waned in the most afflicted towns, while the slightly distressed seemed to increase or decrease their support of the South with the progress on the battlefield of the struggling Confederate forces. The Wigan press early in the war decided that recognition was a necessary step to obtain cotton and was justifiable even in the face of Northern alienation.[32] In the summer of 1862 the *Bury Guardian* was by no means alone in its hope that England would join the obviously willing French in recognizing the South.[33] Articles in the *Ashton and Stalybridge Reporter* suggested that if the same tests of nationhood be applied to the Confederacy as had been used for Italy, it would emerge that by all criteria the Southern states should be recognized.[34]

The press was stimulated in the autumn of 1862 to increase the intensity of pleas for recognition by the darkening shadow of distress and, more esoterically, by the example set by Gladstone's speech at Newcastle.[35] Gladstone's virtual acknowledgment of the South was widely and approvingly interpreted as foreshadowing official recognition.[36]

Roebuck's efforts to secure recognition in mid-1863 were given solid editorial backing. The *Wigan Observer* gave typical support to his Sheffield speech and to recognition itself on 30 May:

> There are many men in this country who, like Mr. Roebuck, deplored the secession and sympathised with the North at the outset of the struggle, but who now wish to see the Confederacy, under Mr. Davis, recognised as an independent nation, and admire the gallant people who have so stoutly defended themselves against a peculiarly cruel foe. . . . Such have for some time been the views of educated and reflecting men which the masses now share.[37]

The faith commonly deposited in Southern recognition was not blind. The *Wigan Observer* was aware that it would take some time before it led to the end of the bloodshed and opening of the ports, while the *Oldham*

32. *Wigan Examiner,* 12 October 1861; 2 May 1862; *Wigan Observer,* 1 March, 3 May 1863.

33. *Bury Guardian,* 19 July, 26 July 1862; *Oldham Chronicle,* 17 May 1862; *Wigan Observer,* 19 July 1862.

34. *Ashton and Stalybridge Reporter,* 21 June, 2 August 1862.

35. Gladstone acknowledged the nationhood of the South in October in Newcastle.

36. *Bolton Chronicle,* 11 October 1862; *Ashton Standard,* 18 October 1862; *Ashton and Stalybridge Reporter,* 11 October, 1862, *Wigan Observer,* 7 November 1862.

37. *Wigan Observer,* 30 May 1863; Sheffield had passed a resolution backing recognition a few days before; see also *Oldham Standard,* 20 June 1863.

Chronicle faced and refuted the possibility that it might lead to war with the North.[38] Hope for recognition flickered slowly on in the autumn of 1863,[39] but was ultimately snuffed out by the inactivity of the government.

As might have been expected, Ashton was the first town to hold a large meeting seeking recognition. At the end of April 1862, six thousand unemployed factory operatives passed by "a considerable majority" William Aitken's resolution

> That, in the opinion of the meeting, it is the bounden duty of the people in the manufacturing districts of Great Britain and Ireland to use every moral means in their power, and to memorialise parliament for the recognition of the Southern confederacy and an alteration in the maritime law of nations that neutral ships of commerce shall pass freely over the waters of the world.

In a supporting speech, John Mathews, of Stalybridge, had acknowledged that "their stomachs" were forcing their brains to try to find a path to recognition.[40] In July a meeting of "Factory Workers Delegates" was held in Ashton. At this, Mortimer Grimshaw, the controversial ex-Chartist from Blackburn, successfully proposed a motion declaring it to be "the bounden duty of her Majesty's government either to recognise the Southern Confederacy" or otherwise save the manufacturing districts from ruin.[41] It was decided that a memorial based on the resolution should be presented to the House of Commons.[42] At a meeting in August, to discuss relief in Ashton, a local man, T. Heginbottom, complained about the bias towards the North that was always heard in the speeches of "our public men" (probably an apt reference to Milner Gibson, Cobden, and Bright). "It was a fact," he went on, "that the North got no nearer the end of the war, and cotton spinners and operatives no nearer their work. . . . He felt convinced that the mills would not be at work until the pressure from

38. *Wigan Observer,* 3 July 1863; *Oldham Chronicle,* 4 July 1863.
39. *Bolton Chronicle,* 8 August 1863; *Wigan Observer,* 9 October 1863.
40. *Ashton Standard,* 3 May 1862; *Rochdale Spectator,* 3 May 1862.
41. The extent and nature of Grimshaw's influence has been much debated. Dickens's portrait of him in *Hard Times* as often disliked but usually respected is probably as accurate as any.
42. *Ashton and Stalybridge Reporter,* 26 July 1862. Only a select number of the petitions presented to the House of Commons were included in the reports of the select committees of the House of Commons on public petitions: none of the petitions from Lancashire seeking recognition were included in 1862 and only a few in 1863 and 1864.

without was made to tingle in the ears of the government, and some action taken on the American question." He ended with an even more explicit plea for recognition very much in tune with the resolutions already passed in the town.[43] A week later Northern supporters from Manchester made a determined effort to see that no further "pressure from without" would be exerted from Ashton. When a meeting of cotton operatives was held at the end of August to discuss the cotton shortage and the war, a sizeable deputation from Manchester, headed by the notorious Northern agitator Thomas Evans, added considerable confusion as well as numbers to the proceedings. James Nield of Mossley proposed a resolution urging recognition as the best means of halting the "degradation of the labouring classes" and was seconded by a workingman, while a cotton operative spoke in favor of the resolution. An amendment preferring arbitration to recognition was only seriously considered because the chairman, Mr. Pilling, put the motion by asking all those in favor of slavery to put up their hands! This aroused a storm of hisses and groans, and cries of "It's not a question of slavery" and "He is not fit to be chairman." Pilling declared the motion to be defeated, although the outcome was by no means clear. An outright victory would have been astounding, considering the loaded way in which the motion was presented.[44] In July a large open-air meeting at Mossley passed a resolution in favor of recognition and petitioning Parliament to make it the official policy of Britain.[45]

During a meeting of the unemployed at Oldham in October, Mr. J. T. Carrodus, the Congregational minister of Oldham's Regent Street chapel, expressed the hope that his fellow townsmen would not recognize the South at any meeting to be held at Oldham in the near future.[46] He was to be disappointed. The very next day a resolution in favor of the recognition of the South was passed at a large and dramatic meeting. This had been called by Josiah Radcliffe, the deputy-mayor, in response to a "numerously-signed requisition of the inhabitants" in order

> to take into consideration the propriety of urging her Majesty's ministers to advise the Queen to be graciously pleased to recognise the

43. *Ashton and Stalybridge Reporter,* 30 August 1862.
44. *Ashton Standard,* 6 September 1862; *Ashton and Stalybridge Reporter,* 6 September 1862.
45. *Oldham Chronicle,* 11 July 1862.
46. Ibid., 25 October 1862.

sovereignty and independence of the Southern States of America, as the only means of putting a stop to the awful bloodshed, waste of life and property, and the horrible civil war, which have so long devastated that suffering land, as well as to relieve the terrible privations and distress of the suffering operatives in the cotton manufactures of England, and the other dependencies of the British Crown.

The Town Hall was packed "to the utmost density" and "thousands" of operatives were unable to gain admission. After some free and open discussion, J. L. Quarmby proposed a motion urging that Britain recognize the independence of the "herioc" Confederacy. Quarmby cited precedents for English recognition of emergent nations and stressed that recognition would renew the rusting links of the cotton trade. Audience reaction to the idea of war resulting from recognition was quick and confident: "We'll punce them into th' Atlantic." Councillor Harrap, seconding the motion, hoped that soon all Europe would recognize the South as the free and liberal nation it was. John Shaw of Oldham's General Relief Committee urged recognition to end the misery and devastation of both the Lancashire operatives and Southern Negroes, who would be freed by an independent South. The motion was passed by an overwhelming majority, and a petition embodying its sentiment was signed by the chairman and "forwarded to London" the next day.[47]

The powerful surge of agitation for recognition that swept over the southeast towns in mid-1863 began by engulfing Mossley in a series of meetings in May and June. In May, one meeting ended with "three hearty cheers for the speedy recognition of the Southern States," [48] while on 1 June the Mossley Southern Independence Association was founded at a meeting which passed a strong resolution for immediate recognition.[49]

It was also in May and June that John Quarmby very successfully spoke at meetings in several of the small towns and villages surrounding Oldham. A resolution urging the government to acknowledge the South and so procure cotton was passed at Crompton, and a petition was sent to the Commons.[50] At Royton, Quarmby was warmly received [51] and at Wa-

47. *Oldham Chronicle,* 25 October 1862, *Oldham Standard,* 25 October 1862.
48. *Oldham Standard,* 16 May 1863; see also ibid., 9 May 1863.
49. Ibid., 6 June 1863.
50. *Oldham Chronicle,* 16 May 1863.
51. Ibid.

terhead the following resolution was carried by an overwhelming majority:

> That we would urge our government, in connection with the government of France and such other European powers as may be disposed to join them, to take the earliest opportunity of recognising the independence of the Confederate States; of bringing the revolting and disastrous war now raging in America to an end; and thus re-opening the trade between the Southern ports of [sic] Europe and supplying cotton to our mills, honest labour to our working population, comfort and plenty to their suffering families, a chance of peaceful emancipation to the slave, and a return of prosperity and happiness to our country and to all the nations of Europe.

On the following evening a similar resolution was passed at Cowhill.[52]

Oldham's increased dedication to recognition was marked by the enrollment of fifty people as members of the Oldham Southern Independence Association on 9 June after a discussion about emancipation and recognition.[53] Two days later a meeting of over fifteen hundred voted overwhelmingly for recognition after an eloquent speech by Joseph Barker, while an amendment supporting neutrality received only fifty votes.[54]

At Mossley on 17 June a petition was adopted with no more than two dissentients at a large meeting called by the Mossley Southern Independence Association, in support of Roebuck's motion for recognition in the Commons:

> Believing that the Confederate States have the right, as they have the power, to sustain their independence, your petitioners deprecate all further attempts of the Federal government to restore the union, such efforts being hopeless, unjustifiable, and outrageous to humanity.
>
> They therefore most respectfully urge the government of this country that—in justice to the Southern confederacy [sic], in the interest of humanity, and in mercy to the myriads of their fellow-subjects, suffering so greatly and unavoidably from the murderous strife—it should, in concert with other European powers, recognise the independence of the Confederate States.
>
> Your petitioners are fully convinced that the moral influence

52. *Oldham Standard,* 13 June 1863.
53. Ibid.
54. Ibid., 20 June 1863.

of such recognition would conduce to an earlier termination of the fatal struggle.

And your petitioners will ever pray.[55]

During that same week Lees passed a resolution urging recognition upon the government by a most decisive majority, at a "crowded public meeting." Efforts of Northern supporters to negate this result by packing further Lees meetings with outsiders failed dismally.[56]

Bury gave its only demonstration of approval for recognition in this crucial period of mid-June 1863 when, after a lecture by Joseph Barker, an ebullient meeting of over six hundred resolved almost unanimously to urge recognition on the government.[57] Barker also lectured at nearby Ramsbottom during the following week and was there faced with opposition from W. A. Jackson, who insinuated that Southern advocates dared not put a resolution to the meeting. Undeterred, Barker did put a motion approving recognition to the meeting. No doubt to Mr. Jackson's chagrin, the motion passed.[58] At Bolton in mid-June Barker successfully proposed a further resoltion seeking official recognition of the South.[59]

The *Oldham Standard* of 27 June contained a list of the members of the Oldham Southern Independence Association. Headed by almost all the councillors and aldermen of the town, the list encompassed men of every class and political and religious creed. The war seemed unique in its capacity to unite men of widely differing beliefs in a common devotion to the South.[60] The strength of this devotion was amply demonstrated at a massive meeting of eight to ten thousand people in the Tommy Field of Oldham. William Steeple proposed:

> That, in the opinion of this meeting, the people of the Southern Confederacy have shown such unanimity, aptitude for self-government, obedience to laws, and heroic courage in defence of their homes and their country, as to justly entitle them to be at once admitted into the family of nations.

55. Ibid., 20 June 1863.
56. Ibid., *Oldham Chronicle*, 27 June 1863.
57. *Bury Guardian*, 13 June 1863; *Bury Times*, 17 June 1863. On 20 June a letter from Mr. Cooper claimed there were only few dissentients.
58. *Bury Guardian*, 20 June 1863.
59. *Bolton Chronicle*, 20 June 1863.
60. *Oldham Standard*, 27 June 1863.

The resolution was passed by a ratio of "eight or ten to one," with strong local support acknowledging a firm link between Southern independence and the welfare of the cotton trade, and was followed up by the adoption of a petition to the House of Commons. The petition made its motivation quite clear:

> recognition will promote the best interests of this country, procure a permanent and plentiful supply of the great staple of our industry, and ultimately lead to the peaceful emancipation of the Negro.[61]

Again the hallmark of an Oldham meeting appeared—the practical desire for cotton expressed, in both motion and petition, alongside concern for the destruction of slavery. The *Oldham Chronicle* pointed out that whereas many meetings were held during the day, so that many of the working class could not attend, "at Oldham, the demonstration took place in the evening, and no one could look at the sea of faces without coming to the conclusion that the great bulk of the people present belonged unmistakeably to the sons of toil." The fact that this was also the largest open-air meeting ever held at Oldham seems proof enough that the motion and petition in favor of recognition were a genuine expression of the beliefs of the people of Oldham. That this in no way influenced the reaction to Roebuck's motion for recognition, though Roebuck actually introduced the Oldham petition before his own motion,[62] was a symptom of the government's disregard of the feelings of its less influential citizens.

A similar and no more effective motion and petition for recognition were passed at Mossley on 9 July by a crowd of about fifteen hundred people. The petition—proposed and seconded by local men, as was the motion—pleaded for recognition out of humane consideration for the local cotton operatives as much as for the Southerners themselves. A telling contrast with the success of this meeting was provided by the abysmal failure of a simultaneously held pro-Northern one at which the presence of a strong Manchester deputation was unable to raise any real support.[63]

On the same evening, at Edgeworth, near Bolton, a strong pro-recognition resolution was successfully proposed by a local man after a speech by Joseph Barker.[64] Barker was to meet with an equally warm re-

61. *Oldham Chronicle,* 4 July 1863; *Oldham Standard,* 4 July 1863.
62. *Oldham Chronicle,* 4 July 1863.
63. *Oldham Standard,* 11 July 1863.
64. *Bolton Chronicle,* 11 July 1863.

sponse when he pressed for recognition at Bury in July and at Heywood and Wigan in August.[65] Mr. Quarmby at Delph and Mr. Kershaw at Lees reemphasized the advantages of recognition, as the summer closed with faith in the effectiveness of resolutions and petitions for recognition fast dulling.[66] From the lack of response, it had become clear that such measures would in no way alter the path the government had already mapped for itself.

A last valiant attempt to change this course by the votes of the people was made at Ashton in June 1864. A letter from "An Ex-Over-looker" in the *Ashton Standard* of 18 June suggested a town meeting that would propose recognition of the South. He, too optimistically, expected that this would enable the "voice of Ashton-under-Lyne" to "be heard effectually in the British House of Commons." [67] A "large" public meeting was held to discuss recognition. A preliminary resolution was proposed by Councillor D. Vernon, who argued that a de facto government ought to be recognized:

> That considering how much calamity has been caused to tens of thousands of families, in the cotton manufacturing districts of England, through the war carried on by the cabinet of President Lincoln, for the subjugation of the Southern States of the old American Union, and which war has now entered upon its fourth year, this meeting considers itself entitled to express an opinion upon the same, in the interests of their suffering fellow townsmen deprived of employment.

The resolution was passed by a large majority. The Reverend F. H. Williams then proposed a successful motion that reappealed for "timely recognition . . . to hasten the conclusion of the unjust and cruel war waged by the Federal against the Confederate government . . . and at least according (as they had always done in similar cases) the just recognition of England to those who have so nobly and devotedly followed her example in defending and maintaining against the aggression of power, their own and their country's rights. That a copy of this resolution be forwarded by the chairman to Mr. Lindsay M.P." Williams explained that Lindsay was chosen to present the motion and a petition as he was about to propose a

65. *Bury Guardian,* 4 July, 15 August 1863; *Wigan Observer,* 7 August 1863.
66. *Oldham Chronicle,* 22 August 1863; *Oldham Standard,* 12 September 1863.
67. *Ashton Standard,* 18 June 1864.

resolution on the subject in Parliament; otherwise Williams would have preferred their own M.P., Milner Gibson, to do his duty, and present their views. That these were the views of all Ashton, Williams felt there was no doubt. All classes were represented at the meeting, which had only been arranged twelve hours before and was in no way packed.[68] Ashton had been the first town to publicly approve recognition. It was fitting that it should in so decisive a manner be the last.

This region bore unique and powerful witness to the activity of Lancashire over recognition. Once it is realized how many towns voted for recognition and petitioned Parliament to bring it about, it is impossible to believe in a silent, quiescent Lancashire. Certainly no riots were roused in the name of recognition, but cool and sensible measures were taken to attempt to attain that end. In this most accessible of areas a sharp contrast was provided by the organization of pro-Northern and pro-Southern meetings. Whereas Northern gatherings were almost always addressed by leading members of the Manchester Union and Emancipation Society and resolutions were formed by them, representatives of the Manchester Southern club were seen only occasionally at meetings in favor of the South and rarely put forward motions. The meetings that demanded recognition in this area were, for the most part, characterized by a spontaneous, indigenous quality that is particularly marked in the framing of the resolutions and petitions wherein the real hope of this widespread movement lay.

MANCHESTER

Manchester was by no means as impervious to the appeal of recognition as has been imagined. The existence of flourishing pro-Southern organizations indicated a source of Confederate sympathy which grew into an important movement as the war advanced. The Southern Independence Association not only helped to expose the existence of a latent desire for recognition in Manchester but also provided a base for more scattered enthusiasts.[69] It was Manchester that published the pamphlets and circu-

---

68. Ibid., 25 June 1864. Lindsay's motion for recognition was forcefully presented on 18 July in the Commons but was withdrawn after a statement had been made by Lord Palmerston. There was a full report in the *Ashton and Stalybridge Reporter,* 26 July 1864.

69. *Manchester Courier,* 10 October, 1863.

lars that helped many in and out of Lancashire to clarify and rationalize their Southern sympathy and in some cases to change from support of the North, or mere apathy, into defense of the South.

Most of the publications of the Manchester Southern Independence Association incorporated implicit, if not explicit, pleas for acknowledging the South. Recognition was usually seen as the essential precursor to Southern emancipation of slaves.[70] The necessity for recognition was also rammed home separately in pamphlets such as that by Thomas Kershaw. Kershaw emphasized that an "honourable recognition" of the South would be in the trade interests of Britain as well as the Confederacy.[71] Other tracts were devoted wholly to arguments for recognition.[72]

One of the more pungent attacks on the refusal of the British government to acknowledge Southern nationhood came in a pamphlet written by "ONE OF THE RUCK" [73] and not published by the association. He complained of the failure of the national leaders to cope with the devastation sapping Lancashire as a result of the Civil War but was gratified to find the operatives themselves clamoring for recognition as a means of ending their distress. This was, he thought, the most rational way to secure a future supply of cotton and loose the stranglehold of distress. He further reasoned that the Confederacy had already won a right to recognition and claimed that "it is an unmistakeable fact that the sympathy of this country has been on the side of the Confederates. Every mail that has brought news of a success to the Confederate cause has produced a feeling of gladness in the majority of English minds." [74]

James Paul Cobbett more specifically claimed that the business interests of Manchester would prefer a separated South rather than a United States.[75] This was most likely true of all but the wealthiest traders, who were making a fortune through the war and would have preferred to

---

70. *Notes on Slavery,* Papers for the People, no. 6, pp. 1, 4. See also pamphlets and broadsheets cited above, chapter 4, Manchester section.

71. Kershaw, *The American Question,* pp. 15, 17, 25, 28, 29, 32, and especially 31.

72. *Ought England to Acknowledge the Independence of the Confederate States?* Occasional Paper no. 5 (Manchester, 1863).

73. "Ruck" was most often taken to mean "common people."

74. "One of the Ruck," *The Cotton Famine; An Attempt to Discover Its Cause, With Suggestions For Its Future Prevention* (Manchester, 1962), pp. 3–5.

75. Cobbett, *The Civil War,* p. 15.

delay the establishment of a separate South. Certainly a petition from
Manchester, sponsored by the Southern Independence Association in July
1864, had many leading Manchester firms among its 5,186 signatories.
The petition asked for the government to take any steps that might lead
to peace on the basis of a free and independent South. It was presented to
the Commons by the local M.P., James Aspinall Turner.[76]

Henry Adams in his "Diary of a Visit to Manchester" in 1861 came
to the conclusion, after talking to a variety of Manchester business men,
that "so far as the cotton interests of Manchester are concerned, our Government will have two months more full swing over the South. At the end
of that time, a party will arise in favor of ending the war by recognising
the insurgents, and, if necessary, breaking the blockade or declaring it ineffective."[77] It took a little longer than he anticipated, but by 1863 and
1864 the "party" had well and truly arrived.

Multiple intimations of the escalation of support for recognition
could be found in the Manchester press.[78] Impatience spilled over in the
summer of 1863 at "the diplomatic concealment of a truth"—the independence of the South—which had long since been generally acknowledged by the nation and specifically backed by the millions contributed
to the Confederate loan. Nonetheless Roebuck's attempts at amateur diplomacy were frowned on.[79] Express and implied refutations of John
Bright's misrepresentations of public opinion were common in 1864 and
1865. It was asserted that the mass of Englishmen recognized the right of
the Southern states to freedom.[80]

The earliest major speech in Manchester to promote Southern recognition was that given by Gladstone to the Manchester Chamber of
Commerce on 24 April 1862. Gladstone himself has a right to be considered as a representative of Lancashire politicians; he was after all born at
62 Rodney Street, Liverpool, and Palmerston said of him, "He grew up to

76. Appendix to the Report of the Select Committee on Public Petitions, Session
1864, p. 226. *Burnley Advertiser,* 16 July 1864.

77. Silver, "Henry Adams," p. 82.

78. *Manchester Guardian,* 8 May 1861; *Manchester Examiner and Times,* 24 October 1861;
Manchester Weekly Express, 11 January 1862; *Manchester Courier,* 28 February, 6 June 1863.

79. *Manchester Courier,* 2, 30 May, 28 March, 1863; *Manchester Weekly Times,* 11 July
1863; *Manchester Guardian,* 3, 4 July 1863.

80. *Manchester Courier,* 1 November 1864; *Manchester Guardian,* 28 July, 20 August
1864; 1 February 1865.

be Oxford, as someone said, on the surface, but Liverpool below." [81] Gladstone made his approval of the South clear and warned against the alienation of "those who may be hereafter a great nation, claiming to enter into peaceful relations with us. (Cheers.)" He compared the fight of the South for independence with that of the original thirteen colonies and hoped that the end in this case would be one of separation.[82] H. S. Gibbs recorded that Gladstone's temerity roused the hope of Southern sympathizers and the fear of Northern supporters that the South would soon be officially recognized.[83]

When Spence visited Manchester in May 1863 he thought that opinion there seemed to have moved towards recognition "mainly owing to the reduction in the stock of goods." [84] A month later, when Joseph Barker lectured to an audience in the Corn Exchange, he indirectly advocated recognition and was rewarded by a majority of hands being raised for the South as well as three cheers being given for Jefferson Davis.[85] Naturally the Manchester Southern Independence Association made several impassioned pleas for recognition.[86]

The Union and Emancipation Society never did succeed in Manchester in raising any really powerful antirecognition feeling, while there were wholehearted efforts made to secure recognition. Nonetheless there is no strong evidence to prove that the mass of Mancunians actively rather than passively wanted recognition; the enthusiasm of a group within the city could never compensate for this.

LIVERPOOL

In mid-1862 Spence felt able to say of Liverpool: "This great city has gone for the South from the first day and the feeling now is at pretty high pressure." [87] There is little doubt that, with a few exceptions, most Liverpudlians were still behind the South when the war drew to a close. Their sympathy reached its height in 1863 when Spence referred to Liver-

---

81. Gladstone papers, 4, 192, quoted in Philip Guedella, *Gladstone and Palmerston* (London, 1928), pp. 24, 29.
82. *Manchester Courier,* 20 April 1862.
83. H. S. G., *Autobiography,* p. 162.
84. Spence to Mason, 4 May 1863, Mason papers.
85. *Manchester Courier,* 6 June 1863.
86. Ibid., 10 October 1863; *Manchester Guardian,* 30 January 1864.
87. Spence to Mason, 23 August 1862, Mason papers.

pool as "the headquarters of Southern sentiment" and the "place where Southern feeling has ever been at fever heat" [88]—and "Southern feeling" meant to Spence an intrinsic desire for Southern recognition.

James Spence himself made his hopes for recognition quite clear in his letters, pamphlets, and book, and spent much time and energy attempting to bring it about. He explained to James Mason in April 1862 that he was writing a pamphlet on the duty of recognition but intended to hold back publication until the time was more favorable towards its reception. He thought June might be a propitious month [89] and he did, in fact, publish soon after, in July 1862. His arguments were clear-cut and forceful:

> Is it a fact that the Southern States form a distinct community, and have over them a government approved by themselves, and reasonably executing the functions of administration? If this be so, the well-established practice of modern times requires us to admit that to be a fact which is a fact.[90]

He had no fears, and hoped to dispel those of others, that a declaration of war from the North might follow British recognition of the South; he was sure the North was far too dependent on the British market for its wheat to allow that to happen.[91]

The chief problem as Spence saw it in his correspondence with James Mason, the Confederate commissioner to England, was to judge the moment when it would be possible to press successfully for recognition. The time had obviously not been right when Spence was called to London in February 1862 to discuss the situation with Palmerston and Russell; but in March 1862 he estimated that, after a period of inactivity while stocks of cotton dropped, recognition might meet the mood of the country. He hoped through his letters to the *Times* to cultivate that mood. By 11 June it was obvious that the time had not yet come—military setbacks for the South had bred caution. On 13 June optimism returned: "On the eve of a battle at Richmond the day does not seem actually come to go for recognition but it may be expedient to begin active measures for

88. Ibid., 12 January, 1 March 1863.
89. Ibid., 16 April 1862.
90. J. Spence, *Recognition*, pp. 4–5.
91. Ibid., pp. 5, 16.

that event." He felt in July a glimmer of abortive hope for a motion Lindsay intended to submit to the Commons, as he thought that public opinion was "ripening fast for recognition," but he was sure that any successful motion in the Commons would have to be preceded by a formal demand for recognition addressed to the government. By 23 August he was certain that at least Liverpool was ripening for recognition. In September he had decided that the time had reached fruition, and he was corresponding "with several men of might on the subject of a public movement," although he felt this would be largely unnecessary because the European governments would act anyway. When this had not happened by October, he surmised that "perhaps the best thing I can do will be to write letters each week on Recognition, argument after argument, so as to keep it constantly before the public." He was obviously despondent later in the month when, because of "the strong and virulent opposition of cotton holders," he could not get a requisition for the Liverpool Chamber of Commerce to memorialize the government for recognition. He gave up early in his attempt because, as always, he feared defeat more than inactivity. However, by January 1863 he was contacting sympathetic M.P.'s and hoping for mass support from the Conservatives so that the matter might successfully be brought to a vote; until set back by the news of the fall of Vicksburg, he was similarly active in July. This changed the possibility of success into a near-certain defeat if Roebuck's motion for recognition had been put to a vote—not because the Commons was basically against recognition (it was thought to be ten to one in favor), but because of the circumstances. Spence accordingly was very nervous. He suggested that Mason advise Roebuck to withdraw and avoid humiliation until either France or Disraeli should lend their full and indispensable support.[92]

The hope that had faded with the summer of 1863 revived in May 1864. Spence, after consultation with Lindsay and the Liverpool Southern Club, asked Mason to seek an interview with Lord Palmerston, "for with this wind tending in our favor [sic], yet hesitating and unsettled, I am of opinion that the effect of an interview with you would be to turn the scales." As Mason obviously was reluctant to press for recognition at this juncture, Spence said he would not normally hustle him, "but the present

92. Spence to Mason, 13 February, 18 March, 11, 13 June, 11 July, 23 August, 15 September, 3, 13 October, 1862, 3 January, 8, 11, 25 July 1863, Mason papers. Roebuck's mission to the French emperor had turned many Southern allies against his motion.

question is that of existence—a life and death struggle. The interests at stake are so vast—the injury to the South if the war is prolonged is so terrible and more than all, the amount of suffering and woe from all this slaughter is so sad that I think these [sic] bid us to stifle feelings of our own and discard the niceties of etiquette if by so doing we may quicken the coming of peace." [93] In July Spence was pleased with the account Lindsay gave him of the interview that Mason did in fact have with Palmerston. His faint anticipation that at least the North might read some significance into the interview[94] was a small aim compared with the difficult and powerful end of recognition he had worked so vainly towards throughout the war. Because his efforts were directed through normal political and diplomatic channels, they had more chance of success than mass appeals; even so, like the mass appeals, they failed as the almost inevitable consequence of representing the effort of a politically impotent minority.

Spence received more than adequate press support from his home city, some of it direct, but most of it indirect in that it was straightforward approval of recognition. This is not to suggest that Spence was responsible for the large amount of Southern feeling in the city. He simply gave exceptionally clear and articulate voice to what the mass of Liverpudlians wanted. The *Liverpool Mail* did go out of its way in February 1863 to support Spence's personal disinterestedness and integrity in advocating recognition.[95]

The *Liverpool Weekly Mercury* gave early approval to recognition, while the *Daily Post* in March 1862 condemned the government for its prevarication:

> The Secessionists have been cruelly used. . . . Our Government led the world to believe that it was favourable to the movement of the Confederates. It indicated as much by a premature recognition, and there was not, we believe, one man in Great Britain or in the United States of America who did not believe that it was the intention of Ministers to acknowledge, on the first opportunity, the independence of the Seceding States. They said virtually as much in Parliament. Earl RUSSELL, in his speech, we think at Newcastle, intimated as clearly as possible that the result of the civil war would

93. Ibid., 31 May 1864.
94. Ibid., 18 July 1864.
95. *Liverpool Mail,* 7 February 1863.

be the establishment of sovereign power on the Mississippi. Public opinion in Liverpool was entirely in favour of the South. To a great extent it was the same throughout England; and although Scotland was adverse, and Ireland dubious, the press of this part of the kingdom was unequivocally adverse to the North.[96]

The *Mail* and the *Albion* echoed this and hoped that recognition would undo the damage, which would please Liverpool and Manchester even if it annoyed John Bright. The Southerners, added the *Albion,* were admired for everything but their slavery and "that their (the Southerners') independence may be speedily acknowledged by France and England is, we are convinced, the strong desire of a vast majority, not only in England, but throughout Europe." [97]

Throughout 1863 the *Liverpool Mercury* published articles by "A" of New York more or less daily; several of these articles urged the recognition that the *Daily Post* in March 1863 felt was illogical of the government to refuse.[98] While the *Mail* gave unqualified support to Lindsay's "unimpeachable" motion for recognition, Roebuck's efforts were sympathized with but thought unlikely to succeed because of his "eccentric," as the *Albion* put it, dealings with the French emperor.[99] The *Mail* and, to a lesser extent, the *Albion* pursued the adoption of recognition unflaggingly to the end of the war.[100]

Meetings designed to stir the government and not the city were held by the Southern Club, and it is not without significance that, at almost all of the very organized meetings held in support of the North, workingmen interrupted the flow of eulogy for Lincoln to demand recognition of the South.[101]

Spence himself addressed a meeting in Liverpool in September 1862 to point out to any of the unconverted the effective value of recognition.[102]

96. *Liverpool Weekly Mercury,* 6 April, 8 June, 12 October 1861; ibid., *Liverpool Daily Post,* 11 March 1862.

97. *Liverpool Mail,* 26 April 1862; *Albion,* 12 May, 23 June, 14 July 1862; *Liverpool Daily Post,* 16 July 1862.

98. *Liverpool Mercury,* 2, 26, 31 January, 18 June 1863; *Liverpool Daily Post,* 16 March 1863.

99. *Liverpool Mail,* 4, 19 July 1863; *Albion* 6 July 1863.

100. *Liverpool Mail,* 13 September 1863, 19 November, 3 December 1864, 28 January, 18 February, 18 March 1865; *Albion,* 23 January 1865.

101. *Liverpool Daily Post,* 24 January, 12 February 1863; *Liverpool Weekly Mercury,* 14 February 1863.

102. Spence to Mason, 2 October 1862, Mason papers.

In October 1862 the Southern Club held a meeting at which it was agreed that a proposition be sent to the government memorializing it for the recognition of the Confederate states.[103] At a large meeting and banquet of the Liverpool Southern Club, Beresford Hope and James Spence stated categorically that recognition had become a duty which should be made impossible for the government to ignore.[104] In July 1864 Spence attempted more directly to influence the government when he went to London as a member of a deputation seeking peace and signed a petition to Parliament on the basis of the recognition "of the independence of the Southern States." [105]

Despondent though Liverpool may have been at the lack of government response to such pleas, it was a city unique in its will and capacity to treat the South as an independent nation. Implicit recognition was demonstrated with the large sums that were lent to the Confederacy by Liverpudlians through the Erlanger loan: fortunes were in fact staked and lost on the independence of the South.[106] More explicit, though less important, were the Southern flags flown by the *Peter Maxwell* and all Mr. Forwood's ships on the Mersey and out at sea.[107] Perhaps most telling of all was that Liverpool acted towards and traded with the South as an independent nation. The blockade was treated as little more than a scrap of paper. Whether officially recognized or not, the Confederacy was regarded in Liverpool as a new and separate country.

THE WEST

This was the area that found the idea of recognition least attractive. There were, admittedly, local branches of the Southern Independence Association in Warrington and Leigh but these seemed to be distinctly lethargic and were exceedingly small. T. B. Kershaw made a somewhat isolated appeal for recognition in this region and met with an icy reception.[108]

103. *Liverpool Mail*, 11 October 1862.
104. *Liverpool Daily Post*, 17 October 1863.
105. *Index*, 21 July 1864; Appendix, "Report of the Select Committee on Public Petitions," Session 1864, p. 224.
106. Spence to Mason, 21 December 1862, 12 January, 17 March 1863, Mason papers.
107. *Liverpool Daily Post*, 1, 4 November 1861; *Liverpool Weekly Mercury*, 16 March 1861.
108. *Warrington Advertiser*, 30 January 1864.

The press was almost as cool. Only lukewarm and temporary support for acknowledging the South was given by the fickle *Barrow Herald* and *Ulverston Mirror*, with a little more consistency being added by the Lancaster press.[109] There was no passionate demand for recognition at any time, and there was a complete lack of the crescendo of feeling that elsewhere singled out the summer of 1863 as being the most likely time for this demand to be heard.

Recognition of the South was unquestionably the most popular way of intervening in the war as far as the cotton towns were concerned. This was particularly true of the worst-hit towns of the southeast, where an unparalleled effort was made to influence the government to abandon neutrality for recognition. The existence of flourishing Southern Independence Associations in Preston, Blackburn, Burnley, Over Darwen, Ramsbottom, Rawtenstall, Middleton, Oldham, Ashton-under-Lyne, Heywood, Bury, Mossley, Bolton, Rochdale, Hyde, Todmorden, Warrington, and Leigh [110] testified to a strong and continuous faith in recognition in almost every town suffering the effects of the dearth of cotton. That the petitions of these associations and of the Manchester Southern Independence Association, together with the advice of prominent Lancashire men, should be unheeded was not unreasonable. When, however, petitions based on resolutions passed by massive public meetings in the distressed towns were totally ignored, Lancashire was made to feel impotent in the face of an arrogant oligarchy.

109. *Barrow Herald,* 31 January, 4 April 1863; *Ulverston Mirror,* 8 November 1862; *Lancaster Guardian,* 8 February 1862; *Lancaster Gazette,* 3 January, 7 February, 2, 13 May 1863, 28 January 1865.
110. *Manchester Guardian,* 30 January 1864.

6

MOVES TOWARD INTERVENTION

> *"I come, then" said she (Britannia), "from a land really*
> *free,*
> *Ruled o'er by a queen, who your pattern should be;*
> *Both she and her subjects are anxious that you*
> *Should agree and be friends. I assure you, 'tis true.*
> *You speak the same language, from their land you spring—*
> *From them, O, Believe me, good wishes I bring;*
> *O imitate them in your own motherland;*
> *And, Abe, do shake brother Jeff by the hand.*
> s.w. of audenshaw cottage, 14 november 1863.[1]

Intervention during the war could change from an intent of mild mediation to one of fierce aggression as the light cast by the fighting and the
famine changed its hue. The role of peacemaker was assumed far more
frequently than that of warmonger because the essential concern was to
stop all hostilities so that the cultivation and exportation of Southern cotton could return to normal. Except perhaps in the northeast of Lancashire, less faith was entrusted to mediation than to recognition as a means
of restocking the cotton mills. Recognition was a clean, swift action with
immediate consequences, whereas mediation might drag on for years.
However, it was realized that the vagueness of mediation might be the
very quality which would allow it to appeal to a nervous government,
while definite recognition would be rejected. Although mediation was the
mildest form of pro-Southern action, it was still intrinsically favorable to
the South since, in Lancashire at any rate, it assumed the existence of two
independent powers to arbitrate between, and precluded the reconstitu-
tion of the Union along pre–Civil War lines.

   Mistrust of the North was pushed to and over the brink of bellicos-
ity in Lancashire only during the *Trent* crisis. Once the North had denied
responsibility, the anger abated. Watchful eyes were kept on Canada but
no substantial demand for war was again heard. Confidence was generally deposited in the capacity of the government to increase troops so that
Canada would be effectively defended in a war. Troops were indeed consolidated and strategically deployed in Canada after the possibility of war

1. In the *Ashton Standard*, 9 January 1864.

134

was laid bare by the *Trent*,[2] but Liverpool and Manchester did have doubts about the adequacy of the measures. The likelihood of war was felt to lie in sudden aggression demanding immediate response from the government. On this Lancashire could have little influence. It was felt that mediation was an ever present possibility and that here pressure might effectively be brought to bear on the cabinet. Resolutions urging government mediation were passed at large public meetings in Lancashire and petitions were sent to the government in an effort to stimulate action. Since it was obvious that English mediation alone was unlikely to be effective, particular enthusiasm was shown whenever France made overtures to Britain for joint mediation. Such overtures were scattered through 1862 and 1863 but were ignored by the British government—to the chagrin of Lancashire editors and operatives alike.

THE NORTHEAST

The weaving towns were far more attracted to the idea of some form of intervention than the spinning centers. Peaceful mediation, always interpreted so as to consolidate Southern independence, aroused at least as much popular support as recognition, whereas it had only a limited appeal in the southeast. Even military intervention was seriously considered by the local press long after the furor over the *Trent* had died down. Here mediation, in all its guises, exhibited its most potent and prolonged attraction.

A "Dignified Remonstrance" from England and France was thought by the *Preston Guardian* in October 1861 to be the most likely way of bringing the conflict to a speedy end.[3] All organs of the Preston press began to urge mediation in 1862 and piled up persuasive arguments during 1863. In particular they attacked the illogicality of Britain generally relying on arbitration and yet ignoring that possibility in the American war.[4]

In the summer and autumn of 1861, the *Burnley Advertiser* and *Preston Chronicle* saw armed intervention as a serious potential weapon in the cam-

2. Bourne, *Britain and the Balance of Power*, pp. 251–52; Robin Winks, *Canada and the United States. The Civil War Years* (Baltimore, 1960), pp. 82–88, 118–19.

3. *Preston Guardian*, 12 October 1861.

4. Ibid., 30 May, 27 June, 4 July 1863, *Preston Chronicle*, 21 May 1862, 5 December 1863; *Preston Pilot*, 25 July, 29 August 1863.

paign to end the hostilities.[5] The *Trent* crisis fanned into flame an inter-
ventionist fire that was here never completely snuffed out. With cautious
exceptions in the *Preston Mercury* and *Preston Guardian,*[6] the press was united
in its demand for a retributive war.[7] The *Blackburn Standard* and *Blackburn
Patriot* were most unconciliatory— "The sooner we cease to be neutral and
become belligerent the better." [8] The desire for military intervention lost
some of its intensity with America's concession to Britain's demands, but
the desire persisted for much of the war. The *Preston Chronicle* and the *Preston Pilot* formulated strong arguments for intervention at intervals
throughout 1862 and 1863, while D. Longworth of Preston suggested to
the *Preston Guardian* that intervention might follow mediation and recognition.[9] Intervention was—even in heavily distressed Preston—always a last
resort.

A couple of meetings in 1862 sought mediation long before it was
contemplated in the southeast. A public meeting organized by the Preston
Peace Society in February 1862 passed unanimously a motion favoring
arbitration in the American war.[10] This was to go as unnoticed as the verdict of a huge meeting of operatives in Blackburn in June 1862 which
proposed, in even stronger terms, that Britain move immediately towards
peaceful mediation.[11] Such a move was forcefully backed in Parliament
by a local M.P., John Turner Hopwood, the Liberal representative for
Clitheroe, who on 18 July 1862 proposed European mediation or lone arbitration.[12]

Popular enthusiasm for such a move was demonstrated far more frequently in 1863. Meetings at Bacup, Rawtenstall, and Rossendale in May
1863 passed motions seeking mediation which presumed that only a recognized South could participate as an equal in peace negotiations. Recognition was clearly approved at the large Bacup meeting before a resolu-

5. *Burnley Advertiser,* 15 June 1861. *Preston Chronicle,* 9 November 1861.
6. *Preston Mercury,* 30 November 1861, *Preston Guardian,* 30 November 1861.
7. *Preston Pilot,* 7, 21 December 1861; *Burnley Advertiser,* 30 November 1861; *Preston
Chronicle,* 4 December 1861.
8. *Blackburn Patriot,* 30 November 1861; *Blackburn Standard,* 4 December 1861.
9. *Preston Pilot,* 26 April, 17 May, 16 August 1862, 25 February, 25 July, 29 August,
31 October 1863; *Preston Chronicle,* 11 January, 20 September 1862; *Preston Guardian,* 19 July
1862.
10. Ibid., 8 February 1862.
11. *Blackburn Standard,* 2 July 1862.
12. *Hansard Parliamentary Debates,* 3d ser., vol. 168, pp. 577–78.

tion was unanimously passed "urging the English Government to take such steps as would bring about a termination of the present struggle in America." The sentiments of the large meetings at Rawtenstall and Rossendale were well summed up in the motion passed at the Rossendale Mechanics Institute:

> Seeing that the two years' bloody and in-human war, waged by the Northern states of America against the Southern Confederacy, has brought woe and desolation into the homes of countless thousands on both sides of the Atlantic without conferring benefit on any portion of the human family, this meeting is desirous that it should be brought to a speedy end, and would urge upon the British government to take such steps as may be best calculated to bring about such a desirable result.[13]

On 17 July 1863 the Reverend A. E. Verity gave an address in Preston under the auspices of the Preston Southern Club and successfully carried a motion to use mediation to terminate the war.[14] A touching and unfounded faith in the power of public opinion to sway official actions was displayed by C.W.C. (Charles W. Chapman.) of Preston in a letter to the local press on 5 August 1863. He warned the operatives of Preston that the government would not move to mediation unless sharply prodded by Lancashire workers:

> Birmingham thrives upon the manufacture of guns, rifles, shot and shell, which it sends in tons to the Northerners, for the slaughter of their brethren in the Confederate States. Are you therefore surprised at Mr. Bright's advocating the continuance of this war when he is the member of Parliament for Birmingham? Birmingham grows fat upon our miseries. Listen no longer to Mr. Bright and his interested followers: they have their own end to serve, but they are not for your interests.[15]

In November the voices of Preston operatives were to be raised in protest but were, as usual, to be unheeded. On 26 November, after "a very numerously signed requisition" was presented to the mayor of Preston, asking him to convene a meeting of the inhabitants to consider adopting a memorial to the cabinet asking for mediation with a view to separation of the states, a public meeting was called in the Corn Exchange. Interest

13. *Bolton Chronicle,* 23 May 1863; *Bury Guardian,* 23 May 1863.
14. *Preston Chronicle,* 18 July 1863.
15. *Preston Chronicle,* 8 August 1863; *Preston Pilot,* 8 August 1863.

was so great that many were unable to gain admittance. The Reverend W. C. Squier submitted a resolution for intercession on the basis of Southern independence; this was ably supported and seconded by C. W. Chapman, who argued that mediation resulting in secession would benefit Americans, white and Negro, as well as the starving Preston operatives. The resolution was passed "by a large majority" over an amendment supporting neutrality. A petition to the Commons was sent, pleading for "the moral influence of Europe" to end the war on the basis of a peaceful separation.[16] A further petition based on a public meeting in Preston, and submitted in June 1864, sought for an end to the war through British intercession—equally ineffectually.[17]

In Burnley, on 20 August 1863, Joseph Barker obtained an overwhelming majority for his resolution, "that we urge our government in conjunction with other powers of Europe, to endeavour by counsels of mediation or other peaceful measures, to bring the horrible war now waging in America to a speedy end."[18]

At a Burnley public meeting convened in December by three hundred inhabitants to discuss the desirability of intervention in the American war, an amendment for neutrality was defeated by a strongly worded resolution for mediation. The implications of mediation were made quite clear when the proceedings ended with three cheers for the South and independence.[19] These cheers were an echo and an indication of what very many in the weaving towns keenly wanted. Mediation was seen as the most simple and inexpensive way of attaining recognition for an independent South and a renewal of the cotton trade. Negotiations for peace were thought to be by far the safest cover for the quest for cotton—a quest that would otherwise have been unacceptably naked and intense.

THE SOUTHEAST

The ephemeral nature of intervention was most apparent in the southeast where enthusiasm drifted from impartial arbitration, through prosouthern mediation, to the final resort of war itself. Peaceful intervention was rarely regarded in the spinning towns as the course most

16. *Preston Guardian*, 28 November 1863; *Preston Chronicle*, 28 November 1863; *Blackburn Standard*, 2 December 1863.
17. "Report of the Select Committee on Public Petitions," 1864, p. 778.
18. *Burnley Free Press*, 22 August 1863; *Burnley Advertiser*, 22 August 1863.
19. *Burnley Free Press*, 19 December 1863.

likely to relieve the cotton famine; however, it was seen as the most viable alternative to recognition. The most distressed areas showed a detached interest in mediation, but elsewhere it was carried to popularity on the backwash of the rebuff of pleas for recognition. War had but a short-lived appeal while indignation over the *Trent* seizure raged; during 1862 the whole idea became abhorrent. Only in the least distressed towns of this district could any form of intervention compete with the overwhelming approval for recognition of the South.

Ironically one of the earliest pleas for arbitration came from Richard Cobden in December 1862. In a letter printed in the *Rochdale Spectator* he suggested that the object of all true and rational patriots should be to enforce upon the government the form of "mediation or arbitration" sanctioned by the Congress of Paris in 1856.[20] Although the *Bolton Chronicle* was gradually to become a devotee of Southern independence, its impartiality in May 1861 seemed in little doubt:

> Would it not be well for some European government to interpose its good offices before it be too late? If the interference of England singly would be looked upon with suspicion, why should not England, France and Russia jointly offer their arbitration, with a view to settling in time, a strife which if continued is likely to assume so formidable a character?[21]

The Chronicle opposed the possibility of France being allowed to intervene alone and gain control of Southern cotton.[22]

The press generally judged the summer of 1862 to be a propitious time for joint Anglo-French mediation; if it failed, discredit would attach only to those who rejected peaceful overtures.[23] That the prime concern was the welfare of the operatives in Lancashire, not the supposed rights of the South, was made abundantly clear by the *Wigan Observer:*

> It will be a slight deference and a great consolation to the men of Lancashire to know that the Government has employed its moral influence for the purpose of terminating the war that deprives them of cotton. . . . If the effort should not be successful, there will be, in the eyes of Lancashire operatives, a merit in the attempt. We con-

20. *Rochdale Spectator,* 21 December 1861.
21. *Bolton Chronicle,* 4 May 1861.
22. Ibid., 22 June 1861.
23. *Bury Guardian,* 19 July 1862; *Wigan Observer,* 20 June, 4, 19 July 1862, *Rochdale Pilot,* 28 June 1862; *Ashton Standard,* 18 August 1862.

ceive it is the duty of our Government to show to the people of this country that every fair and legitimate endeavour has been made to stop a war that indirectly produces starvation and wretchedness, on a broad scale, among millions of honest and naturally industrious people. Viewed from any standpoint we say it is the duty of the British government to join with France in an offer of mediation between the belligerent sections of the once united States.[24]

The same priorities were apparent in November when readers were reminded that "every step towards peace also brings us nearer to four millions of bales of excellent cotton: and who can estimate the value that a suspension of hostilities would have for the starving and famishing people of this district?" As it was also thought that refraining from mediation would earn only the scorn of both North and South in America, anger was felt at the refusal of Russell to accept the French emperor's invitation to join with him in asking America to suspend hostilities and commence peace negotiations.[25]

Throughout 1863 impatience with the government's tardiness in agreeing to joint mediation inflamed the southeastern press.[26] Exasperation bordered on despair in the *Bury Free Press* in May 1864, when the interminable continuation of "barbarities" and "horrid waste and slaughter" was anticipated unless Europe intervened.[27] Even as late as February 1865 the *Bury Guardian* urged Britain to assume the role of mediator.[28] Most editors were conscious by then that the moment for mediation had passed, but indignation that it had simply been allowed to slip away never abated.

Only at one very particular time did press fury spill over into demands for actual war against the North. Before the *Trent* provided this intense provocation, the idea of such a war was rejected as ridiculous;[29] only the *Ashton and Stalybridge Reporter* thought, in early November 1861, that war might be welcomed as bringing cotton.[30] The seizure of the Con-

24. *Wigan Observer*, 20 June 1862.

25. Ibid., 21 November 1862.

26. *Bury Free Press*, 1 January 1863; *Rochdale Pilot*, 3 January 1863; *Bolton Chronicle* 14 November 1863; *Wigan Observer*, 11 December 1863.

27. *Bury Free Press*, 26 May 1864.

28. *Bury Guardian*, 4 February 1865.

29. *Ashton and Stalybridge Reporter*, 6 July 1861; *Oldham Chronicle*, 6 July 1861; *Bolton Chronicle*, 16 November 1861.

30. *Ashton and Stalybridge Reporter*, 2, 23 November 1861.

federate commissioners aroused universal belligerence.[31] The *Rochdale Observer* was alone in pleading for caution.[32] After January 1862, the surge towards military intervention receded, edging only slightly forward again in editorials of the *Bury Guardian* and *Bolton Chronicle* in 1863.[33] Intervention was cast off as too uncertain a way of obtaining cotton.

Meetings and petitions favoring mediation in all its guises sprang up at odd times during the war years. In towns that suffered only moderate distress the popularity of mediation exceeded that of recognition, but in Ashton and Oldham mediation ran a very poor second. Mathew Barton of Wigan made a strong plea for arbitration:

> although the trade of the town was in a very deplorable position, he hoped, ere long, it would be resuscitated, and that instead of pale and emaciated forms being seen in the streets they might see cheerfulness and activity, and that the deplorable struggle in another part of the world which was the cause of their present suffering might soon be ended. He thought the Americans had fought long enough, and that as the police constables in Wigan sometimes interfered between parties who were in contention and had given broken noses, so should the high constables of Europe—England, France and Russia—step in between the Americans and persuade them that they had had enough of fighting, or at all events ask them to stop for a while and draw their breath, and then see if they were in a position to resume their quarrel. (Hear, hear.) He thought if such a course were taken they would soon have their trade revived.[34]

Over a year later a small meeting (between seventy and a hundred) in Wigan Town Hall voted in favor of mediation after a lecture by A. E. Verity.[35]

The Reverend Verity also agitated for mediation in Bury in 1864, and he was heartily cheered when he said that he did not want armed intervention in the war but amiable discussion.[36] In July a petition from seventy-three Bury inhabitants requesting mediation was presented to the

31. Ibid., 30 November 1861; *Bury Guardian,* 30 November 1861, 11 January 1862; *Wigan Examiner,* 30 November, 13 December 1861; *Bolton Chronicle,* 4, 11 January 1862; *Oldham Standard,* 7 December 1861; *Oldham Chronicle,* 7 December, 28 December 1861.

32. *Rochdale Observer,* 30 November, 14 December 1861.

33. *Bury Guardian,* 25 April 1863; *Bolton Chronicle,* 16 August 1863.

34. *Wigan Observer,* 21 November 1862.

35. Ibid., 27 January 1864.

36. *Bury Guardian,* 13 February 1864.

Commons by Bury M.P. Frederick Peel.[37] A mild predilection for British assumption of the mantle of peaceful intervenor was in harmony with the muted impact of the cotton famine.

Bolton was the only town in this region to declare itself to be staunchly in favor of mediation. Early in June 1863 it was announced by placard that two general meetings were called to discuss "Peace versus the American War," and "A Working Man" expressed his satisfaction at the possibility of "peace" being approved by "earnest men" of the town.[38] The meetings did indeed come up to the best hopes of "A Working Man" and opted wholeheartedly for peaceful intervention. A resolution was passed by a large majority at the first meeting asking for British "counsels of conciliation" to end the war peacefully.

Copies of the resolution were sent to Adams and Mason to forward to Washington and Richmond. Approval for the resolution was expressed in several lucid letters to the *Bolton Chronicle* a few days after the meeting.[39] At a meeting in Bolton on 22 June 1863, organized by the Union and Emancipation Society, W. A. Jackson proposed a pro-Northern, anti-Southern motion. An amendment proposing British intervention for peace was backed by operatives and gained the support of half the show of hands at the meeting—a surprising result at this ultra-organised Northern affair—but nonetheless the motion was declared to be carried and copies of the pro-Northern resolution were sent to Palmerston, Russell, and Adams. In this instance they could hardly be blamed for making false assumptions from the inadequate evidence they were given.[40] In January 1864 the Reverend Verity recommended to a Bolton audience a resolution in favor of British and European joint mediation which was passed by an overwhelming majority.[41] Most impressive of all were the 1,914 signatures on the petition presented to Parliament by Captain Gray on 14 July requesting moves to end the war, and backed up by similar petitions from nearby Farnworth and Kearsley.[42]

When compared with the numerous meetings, resolutions, and petitions requesting recognition that emerged from Ashton and Oldham, as

37. "Report of the Select Committee on Public Petitions," 1864, p. 847.
38. *Bolton Chronicle,* 13 June 1863.
39. Ibid., 20 June 1863.
40. Ibid., 27 June 1863.
41. Ibid., 23 January 1864.
42. "Report of the Select Committee on Public Petitions," 1864, p. 846; *Burnley Advertiser,* 16 July 1864.

well as from the "satellites" of Mossley and Lees, mediation won few and then only belated demonstrations in these towns. Not until 1864 did Ashton show any interest in peaceful intervention, and it was not a public meeting but the Church Union Debating Society that passed a resolution asking for official mediation by the Government.[43] Petitions were sent to the Commons from Ashton and Dukinfield in July 1864 also seeking peaceful intervention by the government.[44] There was an organization known as the Ashton and Dukinfield Peace Society which was unique in championing arbitration at the impossible time of February 1865.[45]

Oldham's scant approval of mediation came through a speech by John Tomlinson Hibbert, one of its M.P.'s, at Hollinwood United Methodist Free Church, who declared it impossible "that the north could conquer the south, therefore it would be charitable to interfere and put an end to such cruel work as was going on." [46] Peaceful intercession had rather more appeal in Lees and Mossley. In June 1863 a resolution seeking mediation was passed by "a crowded public meeting" in the People's Hall, Lees, "by a majority of twenty to one," but Mr. Quarmby who proposed it simultaneously made an eloquent plea for recognition. The resolution itself sought to petition Parliament to instigate European mediation to end the war and "to give us a plentiful supply of cotton wherewith to employ our starving operatives"—and to afford an opportunity of peaceful emancipation to the Negro.[47] Lees responded by petitioning for mediation on the basis of recognition. Mossley waited till mid 1864 to approve mediation when a large public meeting passed, with only one dissentient, a resolution pinning faith on ending the war by European efforts at pacification.[48] A petition, signed by 1,260 inhabitants, requesting government initiative in such pacification was presented to the Commons on 15 July by John Cobbett, the senior Oldham M.P.[49] A not unimpressive body of men there campaigned for mediation but always as only a poor alternative to recognition.

The lack of any overwhelming enthusiasm for mediation in the area

43. *Ashton Standard,* 27 February 1864.
44. *Burnley Advertiser,* 16 July 1864.
45. *Ashton and Stalybridge Reporter* 25 February 1865.
46. *Oldham Chronicle,* 3 May 1862.
47. *Oldham Standard,* 20 June 1863.
48. *Ashton Standard,* 2 July 1864.
49. "Report of the Select Committee on Public Petitions," 1864, p. 847. Cobbett also presented a poorly signed petition from Oldham itself.

was demonstrated by the frequency with which meetings were addressed and resolutions suggested by the northeast Lancashire rector, A. E. Verity, rather than by local men. Verity even managed to gain approval for mediation from a Rochdale audience in January 1864, but this vote was close and the attendance thin, as a charge had been made for admission.[50]

No public man or public meeting sanctioned military intervention against the North at any other time than the height of the *Trent* furor. As the *Trent* storm raged, Frederick Peel was given the approval of his constituents at Bury for his willingness to wage war on the offending North, while William Aitken and Edward Watkins at Ashton, John Cobbett and John Platt at Oldham publicly preferred war to loss of English honor.[51] The storm rapidly died down and milder, less painful forms of intervention were favored. Even these were only embraced once the futility of remaining faithful to the more appealing and less equivocal course of recognition had become evident.

MANCHESTER

During the early stages of the Civil War there was no more than a very limited amount of support for any kind of intervention, even from the Manchester press. In 1864, however, there was a rush for peaceful mediation that stemmed from the shifting allegiance of cotton manufacturers and their operatives, merchants and tradesmen, settling on intercession on behalf of the South during the last year of the war.[52]

The *Manchester Courier* was alone in its early and wholehearted championing of mediation,[53] as well as in its unique and bitter suggestion that John Bright and his friends would be the most acceptable mediators to a North whose interests they championed over those of England.[54] Only the most tentative backing for mediation was given by the *Manchester Weekly Express.*[55]

Among its numerous pro-Southern tracts the Manchester Southern Independence Association in 1864 produced two in favor of mediation. A

50. *Rochdale Spectator,* 30 January 1864.
51. *Rochdale Spectator,* 14 December 1861; *Manchester Weekly Times,* 14 December 1861; *Oldham Chronicle,* 7, 14 December 1861; *Rochdale Spectator,* 14 December 1861; *Ashton and Stalybridge Reporter,* 7 December 1861; *Ashton Standard,* 7 December 1861.
52. H.S.G., *Autobiography,* chap. 15.
53. *Manchester Courier,* 17 January, 28 February, 23 May, 6 June 1863.
54. Ibid., 19 July 1862.
55. *Manchester Weekly Express,* 22 November 1862.

pamphlet by C. A. Duval considered that England and France should interpose—preferably peacefully.[56] A poster published by the Southern Independence Association presented clear and succinct arguments for mediation:

STOP THE WAR

THE TIME IS NOW FAVOURABLE. THE EMPEROR OF THE
MOST WARLIKE NATION OF EUROPE HAS PROPOSED A
CONGRESS OF NATIONS TO SETTLE NATIONAL DISPUTES.
LET ENGLAND SECOND THIS PROPOSITION AND SHE WILL
STOP THE WAR.

BRITISH WORKMEN, BE TRUE TO YOUR COUNTRY AND ASSIST
THOSE WHO ARE MAKING EVERY EFFORT TO AROUSE THE
GOVERNMENTS OF EUROPE TO

STOP THIS WAR

GIVE PEACE TO AMERICA

GIVE FREEDOM TO THE SLAVE

GIVE PROSPERITY TO LANCASHIRE.[57]

Nowhere else was so decisive a public statement issued or read.

One of the most heavily signed petitions to the Commons for mediation came from Manchester in 1864. On 15 July James Turner presented a petition from 5,186 Mancunians which assumed

> that the Federal Government cannot subjugate and hold in subjugation the people of the Southern States, and that the present aspects of the conflict afford no hope of its early termination . . . that to protract the contest can only result in a useless destruction of life and property on that continent, and in the infliction of serious injury on our own country.
> Wherefore your Petitioners humbly pray that your honourable House will be pleased to take such steps as may in your judgement most rapidly lead to the re-establishment of peace.[58]

Even more impressive was an address asking the Northern people to start negotiations on the basis of Southern independence. The address was signed by 350,000 people and taken by Joseph Parker of Manchester to

56. C. A. Duval, *Slavery*, p. 20.
57. Southern Independence Association, 26 Market Street, Manchester.
58. Appendix to the "Report of the Select Committee on Public Petitions," 1864, p. 331.

New York in October 1864. This attempt at direct mediation failed because of its unofficial nature, as Seward refused to receive an address that was not approved by the British government. This failure in no way lessens the significance of such a massive Manchester-based demand for English interposition to establish peace between the two nations.[59]

As 1864 drew to a close, an open-air meeting of Manchester operatives passed a resolution asking the government to join with Europe in stopping the destructive American war and so alleviate Lancashire distress.[60] This demand and the large Manchester petition for mediation came too late to affect government policy, even if it had been amenable to public suggestion.

The idea of actual war against the North was more unpalatable, but there was in Manchester a great awareness of the constant possibility of such intervention. Even the *Trent* affair aroused in the press only mild admonitions to the North tempered by the hope that peace would prevail.[61] The strongest reactions came from the *Manchester Guardian* and *Manchester Courier,* which warned that war might result from such ill-considered insults.[62] Manchester merchants tended to accept and use whatever situation existed, and although the *Trent* convinced many that there would be war with the North and a renewed cotton supply from the Confederacy, no efforts were made to see that this happened. A number did go as far as cancelling orders for cotton from India, but more active measures were not adopted.[63]

After indignation over the *Trent* had been appeased, a fear of war mingled with a determination to defend British honor from Northern onslaught lingered on in the Manchester press. Only the *Manchester Weekly Express and Review* actually sought intervention, but editors there were conscious of the danger in clashes with the North that might still detonate war. The *Manchester Courier* envisaged war resulting from the Federal seizure of the *Peterhoff* and its mail, and later of the *Florida,* and severe warnings were issued to the North.[64]

59. Joseph Parker, *For Peace in America* (Manchester, 1865), pp. 3, 5, 9–11, 16.
60. *Manchester Courier,* 5 December 1864.
61. *Manchester Weekly Times,* 14 December 1861; *Manchester Examiner and Times,* 28 November 1861; *Manchester Weekly Express and Review,* 4, 11 January 1862.
62. *Manchester Guardian,* 28 November 1861, *Manchester Courier,* 30 November 1861.
63. *Manchester Examiner and Times,* 10 April 1862; see also Arthur W. Silver, *Manchester Men and Indian Cotton 1847–1872* (Manchester, 1966) p. 167.
64. *Manchester Courier,* 25 April 1863, 3 January 1865.

The most serious threat to peace was seen to be the movement by the Northern General Dix of some of his troops over the Canadian border. The *Guardian* and the *Courier* were tensely aware that only Lincoln's interposition prevented the invasion of Canada and a probable war between England and the North. Concern was subsequently shown for the state of Canada's defenses should war materialize over such an incident.[65]

This perceptive awareness that war might result from fear over Canada's integrity was not found elsewhere. The perception was matched by an intense dislike of the thought of any kind of active interference in the war that made mild mediation seem the most attractive way of influencing events.

LIVERPOOL

In this city where Southern support reigned supreme, the most ardent friends of the Confederacy wanted the adoption of more patently partisan measures than mediation. So much moral and financial sympathy was invested in the seceded states that recognition and the breaking of the blockade were the more favored courses. At times even military intervention was considered. Nonetheless, peaceful interposition did appeal to a not inconsiderable number. In some cases this was simply the first step towards the recognition of Southern independence, but to others it was the limit to which their basic desire for noninterference could be stretched.

The *Liverpool Daily Post* early acknowledged the general Liverpool predilection for a separated South while making clear its own initial preference for an unbroken Union.[66] After a Union victory in September 1861, mediation was advised, and mediation of a special kind. The suggestion was made that Liverpool merchants send a deputation to both Washington and Richmond to see if grounds for healing the breach would be unearthed at a time when defeat might predispose the South to consider peace on moderate terms.[67] Official and peaceful mediation was later advocated, particularly and unusually during the *Trent* crisis.[68]

---

65. In the spring of 1864 General Dix was in fact pursuing into New England Confederates who were using Canada as a base for raising operations. Winks, *Canada and the U.S.,* 302–36. *Manchester Guardian,* 3 January, 25 March 1865; *Manchester Courier,* 30 December 1864, 5 January, 9 February 1865.

66. *Liverpool Daily Post,* 28 May 1861.

67. Ibid., 16 September 1861.

68. Ibid., 9 December, 15 October 1861.

In January 1862 a stronger tone was adopted. "The civil war in America must be stopped—stopped by mediation if possible, by force if absolutely necessary; but stopped it must be, in deference to humanity, in deference to the interests of Europe, and to the preservation of America itself—North and South." Overtures by deputations friendly to each side were suggested as a preliminary to the official mediation that the *Post* continued to press for during most of 1862.[69] The approach of the *Post* was essentially practical, and such intervention was only advocated while it seemed the quickest path to peace and cotton; when Northern victories made the fate of the South less certain, the idea of mediation was abandoned. The fate of cotton was also the prime consideration of the *Liverpool Weekly Mercury*. Intervention of a physical kind was roundly condemned as likely to prolong the cotton famine, but peaceful mediation was approved as a potent means of hastening the end of hostilities.[70] The *Albion* only once, in February 1863,[71] deviated from its fierce devotion to recognition to urge that Britain and France become joint peacemakers, whereas the *Liverpool Mail* consistently and determinedly sought for European efforts to check the war in this way and so further Britain's commercial interests.[72]

Military intervention had for the Liverpool press an uneasy attraction. Warmongering editorials appeared at intervals during the war years. The *Liverpool Weekly Mercury* typified the extreme anger that ran through the press over the *Trent* outrage and itself went as far as to claim that war would have "the hearty and earnest support and approval of all sections of the community." [73] The release of Mason and Slidell won only the most grudging withdrawal from the brink of war.[74] Desire for military intervention then ebbed without totally disappearing. The *Daily Post* still saw provocation for war in the heavy tariffs of 1862; in 1863 the *Mail* saw such provocation in the seizure of the *Peterhoff* mail bags; and spasmodically the *Albion* saw it in the general Northern antagonism and the need of the South for help. The sense of undeserved persecution tended to dis-

69. Ibid., 20 January, 11 March, 12, 20, 23 May, 23 July 1862.
70. *Liverpool Weekly Mercury,* 25 January, 3 May 1862.
71. *Albion,* 9 February 1863.
72. *Liverpool Mail,* 14 June, 12 July 1862, 31 January 1863.
73. *Liverpool Weekly Mercury,* 30 November, 21 December 1861; 4 January 1862; *Albion,* 2, 9 December 1861; *Liverpool Daily Post,* 2 December 1861.
74. *Liverpool Daily Post,* 9, 13 January 1862; *Liverpool Weekly Mercury,* 11 January 1862.

solve in light of the inadequate defenses of Canada, which made hostilities seem suicidal.[75]

James Spence was Liverpool's most persistent advocate of a mediation that he saw as an elementary tool for prying open the door to recognition. His most public championing of mediation was at a meeting of the Liverpool Southern Club in October 1863;[76] his more private effort was in his correspondence with the Confederate commissioner to Britain, James Mason. Spence felt that only recognition would assure the South of its independence but realized that a mildly pro-Southern type of mediation might well be as far as Britain was prepared to go. Without some move from Britain the South, Spence was well aware, had little hope. In a letter written on 15 September 1862 he expected that if the military events reached a crisis the European governments would mediate between the belligerents.[77] On 3 August 1863 even he acknowledged that "I could not advocate Recognition *now* but I have an abundant argument for European mediation as in the case of Poland." [78] A touch of despair was discernible four months later: "I am now clear in my own mind that unless we get Europe to move—or some improbable convulsions occur in the North—the end will be a sad one. It seems to me therefore impossible that too strenuous an effort can be made to move our government." [79] On 31 May 1864, Spence argued that Mason should seek an interview with Lord Palmerston as soon as possible to stress the overriding urgency of European diplomatic mediation.[80] Mason's lack of success did not deter Spence himself from meeting Palmerston in July 1864 as a member of a deputation seeking mediation. The deputation from the Society for Obtaining the Cessation of Hostilities in America had to be content with Palmerston's vague hopes for mediation in the future rather than any promise for immediate action.[81]

Gladstone was the one Liverpudlian who was in a position to in-

75. *Liverpool Daily Post,* 11 July 1862; *Liverpool Mail,* 9 May, 10 October 1863; *Albion,* 23 June 1862, 23 January, 30 January, 6 February, 20 February 1865; *Liverpool Mail,* 25 February, 18 March 1865.
76. *Albion,* 19 October 1865.
77. Spence to Mason, 15 September 1862, Mason papers.
78. Ibid., 3 August 1863.
79. Ibid., 17 December 1863.
80. Ibid., 31 May 1864.
81. *Manchester Guardian,* 18 July 1864.

fluence government policy and did in fact urge mediation with transitory devotion. Russell and Palmerston were aware of the advantages of intervention, and Gladstone's public support for the South at Manchester and Newcastle precipitated a shift towards mediation. Feelers were put out towards France and Russia, and though France was as eager as ever, Russia was reluctant. Unfortunately for the South, victories began to be replaced by defeats, and the cabinet decided to wait for a more propitious moment.[82] This never came, and Gladstone regretted his hasty liaison with the South. Some of the strongest doubts about the value of mediation were cast in Liverpool by Thomas Dudley, who made it evident that mediation would antagonize the North as much as recognition and would lead to a war in which England would lose Canada and ruin herself.[83]

Since war itself might well be attendant on such a mild measure as mediation, many in Liverpool thought it as well to intervene directly through deliberate choice. The seizure of the Confederate commissioners stirred up a whirlpool of vengeful anger that threatened to drag the country into war. Dudley was plainly alarmed by Liverpool's reaction:

> The cry was for war, even before they knew whether the act of Captain Wilkes would be approved or condemned by our government. The great mass of people did not seem to care what we said or did. We had insulted their flag and they wanted to fight us. They desired their government to strike, and at once.[84]

William Lidderdale, S. C. Rathbone's New York agent, plainly expected war to be unavoidable because of public pressure—unless the Federal government totally disowned Captain Wilkes's action.[85]

The high point of the crisis came on 27 November when a meeting of enraged cotton brokers and merchants in the cotton salesroom of Liverpool's Exchange demanded war with the North. This normally cautious body of men passed a violently anti-Northern motion. The belligerent mood only began to soften when it was realized that a war at that mo-

82. Earl Russell to Earl Cowley, 13 November 1862. Correspondence Relative to Mediation, Public Documents, *Annual Register, 1862* (London, 1863), pp. 234–36; Gladstone papers, vol. DCLXVII, 44752 fl 51, DX fl 86; Guedella, *Gladstone and Palmerston,* pp. 64–65, 232; E. D. Adams, *Britain and the Civil War,* 2: 26–27, 73.

83. Dudley, *Diplomatic Relations,* p. 14.

84. Ibid., p. 4.

85. William Lidderdale to S. C. Rathbone, New York, 21 November 1861, Rathbone Collection, University of Liverpool Library.

ment might produce a glut of cotton and a fall in prices.[86] The news of the settlement of the crisis was received with mingled cheers and hisses that reflected the ambivalent attitude prevalent in the city towards a possible war that was known to be unwise yet was still yearned for.[87]

Liverpool went a stage further than any other part of Lancashire in not merely talking about intervention but in actually doing something about it. The Liverpool banking firm of Fraser, Trenholm and Company was the Confederate financial agent in Europe, and it was only through the credit it afforded Major Caleb Huse and James Bulloch that arms, supplies, and ships were able to reach the Confederacy. Bulloch indeed asserts that the success of the battles of Seven Pines and Chickahominy was largely due to credits furnished by Charles Prioleau, the resident partner of the firm, credits which enabled Major Huse to forward the rifles and field artillery that made victory possible.[88] So useful had the services of the company been to the South that at the close of the war the United States thought it justifiable to sue for compensation (the case was settled out of court).[89]

William Forwood was a true ambassador of the city when his pro-Southern talk caused him to be arrested as a political prisoner while on a trip to New York (it was also suspected that he might have money and dispatches for the South). On his release he acted as government agent, noting conditions in Canada which might assist the march of ten thousand British troops across the dominion—troops poised for combat with the North.[90]

Apart from the crews who manned the *Florida* and *Alabama*, it is certain that men from Liverpool fought for the South. How many of the English officers and men in Confederate ranks were from Liverpool it is difficult, if not impossible, to gauge.[91] That many escaped the more professional techniques of the Federal enlisters and remained unimpressed by the greater financial rewards offered by the North suggests at least a

86. *Liverpool Daily Post;* 28 November 1861; *Liverpool Weekly Mercury,* 30 November, 7 December 1861.
87. *Liverpool Weekly Mercury,* 11 January 1862.
88. Bulloch, *Secret Service,* 1: 51–53, 2: 34, 218, 220–23.
89. Ibid., 2: 424.
90. Sir William B. Forwood, P. C., J. P., *Some Recollections of a Busy Life* (Liverpool, 1910), pp. 34–36, 37–39.
91. Ella Lonn, *Foreigners in the Confederacy* (Chapel Hill, 1940), pp. 206, 232, 428–93.

strong personal predilection for the Southern cause. Liverpool craftsmen were also employed by the Confederate government to print its paper money.[92]

Alongside its formidable efforts for mediation and strong desire for official military intervention, Liverpool contributed a unique and effective style of intervention. The ships which the Mersey docks built for the Confederacy almost crippled Northern shipping, while Liverpool blockade runners formed a lifeline between the South and England.[93]

THE WEST

In west Lancashire the lack of personal deprivation led to an inevitable detachment from the problem of what action, if any, should be taken about the American Civil War. Mediation was favored by only a few editors, occasionally and without any real sense of urgency, while even the Trent confrontation roused no genuine warlike spirit, merely a flurry of empty indignation.

To the *Warrington Standard,* the *Barrow Herald,* the *Fleetwood Chronicle,* and the *Southport Independent* it occasionally seemed that England should not refuse to join with France in tendering peace proposals, but, equally, should not assume responsibility for initiating negotiations.[94]

Certainly the only time when a few editors were bestirred enough to hope for war was, predictably, after the arrest of Mason and Slidell. The *Lancaster Guardian,* the *Ulverston Mirror,* and the *Warrington Standard* all expected war to be the outcome and in a half-hearted way looked forward to the opportunity to chastise the arrogant Northerners.[95] The rest of the press was more pacific in tone.[96]

In August 1864 the *Leigh Chronicle* summed up the attitude of the whole region very aptly when it protested that sympathy went out to the Confederacy but not to the point of war.[97] The stance here was never

92. *Liverpool Weekly Mercury,* 8 February 1862.
93. See below, chapter 7.
94. *Warrington Standard,* 27 April 1861, 19 July, 20 September 1862; *Barrow Herald,* 4 April 1863; *Southport Independent,* 4 June 1863; *Fleetwood Chronicle,* 27 December 1861.
95. *Lancaster Guardian,* 27 December 1861, 11 January 1862; *Ulverston Mirror,* 7 December 1861, 4, 11 January 1862; *Warrington Standard,* 7 December 1861.
96. *Southport Independent,* 5 December 1861; *Ormskirk Advertiser,* 5 December 1861; *Leigh Chronicle,* 30 November 1861.
97. *Lancaster Guardian,* 3 May 1862; *Leigh Chronicle,* 20 August 1864.

more alert than that of sometimes interested but never involved bystanders.

The areas in Lancashire which depended on cotton were willing to try any serious measures to bring the war to a close. A large meeting of the Southern Independence Association on 29 January 1864 noted that many Lancashire towns had given their votes for mediation, and petitions had been sent to the foreign secretary or Parliament. In fact far more resolutions were passed in favor of mediation than were cited by the association. At least twelve towns passed one or more such resolutions, while only Ashton, Oldham, Burnley, and Preston, from Lancashire, were mentioned by the secretary in his report.[98] Obviously many towns held meetings without any prior advice or organization from the association. However by July 1864 the association had contacted more of those who wished for mediation, and a collective effort was then made in presenting petitions from most Lancashire towns simultaneously. Petitions were presented to the Commons by local M.P.'s from Manchester, Farnworth, Kearsley, Bolton, Mossley, Bury, Burnley, Preston, Ashton, Oldham, Dukinfield, Rawtenstall, Bacup, "and other places." [99] Added weight was given to this effort to move the reluctant government by the visit on 18 July 1864 of a deputation of factory operatives from Manchester, Stockport, Preston, Oldham, and many other towns with Earl Russell, at the Foreign Office, "for the purpose of presenting to his lordship a memorial signed by upwards of 90,000 persons engaged in the cotton manufacture." The memorial depicted the sad plight of operatives dependent on charity or half pay and inferior cotton, as a result of the war, and then came to the main point:

> And thirdly, considering they had patiently suffered their severe privations, owing to a belief that such a state of things could not last, they were now induced, by the evident hopelessness of the struggle on the part of the North to subdue the Southern States, to represent to his lordship the claims of the factory operatives upon the favourable consideration of Her Majesty's government, and to pray that Her Majesty might be advised to enter into concert with other European powers, with a view to restore peace on the American conti-

98. *Manchester Guardian,* 30 January 1864.
99. *Burnley Advertiser,* 16 July 1864. The Manchester petition was presented by James Aspinall Turner, the Farnworth and Kearsley petition by the Hon. Algernon Egerton, the Bolton petition by Capt. W. Gray, the Mossley petition by J. Cobbett, the Burnley petition by Colonel J. Wilson-Patten, the Bury petition by the Hon. F. Peel, and the Preston petition by Sir T. C. Hesketh, Bart.

nent, and re-establish on a sure basis the industrial prosperity of the manufacturing districts.

Russell soothingly expressed the hope before the deputation departed that the time for mediation would soon come.[100] For most of its adherents mediation provided the one safe and nonaggressive way of helping to end the strife. It was seen as the means of bringing the moral force of Europe to bear on the fratricides while still standing aloof from military combat.

All over Lancashire the arrest of the Confederate commissioners caused consternation and alarm and led to a desire for a retributory war with the North should the prisoners not be released and official responsibility for the affair denied. Once war had been averted by Federal acquiescence with these demands, peaceful cooperation with the South was the course preferred by most in Lancashire. Only in Preston and Liverpool was there any continuous and consistent feeling for armed intervention on behalf of the South, and even then the voices raised were those of a small minority that was stamped with the brand of a generally rejected fringe mania. This peripheral preference for a violent solution could only have spread among the men of Lancashire if intense provocation had been thrown out by the North at a time that corresponded to the period of most debilitating distress. Then war might have seemed an answer to a totally intolerable situation. As it was, pro-Southern diplomatic pressure was hoped for to provide a subtler, speedier, and more successful resolution of the struggle and a renewal of the cotton supply. An essential difference between the cotton areas of Lancashire and the government lay in the willingness to accept the possibility of hostilities resulting from either mediation or recognition. To the impoverished men of cotton the return of a regular cotton flow was worth gambling for, even if the price of losing was war. The government had a responsibility to the entire nation and could not afford to indulge in any game of chance that might involve that same nation in an unwanted war that was unlikely to be won.

100. *Rochdale Spectator,* 23 July 1864; *Manchester Guardian,* 18 July 1864.

♉

BLOCKADE

*One of the first acts of the Government at Washington for
the suppression of the so-called rebellion was to proclaim a
blockade of all the Southern ports.*[1]

The imposition of a blockade made the survival of the South impossible
without some foreign assistance. Any latent British desire to aid the
struggling Confederacy could find its most obvious outlet through her traditional power on the sea. British ports were supremely able to supply the
ships desperately needed by the embryonic Confederate navy. Liverpool
was among those only too eager to fill this need. Theoretically no infringement of official neutrality was involved so long as the ships were not
armed or equipped in British waters. As it was, the mere construction on
Merseyside of the *Alabama* provided fuel for a twenty-year fire of angry
controversy, despite the fact that arms, equipment, and men were supplied outside British territorial waters.

A more fundamental way of furthering the Southern cause would
have been by a denial of the legitimacy of the blockade imposed by the
North on Southern ports. Agitation in Lancashire for government renun-
ciation of the blockade did in fact precede and then run parallel with individual efforts to see that the blockade was ineffective. That a blockade
should have been instigated by the North in 1861 was seen as ironic since
the United States alone had refused to sanction the Declaration of Paris,
which in 1856 laid down definitive regulations for any blockade and abolished privateering. The greatest controversy centered around the final
clause of the declaration, which stated that to be binding a blockade must
be effective. There was no lack of witnesses in Lancashire to claim that, in
the early stages at least, the Northern blockade was not effective and
should be officially ignored. When C. S. Gregory voiced this request in the
Commons in March 1862, and Lindsay, one of Liverpool's largest shipowners, tested Russell's reaction by letter in February 1862, both received
the same reply—the blockade would be officially recognized, for if it were
ineffectual why should Lancashire and Confederate sympathizers generally be so eager to see it denounced!

That the North should declare a blockade of Southern ports in April

---

1. Bulloch, *Secret Service,* 1: p. 299. The proclamation was issued on 19 April 1861 and
a small blockading fleet sent to the Southern coast. The size of the Federal navy swiftly increased and an effective blockade was in force by 1863.

1861 was also seen as an unprecedented breach of international law. The North insisted that the South was merely in rebellion and was not an independent nation; yet it was unknown for a belligerent to blockade its own ports. It could "close" its own ports but only blockade those of an enemy. This misuse of terminology, for which Seward was probably responsible, made it inevitable that Britain recognize the belligerency of the South in May 1861 and gave to the Liverpool shipowners and merchants who chose to ignore the blockade a semblance of indignant justification.

The number of Liverpool merchants and shipowners who broke the blockade was exceedingly large. This was hardly surprising because, apart from the undoubted existence of a great deal of Southern sympathy, the overwhelming stimulus of large fortunes to be made ensured an ample supply of runners and cargo. The profits were so great that a company could afford to lose half its ships or cargoes and still not suffer any overall loss. Ships were built expressly for blockade running, and munitions and supplies were shipped to the South in exchange for badly needed cotton. Ships were also built in Liverpool specifically as men-of-war for the South. The success of the *Florida* and the *Alabama* became notorious, while many in Lancashire mourned the diversion of the *Alexandra* and the Laird rams to more peaceful activities.

THE NORTHEAST

For most people in the weaving towns, breaking the blockade had only a limited appeal as a meandering, danger-strewn path to cotton. It was frequently feared that war between Britain and the North would result; the end, not the extension, of hostilities was expected to be the only way to renew cotton supplies. Blackburn was singularly emphatic in its rejection of blockade-breaking,[2] a means which, in contrast, found fervent support in the editorial and correspondence columns of the Preston and Burnley press.[3] Preston press backing was also given to Liverpool's efforts to unofficially shatter the blockade and provide the Confederacy with badly needed ships in the face of what was judged to be unwarranted government opposition.[4]

2. *Blackburn Standard,* 23 October 1861; *Blackburn Times,* 26 September 1863.
3. *Preston Pilot,* 17 August 1861, 15 February 1862; *Preston Chronicle,* 12 March 1862; *Burnley Advertiser,* 22 February, 15 March 1862.
4. *Preston Chronicle,* 7 May 1862, 27 June 1863; *Preston Pilot,* 2 May, 17 October 1863.

It is possible that the more vital interest in running or breaking the blockade shown in Preston and Burnley sprang from the larger number of spinning firms in these two towns than in Blackburn. Imports of new material were naturally more essential to spinners. So keen were the Burnley firms of Dugdale's, Mark Kippax, and George Slater that they themselves chartered ships to run the blockade. The cotton so imported saved Burnley from being cut by the sharpest edge of the distress.[5]

Surprisingly perhaps, Preston had an even more intense personal concern in the fate of ships that sailed for the Confederacy. In August 1863 an iron ship called the *Cecilia* was completed at the new yard of Mr. Mackern for Messrs. Wilson and Chambers of Liverpool. The ship was ostensibly to provide passage to Australia, but at the launching ceremony subtle allusions added to the definite sense of a double role. The speech of Mr. Edward Haycock provided perhaps the clearest indication of duality, or indeed duplicity:

> As to the vessel, he was sure they would watch her, in the newspapers (laughter) and see an account of her first sailing to Australia, and coming back again, but if they found she was going on a Confederate cruise by mistake, he did not think that any of them would wish her any the less success. (Hear, hear, and laughter)[6]

Whether the ship did in any way ultimately aid the Confederacy is less important than that one could be built in Preston in the hope that she would help sever the constricting blockade. In any case a ship called the *Night Hawk* did successfully run the blockade for several months before capture in September 1864. The *Night Hawk* was built in Preston and may have been the renamed *Cecilia,* but it is more probable that two separate ships built in the town ran the blockade.

Nevertheless, no more than an articulate minority in the area argued that an official explosion of repudiation would shatter the blockade and free Southern and British ships to legally carry cotton to Lancashire. Liverpool blockade-breakers were never thought capable of transporting more than tantalizing foretastes of the bulk of cotton that was needed, while they might just possibly detonate a destructive war with the Union. To the helpless majority in the area, it was war itself which had stultified

5. Bennett, *Burnley,* pp. 121–22.
6. *Preston Pilot,* 8 August 1863.

the cotton trade and must be stopped before adequate cotton supplies could again pour into the northeast.

THE SOUTHEAST

If ships were commissioned to break the blockade by south-easterners, it was without the publicity apparent in Burnley and Preston, but far more agitatory activity for breaking the blockade was generally demonstrated. Meetings as well as editorials and letters asked that the blockade be ignored. Anger at the interference of the government with Liverpool's plans to supply ships to the Confederacy was fierce and widespread.

Rochdale was alone in actually supporting the blockade, and a meeting in 1863 passed a resolution attacking those who built ships for the Confederacy.[7] In the same week John Bright told his wife of his fear that war would follow if all such ships were not prevented from reaching their destination.[8]

The *Wigan Observer* and *Bolton Chronicle* provided solid and consistent opposition to the blockade and thought it "reasonable to look for the mitigation of our people's wretchedness through the opened ports of secession." [9] Mr. Charles Rooks of Bury was a little over-anticipatory when in February 1862, having rejected John Bright's hard advice that the operatives borrow the money they had neglected to save, he predicted that:

> The time is fast approaching when the fortitude and self-denial of the distressed operatives will become exhausted and when the pangs of hunger will burst forth in one universal cry for the intervention of our Government to annihilate the blockade, and let us have cotton.[10]

At Oldham in December 1861 the blockade was twice denounced. On 6 December John Platt, the mayor of Oldham, acknowledged that the people of Lancashire were most anxious for the blockade to be broken so they could obtain cotton.[11] A few days later, John Morgan Cobbett was

7. *Rochdale Spectator,* 2 May 1863.

8. Bright to Elizabeth, 1 May 1863, 25 June 1863, Bright Mss., University College Library, London.

9. *Wigan Observer,* 6 December 1861, 20 February, 2 May 1863, *Bolton Chronicle,* 11 May 1861, 24 January 1862.

10. *Bury Guardian,* 15 February 1862.

11. *Oldham Chronicle,* 7 December 1861.

cheered when he told the crowded meeting of his constituents in the Town Hall that he considered the blockade of the Southern ports quite unjustifiable. The unanimous vote of support at the end of that meeting suggested that Oldham was at one with him in this as in the more general issue of taking a firm stand against the United States, if necessary.[12]

The *Bolton Chronicle* not only attacked the blockade but took pride in the disruptive success of the *Alabama* and her sister ships.[13] In April 1863 righteous indignation was felt for Laird, who was deemed by the *Bolton Chronicle* to have been unjustly accused by Bright of favoring the Southern states in his firm's shipbuilding activities.

> Never since the wolf accused the lamb of muddying the stream was there a more unjustifiable complaint. If the Confederates have sent secret agents to negotiate for the building of here a ship and there a ship, the Federal Government have actually sought to have something like an iron-clad fleet built in this country.[14]

The press of Bury and Wigan gave progressively stronger and more enthusiastic support to the builders of Confederate ships and delighted in noting their success at sea.[15]

The destruction of the *Alabama* by the *Kearsage* was the cause of much sorrow in Lancashire generally, but a unique service was rendered to the crew of the ill-fated Confederate cruiser by John Lancaster of Hindley Hall, Wigan. He was the owner of a yacht, the *Deerhound,* built by Laird along very similar lines to the *Alabama.* The yacht happened to sail out from Cherbourg at the time the battle between the *Alabama* and *Kearsage* took place, and when the *Alabama* began to sink, Lancaster picked up Captain Semmes and his drowning men, who in this way were able to evade capture by the Northern navy. In letters to the *Eastern Daily News* the captain and master of the *Kearsage* accused Lancaster of being in complicity with the *Alabama,* and his ship of being her "consort." Lancaster insisted in his reply that he, his wife, and children happened on the confrontation purely by chance and aided the crew of the *Alabama* out of humanity, although he made no attempt to disguise his strong sympathy

---

12. *Rochdale Spectator,* 14 December 1861.
13. *Bolton Chronicle,* 21 February 1863.
14. Ibid., 4 April 1863.
15. *Bury Guardian,* 18 October 1863, 5 March 1864; *Wigan Observer,* 7 November 1862, 30 October 1863; *Bury Free Press,* 17 November 1864.

with the South. The controversial correspondence was reprinted by the *Wigan Observer* with the valuable addition of the private correspondence that passed between Lancaster and J. M. Mason, the Confederate commissioner. The warmth displayed by both in their communications emphasized the admiration that Lancaster felt for the work of the *Alabama*, but it was equally clear that his had been the spontaneous and personal action of a private individual in no way under the aegis of the Southern government.[16] The sympathy which his action stirred was symptomatic of the general hatred of the blockade in the area that frequently spilled over into tirades directed at governmental inactivity.

MANCHESTER

When the young Henry Adams visited Manchester in November 1861 he was convinced that, before long, a party in the city would demand the breaking of the blockade. This conclusion was partly influenced by the premonitions of a member of a large firm of spinners and the editor of a leading Manchester newspaper (probably the *Manchester Examiner and Times*).[17] There certainly was an effort made by the press of Manchester to move the government to disavow the blockade, but no more demonstrative protests were made. Indeed the only meeting held in Manchester that mentioned the blockade was organized by the Union and Emancipation Society. The society was out in full force, and a resolution was passed that deplored the building of warships for the Confederacy.[18]

The Manchester press made a typical compromise by mildly censuring the blockade but refraining from any comments that might be interpreted as urging its destruction. The *Manchester Weekly Express* was shocked at Federal efforts to reinforce the blockade by sinking stone-laden ships in the channel of the port of Charleston. The newspaper forecast that, far from aiding the "ineffectual blockade," this would secure for the Confederacy the "moral support" of Europe.[19] The *Manchester Examiner and Times* condemned the blockade and considered it might well be broken without causing war, while also anticipating and dismissing the idea of a

16. *Wigan Observer,* 5 July 1864; see also Semmes, *Memoirs,* pp. 370–88, 447–57.
17. Silver "Henry Adams," pp. 82, 87.
18. *Manchester Courier,* 11 April 1863.
19. *Manchester Weekly Express,* 18 January 1862.

change in international law to forbid the capture of merchant vessels.[20] Cobden's letter to the Manchester Chamber of Commerce in April 1862, advocating this change and an end to commercial blockades, was dismissed by the *Manchester Courier* as unlikely to help the cotton crisis and sure to compromise British maritime rights.[21] The legality of building ships for and trading with the Confederacy was mildly defended in the *Courier* and the *Guardian*, but more typical, perhaps, was the preference finally shown by the *Guardian* for the total abstention of English shipping from any part in the war.[22] Breaking the blockade was not really Manchester's answer to the war. For Manchester merchants there was little or no direct gain to be had from running the blockade, and were it officially broken many would have lost the high profits that selling sparse cotton, often to the North, brought in.

LIVERPOOL

Liverpool had a unique stake in the failure of the Federal blockade. Despite the directives contained in the royal proclamation of May 1861 that the Federal blockade was to be respected, not only did private individuals and the press constantly urge that it be officially broken but it was in fact broken frequently by individual Liverpool firms. As Thomas Taylor, the Liverpudlian who ran the blockade for the length of the war, so vividly recalled:

> With due respect to the pain of Her Majesty's displeasure we all knew that to run a foreign blockade could never be an offence against the laws of the realm, nor were we to be persuaded that any number of successful or unsuccessful attempts to enter the proclaimed ports could ever constitute a breach of neutrality. Firm after firm, with an entirely clear conscience, set about endeavouring to recoup itself for the loss of legitimate trade by the profits to be made out of successful evasions of the Federal cruisers; and in Liverpool was awakened a spirit the like of which had not been known since the palmy days of the slave trade.[23]

20. *Manchester Examiner and Times,* 29 October 1861; *Manchester Weekly Times,* 25 January 1862.

21. *Manchester Courier,* 19 April 1862.

22. Ibid., 25 July 1863, 9 February 1865; *Manchester Guardian,* 1 July 1863, 7 February 1865.

23. Thomas E. Taylor, *Running the Blockade* (London, 1896), pp. 9–10.

Lieutenant Warneford added that "an instinctive contempt" for "the bragging Yankee" provided a further incentive to lucratively break the blockade.[24] At least thirty-six blockade runners were built on Merseyside during the course of the war, and they were largely run by Liverpool men. The armed cruiser *Alabama* was a sister of other ships which more subtly but with equal skill sided with the South. Even this was not, in James Bulloch's view, an infringement of the controversial Foreign Enlistment Act. Moreover, he was sure that this was also the official interpretation:

> A neutral may supply either of two belligerents not only with arms and cannon, but with ships suitable to operate in war; and Her Majesty's Government cannot, therefore, interfere with the dealings between British subjects and the "so-styled" Confederate States, whether the object of those dealing be money or contraband goods, or even ships adapted for war. The seizure of the *Alabama* would have been altogether unwarrantable by law. . . . The Foreign Enlistment Act was not meant to prohibit commercial dealings in ships-of-war with belligerent countries, but to prevent what the law regards as the fitting out, arming, or equipment of a ship-of-war within the British dominions, with the intention that she should be employed in the service of a foreign belligerent.[25]

Most Liverpool shipowners supported the South and were pleased that they could demonstrate their support in practical ways within the framework of the law. There were, however, some disgruntled deviators. In July 1863 and May 1864 a memorial was sent to Lord Russell from "Certain Shipowners of Liverpool, Suggesting an Alteration In The Foreign Establishment Act." The memorial pointedly deplored "a state of affairs which permits a foreign belligerent to construct in and send to sea from British ports vessels-of-war." Many of the shipowners, whose names were affixed, were known Northern supporters whose more immediate interests would also have been served by the memorial and by the identical petition sent to Parliament.[26] James Rathbone, for instance, had a strong commercial tie with New York, and his business may well have been damaged by the privateers and Confederate warships. The hallmark of the blockade was, in any case, that all normal business transactions were to some degree upset. For the duration of the war confusion and uncertainty

24. R. Warneford, *Running the Blockade* (London, 1863), p. 1.
25. Bulloch, *Secret Service*, 2: 352–353.
26. *Daily Post*, 17 May 1864; *Albion*, 19, 20 July 1863.

held undisputed sway over the affairs of merchants who traded with both North and South. Fortunes were swiftly made and swiftly lost, but most often lost by those who pinned their faith and financial security on the risky future of the cotton Confederacy. Only those who withdrew early enjoyed any considerable profits.[27] One of the merchants who was almost ruined through backing the South was James Spence; early in the war he condemned the blockade as an act of "arbitrary power" unauthorized by any law and contradicting the principles recently professed by the Federal government. Nonetheless Spence considered that because the blockade had been acknowledged it ought to be respected: "We have maintained the right of blockade when in our favour; it becomes us to uphold it as rigidly when against us." [28]

The most widely read organs of the Liverpool press were unanimous in their hope that the "paper blockade" would be ignored and in their horror at the wanton crippling of Charleston harbor.[29] The *Albion* claimed that the working classes of Liverpool were defying Bright's advice to support the blockade and the North: "We can only observe, that so far as those classes which are suffering most from this war have yet expressed themselves, their cry has been rather in favour of breaking the blockade than of countenancing the North." Certainly the vast majority of Liverpool merchants was felt to be for breaking the blockade.[30]

The building of ships for the Confederacy aroused unease only in the columns of the *Liverpool Daily Post,* where the *Alabama* was singled out for special condemnation.[31] The *Mail* and the *Albion* both firmly defended Liverpool's right to construct ships such as the *Alabama* and to sell them to English purchasers although the ships might be resold to the Confederacy, especially as John Bright's Birmingham constituency sold arms and ammunition to the North through English intermediaries.[32] The legal deten-

27. James Russell Soley, *The Navy in the Civil War* (London, 1898), p. 167; Forwood, *Recollections* pp. 34, 40; Francis E. Hyde, *Blue Funnel: A History of Alfred Holt and Company of Liverpool from 1865 to 1914* (Liverpool, 1956), p. 17, n. 4.

28. Spence, *The American Union,* 4th ed., pp. vii–viii.

29. *Liverpool Daily Post,* 25 June 1861; *Liverpool Mail,* 21 January, 5 February 1862, 3 January 1863; *Liverpool Weekly Mercury,* 4 May, 26 October 1861, 18, 25 January, 1 February 1862; *Albion,* 12 May 1862.

30. *Albion,* 12 May 1862.

31. *Liverpool Daily Post,* 15, 26 March, 5 November 1862, 30 March, 14 December 1863.

32. *Liverpool Mail,* 20 December 1862; *Albion,* 7, 28 September, 30 March, 1863.

tion of the *Alexandra* and the Laird rams was condemned as pandering to unreasonable Northern threats, and the eventual release of the *Alexandra* was greeted with joy.[33]

The Liverpool Chamber of Commerce was naturally most concerned about the blockade. On 20 January 1862 it adopted a resolution approving the remonstrance which the government had made to the North about the blockading of Charleston harbor by vessels laden with stones.[34] In November 1862 discussion about the whole question of commercial blockades became very intense. The council of the Chamber approved a motion to memorialize the government in favor of their abolition. At the full meeting of the chamber this decision was reversed, mainly through Spence's efforts in proposing an agreeable amendment. Spence emphasized that a blockade would be an integral part of British supremacy in a future war.[35] More helpful to the South were his arguments in later meetings for the continuation of the right to capture the merchant ships of enemies. A vote in the chamber secured another victory for an amendment by Spence.[36] A far higher proportion of members voted through circulars (264 by circular, 60 in the meeting), but the results were the same. Spence's amendments for the continuation of commercial blockades and the right to capture merchant ships of the enemy were passed by overwhelming majorities (through the circulars 17 for the motion, 243 for the amendment; and at the meeting 37 for the motion and 223 for the amendment).[37] At a meeting held in January 1863 commercial blockades were again upheld by almost all the speakers, including both local M.P.'s, Thomas Horsfall and John Ewart, who were quietly but implacably pro-Southern in sympathy.[38]

The Chamber of Commerce was impassive and unpenitent in the face of the damage inflicted by the *Alabama* on Northern shipping. A protest to the chamber from New York was no more than formally acknowl-

33. *Albion,* 29 June, 2 November 1863, 18 January, 8 February 1864; *Liverpool Mail,* 8 July 1863, 9 April 1864.

34. *Liverpool Weekly Mercury,* 25 January 1862; *Liverpool Mail,* 25 January 1862. Russell officially protested to Seward through Lyons about the destruction of Charleston harbor on 20 December 1861. The stone fleet had been sunk in late November (see E. D. Adams, *Britain and the Civil War,* 1: 253–55).

35. *Liverpool Mail,* 29 November 1862; *Burnley Advertiser,* 29 November 1862.

36. *Liverpool Mail,* 6, 27 December 1862; *Albion,* 8 December 1862.

37. *Liverpool Mail,* 31 January 1861.

38. *Albion,* 2 February 1863; *Liverpool Mercury,* 27 January 1863.

edged and then passed on to the government. S. G. Rathbone's suggestion that the chamber itself should condemn the *Alabama* won no support, only the somewhat sarcastic retort from A. B. Forwood that if that was done the government should also be memorialized against the sale of arms to the North.[39] The same argument was used in the chamber by Charles Turner, M.P., in August 1863, who simply thought that the same license should be extended to ships as to munitions.[40]

Ships were most definitely sold to the Confederacy by Liverpool shipbuilders throughout the war. Care was always taken not to infringe the Foreign Enlistment Act, and ships were never equipped with arms or crews before they left the port. Despite this, several ships built for the South were detained because of Federal remonstrations, though none of the builders were successfully prosecuted. It is ironic that the North should have made such frequent and angry protests about shipbuilding for the South in Liverpool, when early in the war Laird was approached by the North with a view to building ships for the more powerful side. As it happened, the Laird shipyard could not have fulfilled the conditions stipulated, had they wanted to build ships for the North, and the order was not accepted.[41]

The first ship to be built in Liverpool as a Confederate cruiser was the *Florida* (also known as the *Manassas* and *Oreto*). This was commissioned by James Bulloch, who had been sent to England by the Confederate government specifically to help equip its almost nonexistent navy with sound ships. The builders were W. C. Miller and Sons, who began work on the ship in June 1861. The *Florida* sailed to the Bahamas on 22 March 1862, without any armaments or equipment normal to a ship of war. These were added in the West Indies by transferring them from the *Prince Alfred* in great secrecy, as even in the *Florida's* virgin state she had been indicted for an infringement of the Foreign Enlistment Act in Nassau.[42] Though the ship was cleared, excessive caution had to be exercised in the future.

39. *Liverpool Mail,* 28 March 1863.
40. Charles Turner (1803–75) was a Liverpool merchant, shipowner, and railway magnate of great influence. He was M.P. for Liverpool, 1852–53, south Lancashire, 1861–68, and southwest Lancashire, 1868–75. He was chairman of the Mersey Docks and Harbor Board till 1861; *Liverpool Mail,* 8 August 1863.
41. *Liverpool Mail,* 1 August 1863.
42. Regis A. Courtermanche, "Vice Admiral Sir Alexander Milne, K.C.B., and the North American and West Indian Station, 1860–1864," (Ph.D. diss., London, 1967), pp. 206–7.

Once equipped, the ship was, in August 1862, regularly commissioned and the Confederate flag hoisted for the first time. The *Florida* then went on to destroy or damage numerous Northern ships; she captured and commissioned for the Confederate Navy the *Lapwing* (Oreto), the *Clarence*, the *Tacony*, and the *Archer*. The *Florida*, built in Liverpool and originally manned by a British master, engineer, and crew, had played no insignificant role in the war by the time she was captured in October 1864.

The most notorious ship, the *Alabama*, was built by the Laird brothers in Birkenhead between August 1861 and July 1862. Her exploits under Admiral Semmes, before she was sunk by the *Kearsage* in 1864, were dramatic and incisive in cutting into Northern maritime strength. Among her triumphs were the commissioning and arming of the *Tuscaloosa*, a captured Northern ship which was to be captained by Liverpudlian John Low, and the destruction or disabling of about ninety other vessels. The excessive damage done by the *Alabama* to Northern shipping was dearly paid for by Britain after the war. This was unexpected in that, at the time the *Alabama* was built, it was generally believed that no infringement of the Foreign Enlistment Act was involved; even the Laird Brothers were ostensibly kept in ignorance of the role intended for the ship they were building. But there was little doubt as to the *Alabama*'s fate in the minds of the Liverpool workmen who built the ship and the Liverpool crew which manned her on her first voyage; most of the crew signed on to the ship on a permanent basis. Captain Butcher was entrusted with a fair amount of detail about her destination,[43] and aided in transferring stores and equipment from the supply ship *Agrippina* in the Bahamas. It is undeniable that the *Alabama* left England an unarmed ship, but in the eyes of later adjudicators this did not absolve Liverpool from responsibility for the destruction inflicted by the sturdy cruiser.

Among the other cruisers built in Liverpool for the Confederacy the *Georgiana* was alone successful in reaching its destination unhindered—only to founder on the rocks at Charleston harbor. The *Alexandra* was seized by the British authorities in April 1863 on suspicion of an infringement of the Foreign Enlistment Act. After a series of trials she was cleared and freed in April 1864. Her owners, Fraser, Trenholm and Company, changed her name to *Mary* and she sailed for Nassau, but was again

43. Beaman, *"Alabama Claims,"* p. 69; Bulloch, *Secret Service,* 1: 60–63, 228, 257; Semmes, *Memoirs,* pp. 39–43.

seized and held for trial until the end of the war. The Laird rams were also confiscated by the British authorities in October 1863 and were never released. By May 1864 they had become part of the British navy. More fortunate was the *Shenandoah,* a ship built before the war and bought by Bulloch for conversion to a cruiser, and then equipped with arms by the Liverpool-built *Laurel.* She was unique in that she went on destroying Northern shipping for months after the end of the war, before surrendering at Liverpool.

Consul Dudley's suspicions that ships were being built in and deviously equipped from Liverpool were entirely justified. Adams, indeed, felt able in a letter to Earl Russell to refer to this as "a systematic plan of warfare upon the people of the United States, carried on from the port of Liverpool." [44] No other city in Britain could with so much cause be accused of unofficially fighting on the side of the South during the Civil War.

At an early stage of the war an attempt was made to ensure that the question of running the blockade, which was then ineffectual, was not fraught with confusion or danger. A leading Liverpool merchant, Henry W. Hayman, wrote to Lord Russell in August 1861 informing him that "in conjunction with other merchants, I have it in contemplation to fit out a number of ships for the purpose of trading with New Orleans and other ports of the United States of America." He asked that the ships might either be afforded protection by Her Majesty's ships in the West Indies or have the right to defend themselves. After nothing more than a note of acknowledgment from the permanent undersecretary of state for foreign affairs, George Hammond, Hayman put the merchants' case more strongly:

> It is probably unprecedented, within the confines of international law, that a nation under the strongest terms of amity with another nation (and still remaining so), had, without cause, so far as that nation was concerned, closed her ports and harbours against the legitimate ingress and egress of the ships of such friendly nation [sic]. Contending, therefore, as I do, that the blockade of certain ports of the United States of America as against the ships of this country, *is an infringement of international law, nugatory, and unavailable,* I respectfully

44. Correspondence Respecting the Two Iron-Clad Vessels Building at Messrs. Lairds' Yard, Birkenhead, February to October 1863, Gladstone papers, vol. DXXII (44597), p. 67. See also Dudley, *Diplomatic Relations,* p. 3.

claim the protection of Her Majesty's Government for the mercantile expedition in question;—and at the same time, your lordship's
permission to defend itself in the case of need.

When Hammond replied on behalf of Russell, it was made quite clear
that Britain officially recognized the blockade as effective; any ship breaking it, far from being afforded protection, would be considered open to legitimate capture by the enemy. The deliberate breaking of the blockade,
such as was proposed, would be considered an act of "unjustifiable hostility." Hayman remained unconvinced and expressed further alarm at the
possible intensity of a cotton famine if the blockade was not broken.[45]

Neither he nor most other Liverpool merchants took a great deal of
notice of Russell's directives. So common was the breaking of the blockade by British ships that the sight of the British flag was too often treated
by the Northern navy as an invitation to attack. Forty Liverpool shipowners, in August 1863, memorialized the government for protection
against aggression by Federal ships of war in the Bahama waters. Russell
simply replied that trade between Liverpool and Nassau should be abandoned.[46] In practice, trade with the West Indies continued unabated, but
British officials there, such as Vice Admiral Milne, exercised strict neutrality and afforded no protection to British ships running the blockade.

In the early stages of the war every type of ship was used to break
the blockade. But from 1862 onwards only steamers specially built or
modified could slip through the Federal screen. Jones, Quiggin and Company of Liverpool built at least sixteen blockade-runners between 1862
and 1865. The *Banshee, Lucy, Wild Dayrell, Bat, Badger, Colonel Lamb, Fox,
Georgia, Belle, Hope, Lynx, Owl, Curlew, Hornet, Plover, Snipe,* and *Widgeon*
were all steel or iron paddle steamers of around 400 tons gross weight and
were admirably built to evade the Federal ships. W. H. Potter and Sons in
1864 built two ships of a similar type, the *Deer* and *Dream,* while William
C. Miller and Son created not only the *Oreto/Florida* and the unfortunate
Alexandra but the successful blockade-runners *Phanton, Let Her B, Celia, Abi-
gail,* and *Ray.* Bowdler, Chaffer and Company of Seacombe, in 1864,
launched the *Secret* and the *Stag* and, in 1865, the *Swan.* The Laird Brothers produced not only the wooden-screw *Alabama* (the *Oreto* and *Alexandra*
were also wooden-screw steamers), and the steel rams, but five steel

45. *Liverpool Daily Post,* 26 October 1861. The correspondence was printed in full.
46. *Liverpool Weekly Mercury,* 9 August 1862.

paddle-steamers, the *Wren, Lark, Mary, Isabel,* and *Penguin,* and the *Robert Todd,* an iron screw. All were ships especially suited to the swift maneuvers essential to blockade-running.[47]

Most of these blockade-runners were bought and run by Liverpool trading firms. Edward Lawrence and Company, the firm for which Tom Taylor worked as a supercargo throughout the war, and in which he eventually became a partner, owned the *Banshee,* a notorious blockade-runner with at least seven successful round trips to her credit before capture. A second *Banshee* was built and run by Aitken and Mansell and was again managed by the Liverpool firm. Tom Taylor himself was lauded by Colonel Lamb, commandant of Fort Fisher, for "his coolness and daring" and his generosity with food and luxuries to the poverty-stricken Confederates.[48]

J. Stewart Oxley and Company owned several Liverpool-built ships while Richard Phillips and Company ran the *Curlew,* the *Plover,* the *Deer,* and the *Stag,* which were all built on the Mersey. The *Phantom,* owned by W. T. Mann, was the object of particular suspicion while she was being built. T. H. Dudley was convinced that she was intended for the Confederate government and even obtained false witness to the part supposedly played by James Bulloch in supervising her construction. Bulloch affirmed—and there seems no reason to doubt him—that he had nothing to do with the *Phantom* and that the Confederate government never had any interest in her. She was under private Liverpool ownership on all her trips, carrying various cargoes, from cotton to the celebrated Confederate agent Mrs. Rose Greenlow.[49]

A number of blockade-runners were owned by the ship builders themselves—who no doubt made far more profit from them than would ever have been possible through straightforward sales. William Quiggin of Jones, Quiggin and Company, owned the *Bat,* the *Hope* and the *Colonel Lamb,* which like the *Phantom,* roused Dudley's suspicions when it was being built. The *Colonel Lamb* was in fact sold by Quiggin to J. B. Lafitte,

47. Philip Banbury, "Steamers on the Run," *Sea Breezes,* n.s., 34 (December 1862), p. 402; Arthur C. Wardle, "Blockade-Runners Built on Merseyside and Registered at the Port of Liverpool During the American Civil War, 1861–1865" (Typescript, 23 November 1961, Brown Library, Liverpool).

48. Taylor, *Blockade,* pp. 33–70, 59.

49. Bulloch, *Secret Service,* 1: 256–71; Hamilton Cochran, *Blockade Runners of the Confederacy* (Indianapolis, 1958), pp. 134–35.

of Nassau, but was never the property of the Confederacy, although it was one of the most notorious and successful of blockade-runners under Liverpudlian Captain Tom Lockwood.[50] T. Quiggin also owned the *Owl*, which was sold to Bulloch for the Confederacy, as were *Bat* of the same firm and the *Deer* and the *Stag*—these were among the few blockade-runners owned by the Confederacy itself. The *Owl* was to successfully run the blockade till the end of the war.[51] Josiah Jones the Younger owned another of the ships built by the firm of Jones, Quiggin and Company, the *Badger*. It is extremely unlikely that this ship or any other than those mentioned ever entered the service of the Confederacy. They were the personal stake of Liverpool men in the risky game of blockade-running.

Apart from these ships known to be built in Liverpool for blockade-running, there must have been others made for this purpose which attracted less attention. Certainly many ships were built at other shipyards and then sold to Liverpool merchants. The *Bermuda* (897 tons) first sailed from Stockton-on-Tees in 1861 and was sold to Edwin Naigh, a Liverpool cotton broker, during the same year. He in turn sold her to A. S. Henckel and George A. Trenholm of Charleston. In August she left Liverpool with her first illicit cargo and subsequently made several successful trips before her capture in 1862. Her sister ship, the *Bahama*, was bought by the same brokers, but was later transferred to a London firm. However, it was on the Mersey that she was fitted out and from which she began her career of trading and supplying ships such as the *Alabama*.[52] In April 1862 the iron paddle-steamers *Anglia* and *Scotia*, both built in 1847 at West Ham and Blackwell, were bought by Liverpool merchants—the *Anglia* by Alexander Duranty, the *Scotia* by J. Dorfington and B. Forwood—and sailed from the Mersey. The *Night Hawk*, built at Preston, ran the blockade for several months before capture in September 1864, was owned by E. Lawrence and Company and managed by Tom Taylor, whose death she almost caused.[53]

50. Wardle, "Some Blockade Runners of the American Civil War," *American Neptune* (April, 1943), pp. 135–36.

51. J. Wilkinson, *The Narrative of a Blockade-Runner* (New York, 1877), pp. 233–234, 236, 244.

52. Arthur C. Wardle, *"Blockade Runners,"* p. 135; see also Bulloch, *Secret Service,* 1: 70–73.

53. Wardle, *"Blockade Runners,"* pp. 133, 135; Cochran, *Blockade Runners,* pp. 93–98.

The financial adviser to the Confederacy, Charles Prioleau,[54] of Frazer, Trenholm and Company, bought several ships for trade with the South. The *Douglas,* an Isle of Man packet-steamer, was purchased in 1863 and left the Mersey as the *Margaret and Jessie* under Liverpudlian Captain Tom Lockwood; she became one of the most famous of runners during her brief but spectacular career.[55] Apart from the successful Liverpool-built *Colonel Lamb,* also commanded by Lockwood, Prioleau bought the *Southerner* from Stockton-on-Tees. He entertained a large party on the *Southerner* in the Mersey in June 1863, at which he stated that his firm were active in sending vessels to break the blockade.[56] The *Southerner* was later resold to Fernie Brothers of Liverpool and was purchased "by a syndicate of local merchants and ship owners who, thinking that the prospects of a Confederate victory were certain, planned to establish a direct steamer service from the Mersey to the Southern States, but the fortunes of war decided otherwise." [57] Prioleau also purchased the *Flora,* the fastest steamer of her day, and one which was to be a bane to the North.[58]

Other, less well-documented Liverpool ships ran the blockade alongside their more famous companions. The Liverpool steamer the *Cumbria* was noted only when captured, with two London ships, outside Charleston in June 1862.[59] The Liverpool schooner the *Success* was reported by the *Liverpool Mail* to have run the blockade into Georgetown, North Carolina, with several other vessels in May 1862.[60] The regular lists of ships running the blockade that appeared in the cotton reports of George Holt and C. R. Hall,[61] and in the local press,[62] gave no indication of the home port of each vessel, but it seems fairly certain that many must have come from Liverpool and all used the docks as a base.

---

54. Charles K. Prioleau was a United States citizen who became a naturalized British subject in order to facilitate the financial transactions of the Confederacy in England.

55. Wardle, *"Blockade Runners,"* p. 139; George Chandler, *Liverpool Shipping* (London, 1960), p. 74.

56. *Rochdale Spectator,* 14 July 1863; *Albion,* 29 June 1863.

57. Wardle, *"Blockade Runners,"* p. 140.

58. Ibid., p. 137.

59. *Liverpool Weekly Mercury,* 21 June 1862.

60. *Liverpool Mail,* 10 May 1862.

61. All cotton circulars of George Hold and C. R. Hall, 1861–64, have details of ships bringing cotton into Liverpool.

62. *Liverpool Weekly Mercury,* 7 March, 26 September 1863; *Liverpool Mail,* 5 March, 27 September 1862; *Daily Courier,* daily in April, 9, 18 May 1864.

On the British side of the Atlantic, ships running the blockade eventually reached 588. They shipped 8,250 cargoes, worth $2,000,000, and 1,250,000 bales of cotton were run out from the South to pay for them.[63] Despite the important subsidiary role of Glasgow, there is little doubt that the majority of these ships sailed from Liverpool, and it was on her docks that the valuable cargoes were loaded and unloaded. It was in Liverpool more than any other British city that a flurry of indignation could be whipped up against the smooth surface of official passivity at the same time that the determined practical support given by Mersey shipping interests to the South was undermining that inactivity.

THE WEST

The west, in its apathy toward the blockade, provided the perfect contrast to Liverpool. Not even the local press expressed any predilection for breaking the blockade. The lone voice of the *Lancaster Gazette* defended the building of the *Alabama* and judged the treatment of the Laird rams to be a typical example of the government's one-sided neutrality.[64]

While other regions contented themselves with occasionally urging that the blockade be broken, the west remained silent. For Liverpool, words were not enough; they were supplemented with action. So strong was the action taken by the port in building ships for the Confederacy and defying the blockade that, in Adams' view, it was "virtually tantamount to a participation in the war by the people of Great Britain to a degree which, if not reasonably prevented, cannot fail to endanger the peace and welfare of both countries." [65]

63. Banbury, *"Steamers,"* p. 402.
64. *Lancaster Gazette,* 27 December 1862, 3 June 1865.
65. Adams to Earl Russell, Gladstone papers, vol. DXIIV (44597), p. 68.

8

LINCOLN AND LANCASHIRE

Feeble as he is in argument, mischievous as he is as an in-
strument in the hands of a Seward, whenever he directly ap-
pears, he is indeed, at least, honest. [1]

As president of the disrupted Union Abraham Lincoln exercised a continuing fascination in Lancashire throughout the war. He aroused more
anger and disdain than admiration, but was never dismissed with that indifference allotted to most leading American statesmen. When the virtues
and failings of other men were considered, it was often in contrast or comparison with those of Lincoln. Seward and a few prominent Northern
leaders were occasionally selected to share the disrepute in which Lincoln
was commonly held. Rather more frequently the chief executive was unfavorably contrasted with the mildly esteemed Southern president. The
Marquis of Hartington was typical of Lancashire in respecting Jefferson
Davis far more than Lincoln, of whom he scathingly said, "I shd think he
was very well meaning sort of man, but as almost everybody says, about
as fit for his position now as a fire shovel." [2]

Lincoln was criticized mainly on the occasions of his annual
speeches, his Emancipation Proclamation, and his reelection in 1864. The
Emancipation Proclamation, which was often seen as a concerted attack
on the lives of white Southerners through the possibility of a servile insur-
rection, was almost universally dismissed as an act of hypocrisy. Lincoln
himself was rarely credited with any humanitarian or altruistic motives in
issuing the proclamation. He was thought to be unsure about the morality of slavery and untruthful about its abolition. Even though his men-
tality was often dismissed as low, he was judged as being well aware that
the proclamation was unlikely to free any slaves in the South, and it did
not even attempt to release from slavery those in the border states. Only
occasionally was the proclamation interpreted as an astute political move
by an adept politician. More often it was sneered at as the inept fumbling
of a leader who could not win victory over the South by any more
straightforward means. By only a handful of editors and meetings was
Lincoln ever envisaged as a man of moral status and strength who freed
Southern slaves through personal conviction as well as military necessity.

1. *Wigan Observer,* 19 September 1863.
2. Marquis of Hartington to his father, the Duke of Devonshire, Baltimore, 29 September 1862, Charleston, 21 January 1863, Devonshire papers (Chatsworth).

Lincoln was not so much hated or despised as a personality or a politician but as a symbol of the North's desire to subjugate the South. Until his death in April 1865, judgment on this man of undoubted stature was warped by Lancashire's fear of his tenacious efforts to defeat the cotton-growing Confederacy. Only in the aftermath of his assassination was the abuse heaped on him during his lifetime replaced by high-flown praise.

THE NORTHEAST

Lincoln inspired remarkably little interest in the weaving towns. The man himself was rejected as unworthy of prolonged discussion while his policies generally stimulated only a lethargic condemnation. His Emancipation Proclamation alone drew genuine vitriol. Appraisal in depth became inevitable after the assassination, and there was a dramatic reversal of opinion. Atonement for the years of neglect was made by the spate of adulation that accompanied the mourning for his death.

In 1861 the "timid and incapable hands" of Lincoln were felt by the *Preston Chronicle* to be inadequate for leading the Union.[3] A letter to the same paper accused Lincoln of inconsistency, quoting a speech he had made in 1848 upholding the right of secession.[4] The press of Preston and Blackburn hoped for Lincoln's defeat in the 1864 election; on his success, bitter attacks were made on his trampling of liberty and rights under military despotism.[5] The Burnley press and the *Blackburn Times* were less critical and speculated that Lincoln was more likely to bring the war to an end than McClellan, his opponent.[6] What seemed like informed and certainly influential support was given to this view by Thomas Proctor, a Burnley emigrant to the North's Wappinger Falls. In a letter to his family in Burnley, he insisted that the war would soon end with the defeat of the South if Lincoln was reelected.[7]

Outside of those lectures given in favor of Lincoln's emancipation scheme, only one lecture set out particularly to praise the Northern leader. In October 1861 George Thompson visited Preston and lectured on the

3. *Preston Chronicle,* 4 May 1861.
4. Ibid., 19 September 1863.
5. Ibid., 17 September, 26 November 1864; *Blackburn Standard,* 26 November 1864; *Blackburn Patriot,* 26 November, 24 December 1864.
6. *Burnley Gazette,* 15, 22 October 1864. *Burnley Advertiser,* 26 November 1864; *Blackburn Times,* 26 November 1864.
7. *Burnley Gazette,* 22 October 1864.

war. He was unbounded in his admiration for Lincoln and had implicit faith in his capacity to lead the Northern states successfully.[8]

Instances of praise for Lincoln were no longer isolated after his death. The press suddenly appreciated his moderation, wisdom, and conciliatory spirit, and paid tribute to his honesty and good sense, while his humanity was singled out for unprecedented admiration.[9] The elevated vice-president, Andrew Johnson, suffered unfavorable comparison and was charged with seeking vengeance from an innocent people.[10]

All three major towns gave public expressions of their sympathy. At Preston and Blackburn huge public meetings were gathered, and it was decided to send condolences to Mrs. Lincoln and the American people. At Blackburn Lincoln's life and character were eulogized. Although the mood of the Preston meeting seemed less impressed by Lincoln's achievements than by the tragic way his career had been ended, notable Southern advocates such as W. C. Squier went out of their way to express their sorrow.[11] Over Darwen held a similar meeting and also sent a message to the North.[12] Burnley contented itself with a message, compiled at a meeting of the Town Council, expressing deep regret at the assassination, which was forwarded to the American ambassador in London.[13]

The intensity of the panegyrics which followed Lincoln's assassination was impressive but could do no more than mask the fact that the real heroes of the weaving towns were Jefferson Davis, Robert E. Lee, and the other leaders of the dying Confederacy.[14] It was also obvious that few in this area thought any American personality sufficiently important to provide more than a temporary distraction from the basic problem of renewing the cotton supply.

THE SOUTHEAST

The most constant concern with the American president was demonstrated in the least distressed of the spinning towns of the southeast.

8. *Preston Mercury,* 19 October 1861.

9. *Preston Chronicle,* 29 April 1865; *Preston Guardian,* 29 April 1865; *Preston Pilot,* 29 April 1865; *Blackburn Patriot,* 29 April 1865; *Burnley Gazette,* 29 April 1865; *Burnley Advertiser,* 29 April 1865.

10. *Burnley Advertiser,* 20 May 1865; *Blackburn Patriot,* 13 May 1865.

11. *Preston Chronicle,* 6 May 1865; *Blackburn Patriot,* 6 May 1865.

12. *Blackburn Patriot* 6 May 1865.

13. *Burnley Gazette.* 6 May 1865.

14. *Preston Guardian,* 26 April 1865.

Ashton and Oldham were too involved with finding ways of ending the cotton famine to concentrate on analyzing Lincoln's character, or even his policies, except where the latter more obviously impinged upon the vital questions of ending either the war or slavery. Editors of the rest of the local press made frequent attempts to fathom Lincoln's complex personality and to interpret his sometimes ambiguous public statements. Emphasis was still placed primarily on his emancipation policy and his assassination.

It was consistent with its general attitude that the Rochdale press should mildly praise Lincoln's personality as honest and sincere and include reports illustrating his warmth and compassion for individual hardship. Noted with special approval was the occasion when Lincoln acceded to the request of John Bright to pardon a young Birmingham man who had been imprisoned for aiding Confederates.[15] Bright and Cobden themselves were always unequivocally complimentary about Lincoln's personal integrity and political ability. Bright's respect for Lincoln was as great while the latter was alive as when he was dead. In his diary for 29 April 1865, Bright echoed remarks he had made in an 1863 speech at Rochdale and in an 1864 letter to Horace Greeley:

> In him I have observed a singular resolution honestly to do his duty, a great courage, shown in the fact that in his speeches and writings no word of passion or of panic, or of ill-will has ever escaped him; a great gentleness of temper and nobleness of soul proved by the absence of irritation and menace under circumstances of the most desperate provocation, and a pity and mercifulness to his enemies which seemed drawn as from the very fount of Christian charity and love. His *simplicity* for a time did much to hide his *greatness,* but all good men everywhere will mourn for him, and history will place him high among the best and noblest of men.[16]

Cobden defended Lincoln against his many attackers when, in his annual speech at Rochdale on 24 November 1863, he turned the president's railsplitting background into a symbol of the power of democracy in America.[17]

The only really flattering appraisal of Lincoln to be made before his

15. *Rochdale Spectator,* 26 December 1863, 28 March 1864; *Rochdale Observer,* 26 November 1864.
16. John Bright, *Diaries,* p. 290.
17. Cobden, *Speeches,* p. 363.

death by someone other than Bright or Cobden appeared in the *Bury Guardian* but was written by an inhabitant of Lancaster, a Mr. Fowler, who purported to be an expert on phrenology. He discovered from this particular craft that Lincoln was a man of "unusual prudence, fore-thought, justice, integrity, firmness, stability, and perseverance. He is largely developed in veneration and benevolence and the forehead in-dicates an unusual degree of perceptive power, talent to acquire knowl-edge, and ability to become acquainted with men and things, to gather up facts, to remember actions and occurrences and to use knowledge as the occasion requires." He was generally accredited with every excel-lence.[18] The *Ashton and Stalybridge Reporter* was the only other newspaper to commend Lincoln's liberality while condemning Jefferson Davis's "ag-gressive insolence." [19]

Lincoln was also praised at a couple of meetings which were held to support him as a person rather than for his abolition plans. In January 1863 George Thompson lectured on the war at Heywood, and succeeded in obtaining a vote of confidence in the Northern leader.[20] In July the American lecturer Peter Cooper represented the Manchester Union and Emancipation Society in Middleton and extolled Lincoln's virtues at great length. He found an unresponsive listener in J. Wolstencroft, a local man, who charged Lincoln with dishonesty, hypocrisy, and inconsistency. The meeting had been expected to give Lincoln solid support but instead ended riotously with at least as many against as for him; it closed with three cheers for both President Lincoln and President Davis.[21]

The press of the region was almost as one in its skepticism about Abraham Lincoln. The *Bury Guardian* followed up scornful references to his "mediocrity of mind" with denunciations of his tyranny and oppres-sion and his "scorpion rule." He and Seward were branded together as to-tally deficient in self-control and diplomatic courtesy.[22] The *Oldham Stand-ard* simply did not think that Lincoln was equal to the situation that existed in America at the time, while the *Ashton Standard* was conscious

18. *Bury Guardian,* 27 May 1865. Despite its late appearance, this was written on 25 April 1865, before news of Lincoln's assassination reached Lancashire.

19. *Ashton and Stalybridge Reporter,* 26 December 1863.

20. *Heywood Advertiser,* 3 January 1863.

21. *Middleton Albion,* 4 July 1863.

22. *Bury Guardian,* 3, 30 January 1863, 7 November 1863, 20 February 1864.

only of his selfishness and hypocrisy.[23] The *Wigan Observer* condemned his
"querulous vapouring and ill-natured rebuke." His "illogical" attempt to
answer his critics was thought to demonstrate a singular lack of humanity
and sensibility about America's problems, and he was sharply condemned
as being driven by a compulsion for personal domination. If he fulfilled
his ambition, "the South will be overrun, its white people exterminated,
its political entity squelched, and all the earth between the Atlantic and
the Pacific shall acknowledge the rule of Autocrat Lincoln." [24] In the view
of the *Bolton Chronicle* Jefferson Davis was definitely superior to Lincoln,
who was not thought worthy of any respect; any apparent support for
Lincoln in the area was discounted as the work of paid Federal agents.[25]

Admiration was reserved almost exclusively for Jefferson Davis, who
triumphed in the comparison made between the two leaders. The *Bury
Guardian* considered him "the most remarkable man of the age." He and
other leading Southerners were felt to embody "determination, ability,
courage, and a love of truth." [26] Lincoln's annual message to the nation at
the close of 1863 was most unfavorably contrasted by both the *Bolton
Chronicle* and the *Wigan Observer* with that delivered by Jefferson Davis to
the South: "The one is full of brag, and is toned by the wretchedest gasco-
nade; the other is calm and earnest, and exhibits a lofty purpose." Lincoln
was condemned as blind to and unappreciative of Britain's "exceeding
friendliness," while Jefferson Davis was thought to be justly indignant at
the biased and wrong nature of British neutrality.[27]

The 1864 election did not in any way mitigate the harsh picture
painted of Lincoln by the press of the area. Having pondered the possibility that McClellan might be an even more undesirable president than
the existing one, the *Wigan Observer* indulged in a mammoth attack on
Lincoln as well as on Seward. Lincoln was underestimated to the extent of
being regarded as a "grotesque puppet" of Seward the "wirepuller," a
simple, docile servant of a great political necromancer.[28] Regret for the
defeat of McClellan was expressed after the election by the *Wigan Observer,*
the *Bolton Chronicle,* the *Bury Guardian* and the *Oldham Chronicle,* and fear

23. *Oldham Standard,* 20 July 1861; *Ashton Standard,* 18 October 1862.
24. *Wigan Observer,* 19 September, 30 October 1863.
25. *Bolton Chronicle,* 26 December, 14 February 1863.
26. *Bury Guardian,* 31 January 1863.
27. *Wigan Observer,* 26 December 1863; *Bolton Chronicle,* 26 December 1863.
28. *Wigan Observer,* 10, 24 September 1864.

that Lincoln and Seward's belligerency would deepen the rift between North and South was explained, together with the irony of such a despot being elected to rule over what had recently been upheld as the freest land on earth.[29]

Few of Lincoln's press detractors shared "the curious amnesia"[30] that marked the general reaction to Lincoln's life once it had been violently ended. The cool tone of the anti-Lincoln newspapers was warmed only by the inevitable respect awarded an assassinated leader. It was extremely rare to find hostility replaced by eulogy.

The *Bury Guardian* was totally consistent in its regret that Lincoln had been killed with "all his sins and imperfections upon him" and was more concerned that Richmond should have fallen and Lee surrendered. The *Rochdale Pilot* was no more generous.[31] The Wigan, Ashton and Oldham press continued to deny Lincoln any outstanding political ability or qualities of leadership but suddenly appreciated his personal virtues of integrity, charity, will-power, insuperable honesty, and his "unbending and uncompromising spirit."[32]

The *Bolton Chronicle,* the one newspaper that had previously made piercing attacks on Lincoln and greeted his demise with honeyed praise, provided careful justification for its change of heart:

> President LINCOLN, whose elevation to the Presidential seat was considered a fit subject for laughter, and whose earlier speeches and proclamations were received with the sort of contempt that one accords to a well-meaning idiot, has come in these latter times to be thought the chief hope of those who regard the civil war in America as an unmitigated evil which can only be removed by wise and impassioned counsels. . . . At first it was thought that the simple rail-splitter from the Far West would be a mere puppet in the hands of the older and more practised men in his Cabinet. Gradually, however, it has come to be known that this man of humble origin and without pretension of any kind had a will and thought of his own. That his education was not a liberal one he himself was readiest of all to admit. That about him and his family there was little of the

29. Ibid., 25 November 1864; *Bolton Chronicle,* 26 November 1864; *Bury Guardian,* 26 November, 24 December 1864; *Oldham Chronicle,* 26 November 1864.

30. Christine A. Bolt, "British Attitudes to Reconstruction in the United States, 1863–77," (London, 1966), p. 50.

31. *Bury Guardian,* 29 April 1865; *Rochdale Pilot,* 29 April 1865.

32. *Wigan Observer,* 29 April, 5 May 1865; *Ashton Standard,* 29 April 1865; *Wigan Examiner,* 28 April 1865; *Oldham Standard,* 29 April 1865.

polish and refinement of the higher classes of society he never attempted to conceal. But gradually it became clear that his was a
commanding mind; that the errors he made were when he weakly
submitted to those whose learning and acquirements he admired.
He himself was an honest-hearted, clear-headed, truth-loving,
honourable man. Looking back through the four years in which he
has held a position that the proudest Emperor of Europe might
have been glad to fill, we can recall no act of his which can give
those who love him now that he is laid in the grave regret, and no
word of his to which can be charged the prolongating of the murderous war which he had just lived to see concluded.[33]

Such magnanimity was unnecessary for those editors who had for
some time been convinced of Lincoln's virtues and ability. These were
simply faced with the task of mourning one whom they already acknowledged as a great man. The *Rochdale Spectator* was certain "that the fame of
Abraham Lincoln will live so long as the world endures, that his magnanimity and statesmanlike ability will bear comparison with that of any
man that ever lived," and his contribution to emancipation was lauded as
unparalleled.[34] The *Bury Times* and the *Ashton and Stalybridge Reporter* paid
tribute to the human warmth and great statesmanship and foresight of
the defunct leader, deeply regretting his loss to the future.[35]

Condolences to the widow and the American people in their be-
reavement were sent from almost every town in the area. Meetings were
speedily gathered together to express sorrow and compose messages of
sympathy. Propelled by the shock of the assassination, such meetings were
more often guided by a desire to compensate for the harsh condemnations
passed on Lincoln than by basic admiration for his leadership. Rochdale
most probably was moved by genuine regret at the passing of a notable
man when it held one of the earliest meetings of mourning. The dead
President was paid the undoubted compliment of being linked with Richard Cobden, whose recent death was deeply regretted.[36] Lincoln had followers in Bury who joined with those saddened by the deed, not by the
loss of the man, to form a vast public meeting in the Athenaeum at which
several resolutions of sympathy were passed.[37] Bolton was in turn stirred

33. *Bolton Chronicle,* 29 April, 6 May 1865.
34. *Rochdale Spectator,* 29 April 1865.
35. *Bury Times,* 29 April 1865; *Ashton and Stalybridge Reporter,* 29 April, 1865.
36. *Rochdale Pilot,* 6 May 1865.
37. *Bury Guardian,* 13 May 1865.

to pass a resolution of condolence for the Northern states at a meeting of the town council.[38]

At Ashton and Stalybridge the initiative in paying tribute to the assassinated President was taken by men who had opposed him in life. The Reverend S. A. Steinthal, the celebrated Liverpool "Southerner," commemorated Lincoln's martyr spirit and his tender, peace-loving soul in the Platt Chapel at Ashton and in Ashton Town Hall.[39] At a large meeting in Stalybridge, the Reverend John Page Hopps, always active in the Southern cause, proposed a motion of sympathy with the North.[40] Hopps also personally organized a meeting in his own Old Chapel at Dukinfield to express his sorrow over Lincoln's death. He even admitted that he might well have been wrong in condemning Lincoln as inconsistent and one-sided.[41]

The most volatile meeting in the southeast to ensue from Lincoln's assassination was the last, held in Wigan on 17 May. The town had always housed a curious mixture of people, utterly dependent on cotton, whose fortunes rested on the outcome of the war, and others (mainly coal miners) who were without any economic involvement in the war. It is likely that the uninvolved had remained aloof from previous meetings which passed resolutions favoring the South, but they now turned out in force to champion the Illinois rail-splitter and attack the supposedly murderous aristocratic Southerners. Despite some working class opposition, it was successfully proposed:

> That this meeting tenders its heart-felt sympathy to Mrs. Lincoln upon the loss of her noble and devoted husband, and to the people of the United States in their sudden deprivation of a wise, just, and merciful head. That, expressing its utmost abhorrence and detestation of the foul and treacherous assassination of President Lincoln and the attempt upon the life of Mr. Secretary Seward, it at the same time expresses its conviction that it was but the culminating point of a crime, if possible, of still darker hue—the attempt to perpetuate the bondage of millions of men and to achieve the destruction of a great nation.[42]

38. *Bolton Chronicle*, 13 May 1865.

39. S. Alfred Steinthal, *Address on the Assassination of Abraham Lincoln* (London and Manchester, 1865), pp. 14–15.

40. *Ashton and Stalybridge Reporter*, 6 May 1865.

41. Ibid., 29 April 1865.

42. *Wigan Observer*, 20 May 1865.

In this area the most clear contrasts were apparent between those few who admired Lincoln in life and mourned him in death and those whose honesty forbade the clouding of their judgment by the enveloping fog of regret. The contrasts were blurred only by the existence of new praise from erstwhile enemies who, on his assassination, abruptly appreciated the value of his moderation for a defeated South. Even more obvious was the line of demarcation between those towns whose relative lack of distress enabled them to ponder coolly, if antagonistically, the inadequacies and merits of the Northern president and those towns whose involvement with the war was so total and acute that such analysis would only be attempted when the very outcome of the war seemed at stake.

MANCHESTER

Manchester was remarkably lacking in sympathy for a president whose abundant store of good sense should have made him dear to its practical heart. The support that was given can only be described as mild and perfunctory. Supple contortions of attitude were made once Lincoln no longer provided a live target for attack. Suddenly his attributes seemed laudable and his leadership of unrealized value.

His initial election was an occasion for special rejoicing in the editorial columns of the *Alliance Weekly News,* as it was not often that a teetotaller, and a genuine and earnest one at that, was elected president.[43] Consistent but lukewarm deference was awarded Lincoln by the *Manchester Examiner and Times.* His plans for reconstruction were hailed as the onset of a political revolution, and he himself was commended as a strong and "solid" man with clear aims and moral impulses which would earn him honorable mention among American presidents.[44]

Press criticism sprang up early in the war and flowed in a widening stream till his death. To the *Manchester Weekly Penny Budget,* in June 1861, Lincoln was already guilty of abolishing freedom in America and had committed treason—he had levied war, suspended habeus corpus, misspent public money, and saddled the state with debt.[45] In 1863 the *Manchester Guardian* accused him of talking arrant nonsense and assuming the

43. *Alliance Weekly News,* 26 January 1861.
44. *Manchester Examiner and Times,* 23, 28, 29 December 1863; *Manchester Weekly Times,* 4 May 1861, 24 December 1864.
45. *Manchester Weekly Penny Budget,* 29 June 1861.

role of a despot; for the *Manchester Courier* he lacked sagacity and human-ity.[46] Jefferson Davis was praised at Christmas as being candid and full of hope while Lincoln was denigrated as affected and boastful.[47] During the 1864 election the president was denounced as a warmonger who wanted only to spill blood to further his personal ambition.[48] Even at the Hamp-ton Roads peace conference he was judged too much the tough politician, too little the seeker of peace.[49]

After Lincoln's assassination, the Manchester press made only mild compensation for the lack of warmth it had previously shown him. The *Manchester Examiner and Times* paid tribute to his calm wisdom, his sim-plicity and homeliness, and regretted that his death had been violently engineered just when he was most needed as a fair and consistent pacifica-tor.[50] Neither the *Guardian* nor the *Courier* reversed their poor opinions of the president, the former still regarding his rule with abhorrence. Their only praise was for the conciliatory spirit towards the South he had re-cently shown, which might not be shared by his "rowdy" successor.[51]

Meetings that supported Lincoln and his policies in Manchester, in-cluding that famous delusory gathering of workingmen in December 1862, concentrated on his emancipation scheme.[52] Not until his death were his virtues acclaimed in a wider context. As soon as news of the assas-sination reached Manchester a meeting was gathered together in the Free Trade Hall by the Union and Emancipation Society. The impressive achievements of the late president were recounted and his personality was unstintingly praised and sadly mourned. Condolences were sent to the widow and the American people.[53] At the meetings of the council and the city that followed sympathy was not boosted by retrospective adulation.[54] Though adulation might be absent, respect had become entrenched. Dur-ing the war the Southern Independence Association had denounced Lin-

46. *Manchester Guardian,* 5 January, 1 June 1863; *Manchester Courier,* 21 March, 19 Sep-tember 1863.
47. *Manchester Courier,* 26 December 1863.
48. Ibid., 13 September 1864; *Cotton Supply Reporter,* 1 December 1864.
49. *Manchester Guardian,* 17 February 1865.
50. *Manchester Examiner and Times,* 28 April 1865.
51. *Manchester Guardian,* 27 April 1865; *Manchester Courier,* 29 April 1865.
52. *Manchester Weekly Express,* 3 January 1863.
53. *Manchester Courier,* 29 April 1865.
54. *Manchester Examiner and Times,* 4, 5 May 1865.

coln's policies and principles,[55] but after his death even such opponents "had come," as an anonymous pamphlet claimed, "to admire his firmness, honesty, fairness, and sagacity." [56]

Manchester in actuality did not live up to its ill-drawn image as a city that steadily sanctioned Lincoln's actions and singularly appreciated his greatness as a president and a personality. One farcical meeting and a few pronouncements by prominent men were a spurious basis for such a picture. The image only began to reflect reality once regret at the passing of a man of stature began to seep through the shock of his assassination.

LIVERPOOL

It was not surprising that a city which had little respect for the North should persistently underestimate the worth and ability of Abraham Lincoln. For some, he was a good-natured nonentity; others depicted him as a wicked despot. Liverpool gave most of its attention and admiration to Southern leaders. Not only was Jefferson Davis judged superior to Lincoln, but Lee and Stonewall Jackson were singled out for unqualified adulation.

The press gave a spectacularly uniform underestimation. Even the unprejudiced *Daily Post* dismissed Lincoln as inferior to Jefferson Davis and from a vastly poorer mold than the great presidents and statesmen of the past.[57] As the war advanced the adverse verdict hardened. The American president was depicted as impolitic, uncivilized, and without cultivation or intellect. He was seen as kind and good but totally inadequate for the task of leadership; far from being a genius, he was a complete incompetent whose common sense was better suited to farming or the law than politics.[58] The *Liverpool Mail* sourly regretted that he had given up log-splitting.[59] *Liverpool Mercury* and the *Albion* attacked Lincoln as an incapable military despot, reliant on force for his power. They rejected his proposals for "sham" governments for a reconstructed South and denied he sought a peaceful settlement, because the total submission he de-

---

55. In *The Principles and Policy of President Lincoln.*
56. *A Concise History of the . . . Civil War in America.* (Manchester, 1865?), p. 2.
57. *Liverpool Daily Post,* 4 March, 11 April 1861.
58. Ibid., 25 April, 17 November 1862, 11 February 1863.
59. *Liverpool Mail,* 31 January 1863.

manded was a "wanton insult." He was dismissed as irrevocably inept and impractical.[60]

The 1864 election aroused general hope that Lincoln might be defeated and peace attained, which was followed by unanimous despondency when the reelection of the incumbent was known. His warmongering, vulgarity, and general ineptitude were thought adjuncts of a character "thoroughly and irredeemably bad." [61]

The Liverpool press shared the universal horror at Lincoln's violent end but remained faithful to the idea of a man honest and kind but inadequate for the role of president. *The Albion* expressly renounced the hypocrisy of praising someone simply because he was dead. The *Liverpool Weekly Mercury* grudgingly admitted that Lincoln had developed the commendable qualities of moderation and conciliation just before he was struck down. The *Mail* admitted that Lincoln had at least had common sense and self-control even if he lacked more generous and noble attributes.[62] Reparation was made at a Liverpool meeting to mourn the assassination. Six thousand Northern and Southern sympathizers met in St. George's Hall at the instigation of the mayor, Edward Lawrence, on 27 April 1865, and the large audience unanimously passed the motion of sympathy proposed by William Rathbone. Northern supporters eulogized Lincoln's achievements, particularly as far as emancipation was concerned. James Spence, in a written message from London, where he had been unavoidably detained, declared Lincoln's death to be even more of a loss to the South than to the North.[63] Meetings were also held by the town council and the Liverpool Chamber of Commerce to discuss the tragedy; messages of condolence to the widow and the American people were agreed on and sent to Adams in London.[64]

In contrast to the cool tone which marked the posthumous appraisal of Lincoln and the bitterness that attended him in life, the Southern lead-

60. *Liverpool Weekly Mercury,* 5 October 1861, 26 December 1863; *Albion,* 22 July 1861, 22 December 1862; *Liverpool Mail,* 2 January 1864.
61. *Liverpool Mail,* 10 September, 29 October, 19 November 1864; *Albion,* 21 November 1864; *Liverpool Weekly Mercury,* 26 November 1864; *Daily Courier,* 4 June 1864.
62. *Albion,* 1 May 1865; *Liverpool Mail,* 29 April, 6 May 1865; *Liverpool Weekly Mercury,* 29 April 1865; *Liverpool Daily Post,* 27 April 1865.
63. *Liverpool Daily Post,* 28 April 1865; *Liverpool Mail,* 29 April 1865; *Liverpool Weekly Mercury,* 29 April 1865; *Albion,* 1 May 1865.
64. Liverpool Town Books, 3 May 1865; *Liverpool Mail,* 6 May 1865.

ers won consistent high praise. Tributes were paid to the dignity and steadfastness of Jefferson Davis and his superior ability as a leader.[65] Lee was praised by the press for his skill, bravery, and gallantry,[66] and James Spence was deeply saddened by the death of Stonewall Jackson, claiming that through him "the South in a lifetime of two years has given to the world a name that will live and be cherished in the hearts of men more warmly than any the Union produced in 80 years." [67]

Lincoln was never revered in Liverpool. He was criticized instead to a degree proportionately greater than anywhere else. Little hope was extended for him at the beginning of his office even by a Northern supporter such as George Alexander Brown, who considered his first speech vague and inferior.[68] Only scant and dubious praise was awarded his work as an emancipator.[69] After his death there was a marked absence of panegyrics; it was mourned as a shocking event but not as the end of a great man.

THE WEST

When compared with the general lack of concern in West Lancashire over the war, the interest taken in Abraham Lincoln was exceptional. Unlike in the rest of the county, approval there was as strong before as after his death.

Press reaction to Lincoln was here almost completely favorable. Only the *Warrington Advertiser* and *Lancaster Gazette* carried any real criticism.[70] In other newspapers his ability and character were fully appreciated, with his shrewdness and political acumen obtaining as much acclaim as his celebrated honesty and conciliatory spirit.[71] His reelection in 1864 was greeted with particular delight; it was assumed that a man of

65. *Liverpool Mail,* 17 October, 24 December 1864, 1 April 1865; *Liverpool Daily Post,* 4 March 1861.

66. *Albion,* 24 April 1865; *Liverpool Mail,* 22 April 1865.

67. Spence to Mason, 23 May 1863, Mason papers.

68. George Alex Brown Diaries (1803–70), 18 December 1861, Brown Library, Liverpool. Brown was a wealthy Liverpool merchant and shipowner who befriended the Northern consul, Thomas Dudley.

69. *Liverpool Daily Post,* 20 February 1863.

70. *Warrington Advertiser,* 17 January 1863; *Lancaster Gazette,* 7 February 1863.

71. *Southport Independent,* 24 December 1862, 27 December 1864; *Lancaster Guardian,* 20, 27 July 1861; *Barrow Herald,* 19 September, 26 December 1863; *Warrington Guardian,* 26 December 1863.

such unmatched calibre would be the most likely leader to end the current bloodshed.[72]

Eulogies, with only a couple of exceptions,[73] accompanied the reports of Lincoln's assassination, which was considered as great a loss to the South as to the North.[74] The *Lancaster Guardian* even apologized for the unjust way that he had been reviled by the British press.[75]

Despite press enthusiasm for the president and the sense of deprivation pervading editorials after his death, only one massive memorial meeting was held in this area. On 23 May, Leigh paid glowing tribute to the lost leader and sent condolences to his widow.[76] Interest in the west was too uninvolved, too academic to stimulate further public demonstrations of approval and sympathy, but it was because of this very aloofness that, only there, could press judgment of Lincoln be fair and unprejudiced.

Lincoln was almost totally ignored in the towns suffering acute destitution, and imaginatively described as an honest nonentity or a villainous despot in those where distress was less pervasive. However, the essentially practical men of Lancashire were aware that no amount of adverse judgment passed on the president could affect the outcome of the war. They consequently diverted their energies to advocating courses of action that would help to secure peace and cotton. His death came at a moment when all but the most blind knew that the war was over and cotton would again flow from a reunited Union. Those who had expressed the most rancorous animosity towards the leader of the South's enemies could then afford to make abject atonement on his death. Others who had always been able to appreciate his more homely qualities sturdily continued to emphasize these to the exclusion of any more powerful political abilities. That posterity would afford Lincoln considerable admiration would have seemed curiously inexplicable to most of the men who felt the impact of the Civil War in Lancashire. Only the vocal minority which supported

72. *Barrow Herald,* 26 November 1864; *Leigh Chronicle,* 26 November, 24 December 1864.
73. *Leigh Chronicle,* 29 April 1865; *Fleetwood Chronicle,* 29 April 1865.
74. *Southport Independent,* 4 May 1865; *Warrington Guardian,* 29 April 1865; *Ulverston Mirror, Barrow Herald,* 29 April 1865.
75. *Lancaster Guardian,* 29 April 1865.
76. *Leigh Chronicle,* 27 May 1865.

the North appreciated his stature and made support of his policies, especially his emancipation policy, a prime component of their campaign for nonparticipation in the war. To the majority Lincoln was no more than an obstacle to the independence of the South and the renewal of the cotton supply. His efforts to maintain the Union were classed as a worthless and indeed dangerous expenditure of energy. In death he was no danger; nothing could be lost and peace of mind could then be gained by lauding his neglected virtues.

THE MYTH OF SILENCE

War's clamour and civil commotion
Has stagnation brought in its train;
And stoppage brings with it starvation,
So help us some bread to obtain.
The American War is still lasting;
Like a terrible nightmare it leans
On the breast of a country now fasting
For cotton, for work, and for means.

W.C.[1]

The American Civil War had a cataclysmic effect on Lancashire life everywhere except in the agricultural west. For four years it dominated the thought and conversation of men from all walks of life. News of battles and prospects of peace were avidly discussed, for on them depended the fortunes of the speculators, the livelihood of the manufacturers and the operatives alike. In a town like Ashton the newspapers were avidly read aloud. "But no kind of news seems to take with the multitude but American. 'The greatest nation in the world' seems to have become the centre of attraction of high and low, rich and poor. It is the source of light, heat, and life, with so many people. All their hopes are centred on the American struggle. On its continuance or sudden cessation depends the future position in life of thousands upon thousands of honest industrious working men. No wonder then that this eager anxiety after news should crop up every morning at every street end, in every alley, and on every hill top. No wonder it should bud and blossom all around you— above, below, and on every side, with the momentous question, 'Owt fresh?' Should a kind and good-hearted neighbour commence reading for you the morning's news, a crowd gathers immediately; it soon becomes a little public meeting. Carts will stand stock still in the middle of the street, and the horses will prick their ears, as if eager to catch something fresh." [2] Symptomatic of the intense concern felt about the war in the cotton towns was the appearance of a column devoted to the progress of the war and an editorial analyzing its problems in almost every issue of each local news-

---

1. "The Millhands' Petition," part of a song printed as a broadsheet at Ashton-under-Lyne and sung in most towns of South Lancashire.
2. *Ashton Standard,* 18 June 1864.

paper.[3] The importance of such editorials in influencing and reflecting public opinion was fully acknowledged by contemporaries.[4] The vast majority of editors from those parts of Lancashire dependent on cotton firmly supported the South and in so doing seemed to give coherent expression to the views of entire communities, not merely educated elites. Instances where press enthusiasm for some form of intervention to aid the South outran popular feeling, as expressed in public meetings, were extremely rare.[5] More commonly, press reaction paralleled public meetings whose sheer size and frequency excluded the possibility that they were gatherings of unrepresentative minority groups. When resolutions and petitions seeking recognition and mediation were voted for by a third of a town's population (8,000–10,000 voted for recognition at one Oldham meeting), they cannot be dismissed as the work of a handful of fanatical agitators. In the cotton towns, at least, 82 sizeable meetings favored either recognition or mediation, with a minimum of 66 resolutions and 40 well-supported petitions attempting to force the government to aid the Confederacy (see table 9). Considered together with the more diffused pro-Southern activities of Manchester and Liverpool, these impressive efforts of the distressed towns make the idea of a passive Lancashire meekly approving Northern policies seem utterly ridiculous. Behind the apparent quiescence lay a complex fabric of Southern sympathy dependent for its design on the condition of the cotton industry and the imprint of distress on each area and each town.

As the war dragged on into the second half of 1864, a clear pattern emerged from the complex interweaving of meetings, with their resolutions and petitions, editorials, and isolated individual stands. It became evident that mediation was most favored in the weaving towns of the northeast. Rapid ruin had induced operatives and manufacturers alike to seize upon the course of nonviolent intervention as most likely to produce

3. See ibid., for the dramatic focus placed by the operatives on the events of the war as late as 1864. The main, if not sole, appeal of the local press lay in these details and in editorial comments on the war; see also *Liverpool Mercury*, 2 January 1863. The *Preston Chronicle* and the *Oldham Chronicle* amply demonstrate the monopoly exercised by the Civil War over editorial space in deeply distressed towns; the *Bury Guardian* and the *Bolton Chronicle* commented on the war in over two-thirds of their editorials and were typical of the press of more lightly affected cotton towns.

4. *Bury Times*, 17 May 1862; Edward Baines speech on the Franchise Bill, *Parliamentary Debates* 3rd ser., vol. 162, 2 (1861), pp. 372–4.

5. Possibly the *Wigan Observer* was more demonstrative than the town itself.

peace, but recognition of the South had almost as much appeal. The slight deferment of the distress in spinning towns, which were ultimately to suffer greatest hardship, gave them time to realize that arbitration is only feasible when both parties genuinely want a just solution. Such a solution would always have given more independence to the South than the North was prepared to part with, even if Negro emancipation was assured. To the impoverished spinning towns recognition was a far more certain path to peace and cotton. Only as it became evident that this was too strong and dangerous a stand to be palatable to the British government was mediation sought after. Even then the idea of recognition was not abandoned.

Intervention had in both regions only the most cursory appeal, while indignation continued to rage over the seizure of Mason and Slidell. There was always the risk that war would add to and prolong the hardship inflicted by the cotton famine. Manchester, apart from the Southern Independence Association, was hypersensitive to this risk, and many in the city feared that any show of Southern sympathy might lead to war. Despite this, peaceful intervention and, to a lesser extent, recognition found impressive public and press support. Only Liverpool tended to hanker after not only recognition but more active participation in the Southern fight for freedom, and the city found its own ways of bypassing official sanctions for such support. The constant breaking of the blockade and the provisioning of warships for the Confederacy were so effective as tools of war that the United States felt justified in suing Britain for heavy compensation. An award of $16.5 million was made for damage inflicted by the *Florida, Alabama,* and *Shenandoah,* and international neutrality laws were amended to preclude the possibility of such intervention by a neutral in the future.[6]

The absolute passivity that the Northern States sought was only favored by a majority in the west and in Rochdale. These were also the only places to pinpoint slavery as the chief cause of the war and to herald Abraham Lincoln as an abolitionist crusader. The failure of the Union and Emancipation Society is demonstrated by the prevalence elsewhere of the belief that the South was fighting for a freedom which would ultimately encompass Negroes while the North wanted to clap that freedom

6. Adrian Cook, "The Way to Geneva: United States Policy and Attitudes Towards Great Britain, 1865–1872" (Ph.D. diss., Cambridge, 1964) pp. 588–99.

into Union chains. Lincoln was generally seen as a sad instance of a man whose native honesty had disintegrated into the hypocrisy of the Emancipation Proclamation. He totally lacked charisma in Lancashire eyes. The death of Lincoln did not initiate any swift abandonment of the Southern side by Lancashire men. Defeat was acknowledged as imminent but it was seen as the defeat of a noble and worthy cause. Only those few whose allegiance was never firmly aligned with the Confederacy could see the victory as one where both might and right had triumphed. To the rest it was a sad destruction of freedom by the arrogant use of force.[7]

It was by an odd twist of circumstance that the lack of work created by the war made possible the formation of many of these judgments on the situation in America. It was at schools set up in almost every Lancashire cotton town that thousands of illiterate operatives became capable of assimilating the fruits of the local press. These schools provided an invaluable outlet for the frustration of idleness but, by making possible greater political awareness, fostered a new kind of frustration. The desire to act politically and help influence the nation's course found a double outlet. Direct franchise reform was sought with increasing enthusiasm as the war advanced,[8] while the carefully written resolutions and petitions sought to alter the diplomatic policy of the country for the immediate economic relief of the cotton towns.

Those who lost faith in their power to influence their fate by legiti-

7. *Wigan Observer,* 5 May 1865; *Ashton Standard,* 5 May 1865; *Oldham Chronicle,* 4 May 1865; *Bolton Chronicle,* 13 May 1865; *Preston Chronicle,* 14 May 1865; *Blackburn Patriot,* 13 May 1865; *Burnley Advertiser,* 20 May 1865; *Ashton and Stalybridge Reporter,* 6 May 1865; *Manchester Courier,* 5 May 1865; *Manchester Weekly Times,* 6 May 1865; *Liverpool Mail,* 6 May 1865; *Albion,* 8 May 1865; *Leigh Chronicle,* 27 May 1865.

8. *Manchester Courier,* 1 March, 24 May 1862; *Bolton Chronicle,* 15 October 1864; *Rochdale Pilot,* 18 March 1865; *Burnley Gazette,* 20 May 1865; *Burnley Advertiser,* 20 May 1865; *Bury Guardian,* 29 April 1865. The responsible attitudes of these operatives during the Civil War favorably influenced both Gladstone and Derby towards suffrage extension (see W. E. Williams, *The Rise of Gladstone to the Leadership of the Liberal Party 1859–1868* [Cambridge, 1934], pp. 104–7; W. D. Jones, *Lord Derby and Victorian Conservatism* [Oxford, 1956], p. 323), but Gertrude Himmelfarb has lucidly argued that the Civil War did not effect a radical "change of heart" towards democracy in England ("The Politics of Democracy: The English Reform Act of 1867," *Journal of British Studies,* 6, no. 1 [November 1866]: 97–139, especially p. 100). Certainly the outbreak of a fratricidal war in the "home" of democracy alienated many from the whole idea. (*Liverpool Daily Post,* 21 November 1861, 18 February 1863; *Manchester Courier,* 17 January, 7 July 1863; *Blackburn Standard,* 22 May 1861; *Burnley Advertiser,* 29 November 1862; *Bury Guardian,* 2 January 1864; *Blackburn Patriot,* 20 April 1861; *Oldham Standard,* 27 April 1861; *Barrow Herald,* 2 May 1863.)

mate political means chose not to protest violently but to leave the county and the country. Emigration to America and the British colonies of Australia, New Zealand, and Canada increased dramatically during 1863 and 1864 (see table 6). At least two thousand spinners and weavers left Lancashire for America alone in 1864; [9] many more used generous aid from Australia and New Zealand to emigrate to those underdeveloped countries.

Agents were sent to Lancashire by the Federal government and private Northern companies to popularize the idea of emigration and help fill the acute labor shortage. Enthusiasm for the idea of a new life in a civilized land with similar conditions of labor [10] was marred by the widespread and sometimes justified fear that jobs and fares were bait for luring men into the depleted ranks of the Union army. [11] Not unexpectedly, it was the deeply impoverished men of Preston and Ashton that were most willing to risk such hazards. [12] Far more popular was emigration to Australia, New Zealand, and Canada. [13] This was heavily subsidized by donations from these colonies, which were eager to attract skilled operatives sickened by the degradation and poverty attendant on living off relief. [14]

9. According to W. O. Henderson, *The Lancashire Cotton Famine 1861–1865* (Manchester, 1934), p. 118, over 18,000 cotton operatives emigrated from Lancashire in 1862 alone. The emigration from Lancashire is mirrored in the drop in the cotton operative population from 534,000 in 1861 to 450,000 in 1865 (Ellison, *Cotton Trade,* p. 95). Return of S. Walcott, Government Emigration Officer, quoted in Watts, *Facts,* p. 214.

10. Charlotte Erickson, "The Encouragement of Emigration by British Trade Unions, 1850–1900," *Population Studies* 3 (1949–50): p. 257; Arnold, *Cotton Famine,* p. 8; Rowland Bertoff, *British Immigrants in Industrial America 1790–1950* (Cambridge, Mass., 1953), p. 32.

11. *Blackburn Patriot,* 14 January 1865; *Blackburn Standard,* 22 April 1863; *Blackburn Times,* 19 November 1864; *Bury Guardian,* 4 July 1863, 6 August 1864; *Ashton and Stalybridge Reporter,* 21 February 1863; *Ashton Standard,* 19 November 1864; *Oldham Chronicle,* 16 May 1863; *Preston Guardian,* 31 January 1863.

12. *Ashton and Stalybridge Reporter,* 12 March, 14 May 1864; *Ashton Standard,* 2 July 1863; *Preston Chronicle,* 10 January 1863, 12 November 1864.

13. *Wigan Observer,* 27 February, 24 April 1863, 2 July 1864; *Oldham Standard,* 11 April 1863; *Bury Times,* 14 February 1863; *Bury Guardian,* 16 May 1863; *Preston Guardian,* 9 May 1863; *Bury Times,* 22 August, 30 May 1863; *Bolton Chronicle,* 9 May 1863; *Bury Guardian,* 25 April 1863; *Wigan Observer,* 9 May 1863; *Rochdale Spectator,* 25 July, 15 August 1863; *Bolton Chronicle,* 25 April 1863; *Albion,* 14 July 1862; *Lancaster Guardian,* 11 April 1863; *Warrington Advertiser,* 7, 21 February 1863.

14. Arnold, *Cotton Famine,* p. 236; *Bury Times,* 14 February, 2 May 1863; *Bolton Chronicle,* 11 April 1863. *Companion to the Almanac; or Year Book of General Information for 1865* (London, 1865), pp. 223–24.

Those whose hope of stable conditions through government intervention
in the war had faded, felt their only chance of survival lay in a fresh start
in new lands. Local emigrants' societies, the Manchester Emigrants' Aid
Society, and the National Colonial Emigration Society helped this chance
to become a reality for thousands of operatives not subsidized by the colonies themselves.[15]

The exodus and the agitation alike would have been totally unnecessary if the Lancashire cotton industry had not been so utterly dependent
on Southern raw cotton. Fear of the consequences of relying almost solely
on this one source had long existed, but efforts made before the war by the
Manchester Chamber of Commerce and by the Cotton Supply Association to secure adequate supplies of good raw cotton from other areas had
proved abortive.[16] Once the cotton famine had become a reality, such efforts were dramatically intensified and spread beyond Manchester to the
distressed cotton towns.[17] That only temporary and inadequate organization was given to Indian cotton production and other potential sources of
supply can be blamed largely on the unwillingness of most concerned to
devote more than words of encouragement to such schemes. Merchants,
manufacturers, and operatives alike treated non-American cotton supplies
as no more than an expedient; their hopes rested on a restoration of peace
and prosperity in the Southern states.[18] The operatives actually developed

15. *Bury Times*, 6 September 1862, 20 June 1863; *Bolton Chronicle*, 11 April, 2, 9 May,
26 December 1863; *Ashton and Stalybridge Reporter*, 12 March 1864; *Preston Chronicle*, 25 April
1863; *Preston Guardian*, 2 May, 4 July 1863; *Preston Pilot*, 4 July 1863; *Burnley Free Press*, 7, 14
February 1863; *Bury Guardian*, 18 April 1863; Arnold, *Cotton Famine*, p. 236. Thomas Banks to
George Melly, George Melly, Private Correspondence, vol. 7, 16 July 1863 (1714), 7 December 1863 (1797), vol. 10 (2371), Brown Library, Liverpool.

16. Proceedings of the Manchester Chamber of Commerce, 30 January 1861; Silver,
Indian Cotton, p. 301. *Liverpool Weekly Mercury*, 26 January 1861. The Cotton Supply Association was founded in Manchester in 1857 to stimulate cotton production in India and any
other suitable places.

17. Peter Harnetty, "The Imperialism of Free Trade; Lancashire, India, and the
Cotton Supply Question, 1861–1865," *Journal of British Studies* 6, no. 5 (November 1966):
73–74, 77, *Indian Cotton* 82, 84; Silver, *Indian Cotton*, pp. 177, 180–82, 301, 309–11; Henderson,
Cotton Famine, p. 40; The *Times* (London), 14 August 1862; *Manchester Weekly Express*, 1 February 1862; *Manchester Courier*, 31 January 1863; *Ashton and Stalybridge Reporter*, 15 March, 6
September 1862; *Preston Chronicle*, 5 February, 29 March 1862; *Burnley Advertiser*, 12 February
1862; Bennett, *Burnley*, p. 21.

18. A Cotton Manufacturer, *An Inquiry Into the Causes of the Present Long Continued
Depression in the Cotton Trade* (Manchester and Bury, 1869), p. 9; *Manchester Examiner and
Times*, 10 April 1862; *Liverpool Daily Post*, 23 May 1863.

an unrestrained hatred of the coarse, quick-to-break Indian Surat and when praying for cotton added, "But not Surat." [19] Any hopes that the war might free Lancashire from dependence on Southern cotton died with the return of peace.[20] Not surprisingly, these hopes only developed in the least depressed cotton towns. Those with the highest consumption of cotton, such as Ashton, Oldham, and Preston, knew that only the Southern States could provide them with the quantity and quality of raw material that would enable their numerous mills to rumble into full production again and end the distress. Once the war was over, American crops quickly reasserted their powerful hold over the Lancashire cotton industry (see table 5).

Operatives and editors were among those who straightforwardly declared their concern for the South to be based on hope for a swift inflow of cotton.[21] Others identified with the South over specific issues and made barbed denunciations of the policies of the North without ever mentioning a need for cotton. The difference lay only in the degree of sophistication and rationalization. The quest for cotton moved almost all those who supported the South in any way, whether through words, money, or agitation directed at Parliament. The alignment of most Southern sympathizers involved such convinced commitment, superimposed on the economic interest, that it was tenaciously clung to in the face of inevitable Northern victory and then sublimated into concern for the fate of the overpowered Confederates.[22] Involvement had been too deep to be abandoned simply because the Union had become once more the home of cotton. Desire for cotton was the prime motivating factor of support for the South, but that support was then padded with so much emotional as well as rational justification that it was not easily withdrawn. Only a tiny minority of the more astute pragmatists understood that cotton would be

19. H.S.G., *Autobiography*, p. 170; Bowman, *Ashton.*, p. 450; *Oldham Standard*, 21 February 1863; Moses Heap Diary, R.P.L., p. 44.
20. *Bolton Chronicle*, 15 June, 28 September 1861; *Wigan Observer*, 13 September 1861, 14 March 1862; *Rochdale Pilot*, 4 January 1862; *Manchester Weekly Express*, 1 February, 15 March 1862; *Manchester Courier*, 12 July 1862, 11 October 1864; *Liverpool Weekly Mercury*, 18 January 1862; *Liverpool Daily Post*, 28 July 1862; *Cotton Supply Reporter*, 1 May 1865.
21. *Preston Guardian*, 4 July 1863; *Wigan Observer*, 1 March 1862.
22. *Wigan Examiner*, 21 April 1865; *Ashton Standard*, 29 April 1865; *Blackburn Patriot*, 22 April 1865; *Manchester Courier*, 19 December 1863, 24 May 1864, 10 January 1865; *Liverpool Weekly Mercury*, 22 April 1865; *Liverpool Mail*, 13, 27 May, 10 June 1865; *Manchester Examiner and Times*, 3 May 1865; *Barrow Herald*, 29 April 1865; *Wigan Observer*, 26 May 1865.

obtained through a speedy Northern conquest.[23] To most Lancashire
minds, the fate of the South and of cotton were inextricably linked and
identification with both was firmly made.

It is not surprising that the essential reaction of Lancashire to the
war was purely practical. There is a beautiful logic about the unswerving
support given to the South by the most distressed cotton towns. This is en-
hanced by the symmetry with which the degree of distress matched the
enthusiasm for recognition and intervention and rejection of Lincoln and
his policies. The deviance of Rochdale serves only to make the general
pattern more valid. It is to be expected also that the diversity of interests
in the two trading centers should result in mixed alignments, with an always dominant commitment to the South. The chances offered for Liverpool shipping and Manchester trade were never overlooked.

What is almost astounding is the degree of sophistication that attended this simple acknowledgment of economic interest. The war was
seen in abstract terms as a bid for freedom against oppression; com-
parisons were drawn with Greece, Poland, and Italy. The fate of the Negro was rarely dismissed as secondary to the operatives' welfare. Instead it
was constantly asserted that the independence of the South would benefit
blacks as much as the Lancashire cotton workers. A free South would be-
stow liberty on the slave and outdo the hypocritical North by introducing
full integration. Recognition and intervention would, it was assumed,
positively aid and certainly not hinder the cause of assimilation. Such
logic was breathtaking in its audacity; it might have been improbable but
could only have been proved wrong in the event of a Southern victory.

The need shown by Lancashiremen to satisfy not only their economic necessities but also their consciences was a significant advance in
political development. It demonstrated a sense of responsibility that was
in no way negated by the conclusions reached. The decision that support
for the South was not just expedient but right, was arrived at only after
all facets of the war had been given unparalleled consideration. Yearning
for the Southern staple predisposed cotton-dominated Lancashire towards
the South, but genuine conviction was necessary to elicit active agitation
on the South's behalf. After all, had the military, political, and moral
data available been read differently, it could have seemed obvious that
the speediest path to Southern cotton was through the gate of Northern
victory.

23. *Liverpool Daily Post,* 26 February 1863; *Ashton and Stalybridge Reporter,* 29 April
1865.

EPILOGUE

PETER d'A. JONES

THE HISTORY OF A MYTH
British Workers and the American Civil War

For over one hundred years now the historical myth has persisted that during the American Civil War the Lancashire cotton workers, though starved by the Union blockade of Confederate ports, stubbornly and nobly supported the North. The British working class in general, so the story goes, driven by a deep hatred of slavery and a yearning for the creation of American-type democratic government at home, formed a massive bloc of opinion that restrained the pro-Confederate, "aristocratic" leanings of the English governing class.

Dr. Mary Ellison has effectively demolished this century-old belief. She finds, mainly from a study of the local press, that Lancashire opinion was generally pro-Southern and motivated by a mixture of moral conviction and economic self-interest. Its moral conviction was anti-Yankee as much as pro-Confederate: suspicion of Lincoln's war aims, doubts about the true meaning of the Emancipation Proclamation when it finally appeared, general distrust of things Yankee, as well as sympathy for the Confederate cause as a test-case in the sacred Radical-Liberal struggle for national self-determination. To be pro-Southern was not necessarily to be pro-slavery.

Even more important for Dr. Ellison's brief is economic self-interest. A fairly clear geographical pattern emerges from her research: support for the South varies directly with the degree of felt economic distress, being highest where unemployment among textile workers is greatest. The fundamental issue, she discovers, is economic survival. It cuts across the rather fluid social class lines of industrial Lancashire; and it is relatively unaffected by the so-called "Nonconformist conscience," that catchall phrase by which historians have explained too much of the British nineteenth century. For instance, Liberal, Nonconformist Ashton-under-Lyne proves more sympathetic to the Confederacy than heavily Tory, Catholic Preston. In sum, self-interest lay clearly in official British recognition of the Confederate states and speedy lifting of the blockade. Here was a foreign war, the military outcome of which was uncertain; it did not have the appearance of an antislavery crusade to outside observers even after the final Emancipation Proclamation. Why should anyone have ever thought that British textile workers would allow themselves to be sacrificed to save the American Union? Dr. Ellison's evidence makes us now abandon the myth of worker support for the North. But how did the

myth originate in the first place? And why has it been faithfully trans-
mitted over ten decades, from the earliest accounts down to the latest textbooks of English and U.S. history?

My own tentative answer, after some historical tracing, is that the
myth was born in propaganda and survived because, like all myths that
endure, it told people what they wanted to believe. The structure of this
particular myth is modestly complex. It has at least three sides, three satis-
fied audiences: the English Radical-Liberals who needed the myth to help
them fight the battle for parliamentary reform at home; Marx and Engels, for whose world view the myth was expedient and fitting; and Americans, deeply concerned, as always, with their national identity. I shall
have something to say about all three in this brief essay, but the American
side is the most important in sustaining the myth.

The myth of the noble worker, supporting the Union against the
slave-power despite the distress caused by the cotton famine, was born on
the spot and at the time. It did not have to be created after the event, like
many myths, though the victory of the North did strengthen the myth
enormously. Presumably, if the South had won, the myth would have
been a political embarrassment to both nations, and the British would
have more readily remembered their pro-Confederate tendencies. The
myth of the noble workers would have conveniently withered away. Abolition of slavery and Northern military victory were the necessary pre-
conditions for the myth to flourish.

Beyond this pragmatic need to accept the outcome of battle and to
play down formerly pro-Confederate sympathies, one finds a more profound American need to believe in British lower-class love for the Union,
a need and a belief founded on a simplistic view of British social structure.
There was a crude polarization in this view between "aristocrats" and
"lower classes," flattering to the American democratic self-image. Lincoln
himself, as John Hope Franklin's study of the crucial Emancipation Proclamation shows, was very anxious to court the British workers, going so
far as to write his own resolutions for them to adopt, it was hoped, at
spontaneous mass meetings in England.[1] As is well known, Lincoln did
successfully communicate with workers' groups.[2] Where did the president

---

1. John Hope Franklin, *The Emancipation Proclamation* (New York, 1963), pp. 148–49.
2. J. R. Pole, *Abraham Lincoln and the Working Classes of Great Britain,* pamphlet (London, 1959); further evidence of Lincoln's awareness of pressures from abroad is given in R.
F. Nichols, *The Stakes of Power* (New York, 1961), pp. 125–26.

acquire his view of the British workers? As a harassed wartime executive he was dependent on certain sources for foreign intelligence. We know he studied diplomats' reports carefully, especially those of Charles Francis Adams in London. In addition the noisiest segment of British opinion would manage to get through to him—the rabidly pro-Confederate and anti-Yankee London *Times* contrasting starkly with the steady, emollient stream of antislavery, pro-Union propaganda coming from people like John Bright, who was in himself a potent force. If the creation of the myth could be ascribed to individuals, then the names of John Bright on the English side and the Adamses (C. F. and his son Henry) on the American would be the ones mentioned.

While it was the reports and letters of C. F. Adams, Sr., that were read in Washington in the early 1860s, many of the ideas that went into them came from his son and private secretary, Henry. The latter's famous autobiography, *The Education of Henry Adams,* printed privately in 1906 and released generally in 1918, helped sustain the myth in the twentieth century. Father and son alike were angered by the patronizing, arrogant attitude towards the United States of London high society, the sneers at every military setback for the North, the implied wish that the South would win. Both men were ardent patriots; Henry went so far as to regard Confederate leaders as ignorant provincials, even mentally sick men. He was outraged at British assumptions that the South would win the war, especially after first Bull Run. Over forty years later he recalled his bitterness, his painful sense of social ostracism in London society, his hatred of the "impenetrable stupidity of the British mind," the "slowest of all minds," and his desire at one depressed moment to "wipe the English off the earth." [3]

The belief in the implacable hostility towards all things American of the English "upper classes" is to be found deeply imbedded in Henry Adams. Yet, curiously enough, Adams was himself more of a genuine "aristocrat" in his native American setting than several of the leading politicians of Britain were in theirs. Lord Palmerston aside, neither Gladstone nor Disraeli, whose great duel was to dominate English political life in the years after the Civil War, were by any English definition "aristocrats." Disraeli was of course a baptized Jew from a literary family,

---

3. *The Education of Henry Adams,* Sentry edition (Boston, 1961), pp. 114–15, 122, 128, 170. For his father's impressions, see M. B. Duberman, *C. F. Adams, 1807–86* (Cambridge, Mass., 1961), p. 275.

middle-class and not especially well-placed financially; Gladstone's slave-trading Lancashire forebears were much closer to the Yankee trader in type, and far removed from the would-be Cavaliers of the plantocracy. As for Palmerston, in a magnanimous chapter of the *Education* dealing with the Anglo-American war-scare over the British building of armored vessels for the Confederacy (the "battle of the rams" of 1863), Henry Adams himself was forced to recant his earlier views of the man and admit publicly that this English lord behaved with remarkable restraint and statesmanship.[4]

But the irony goes even deeper. Henry always excluded Yorkshiremen, whom he admired, from his general tirade against the British. In November 1861 he visited Manchester to investigate the cotton trade and there found other Northern Englishmen—Lancashiremen—with whom he could relate more easily. Though they were unsympathetic to the Union, he felt the Manchester folk would change their tune when cotton inventories ran out and the tide of war changed in Lincoln's favor. He published a long article about the trade in a Boston paper, and English journalists picked it up for severe criticism. The London *Times* seized on one paragraph in which Adams compared London society unfavorably with that of Manchester; so did the *Examiner* (11 January 1862): "He complains that at evening parties he was not allowed a dressing-room. . . . He was regaled with hard seed-cakes and thimblefuls of ice-cream." And the paper added, I think very shrewdly indeed: "That hard seed-cake runs through and embitters all the young gentleman's reports of us."[5] Perhaps it is not too fanciful to say that the treatment young Henry received, or thought he received, at the hands of the London hostesses he names—"that hard seed-cake"—had much to do with the creation of the myth we are investigating.

So much for American suspicion of English "aristocrats," as disseminated by the Adamses. What of the workers? Henry's only remark about them in his 1861 article was very critical: "The operatives," he wrote with disgust, "were dirty, very coarsely dressed, and very stupid in looks; altogether much inferior to the American standard."[6] Yet else-

---

4. *Education,* chap. 11.
5. A. W. Silver, "Henry Adams' 'Diary of a Visit to Manchester,' " *American Historical Review* 51, no. 1 (October 1945): 74–89 (see p. 78, n. 19).
6. Ibid., p. 84.

where, and later, he approaches nearer to the myth. In his correspondence, especially after the Emancipation Proclamation of 1 January 1863, he finds a great change in English opinion—a swing towards the Union, with all the "symptoms of a great popular movement, peculiarly unpleasant to the upper classes here, because it rests on the spontaneous action of the laboring classes and has a pestilous squint at sympathy with republicanism." [7] And in March he writes to Seward, describing the London labor meeting apparently engineered by Marx, at which Bright gave of his most Radical best: "The meeting was a demonstration of democratic strength and no concealment of this fact was made. . . . Every hostile allusion to the Aristocracy, the Church, the opinions of the 'privileged classes' was received with warm cheers. Every allusion to the republican institutions of America, the right of suffrage, the right of self-taxation, the 'sunlight' of republican influence, was caught up by the audience with vehement applause." Adams saw the close link between British attitudes to the American Civil War and their own internal political battles. Triumphantly he asserted: "the class of skilled workmen in London—that is the leaders of the pure popular movement in England—have announced by an act almost without precedent in their history, the principle that they make common cause with the Americans who are struggling for the restoration of the Union." [8] By March 1863 Henry Adams had formulated the myth complete, in both its sections: the upper classes were hateful and the lower noble.

But behind Henry Adams was John Bright. Adams and his father may have formed their own opinions of the English ruling classes (in fact they inherited them, and travelled to England in 1861 already nursing such views); but Bright was the chief source of Henry's views of the workers. Bright came to believe his own propaganda; forever cajoling his fellows on the need to support the Union, he ended up believing he actually spoke *for* the broad mass of lower- and middle-class opinion. In view of the traditional hostility between the middle-class, free trade, anti-Corn-Law types represented so perfectly by Bright, and the working-class leadership, his hopes were misplaced. Yet his impact on Adams is seen in the *Education,* where the American summarizes and quotes Bright, and lays

7. W. C. Ford, ed., *A Cycle of Adams Letters, 1861–65* (Boston, 1920), 1:243.
8. E. D. Adams, *Great Britain and the American Civil War,* 2 vols. (New York, 1925), 2:293.

bare the simplistic class-division hypothesis on which the myth rests, an hypothesis which he swallowed.[9]

The most recent biographer of Bright, Professor Herman Ausubel, points out that the Civil War took Bright by surprise. He quickly recovered, however, and conceived of the war as "God's instrument for the destruction of slavery," which institution was America's "only major evil." Intensely anti-aristocratic and class-conscious, Bright grasped the true meaning of the Civil War for British politics: the defeat of the Union and the dissolution of the United States, that real "home of the working-man," would set back the movement for parliamentary reform and the extension of the franchise in England. Victory for the Union and abolition of slavery (in both North and South, it was hoped—a matter left open by the Emancipation Proclamation), would vindicate democracy and provide a telling argument for a new Reform Bill at home. For if the American people were ready for democracy, why not the English? (Especially, one might add, if they had been foresighted enough to back the winning side in the Civil War). Bright could not be fairly faulted for ignoring the needs of his own local people; he had deplored English dependence on U.S. cotton supplies in pre-Indian-Mutiny days and suggested an expansion of Indian output to vary the source.[10]

The remarkable power of Bright's class prejudice is seen in the way it captured his famous biographer, G. M. Trevelyan. Generally overpraised, the biography commits the cardinal sin of accepting the propaganda of its subject; it thereby further extended the life of the myth by lending it Trevelyan's cachet of great historian. As far as English reaction to the Civil War is concerned, wrote Trevelyan in 1913, it was "only the wealthier classes that went wrong; but at that time they nearly monopolized the press, as well as political power." What of representation? "The House of Commons, Whig and Tory, represented the attitude, not of England, but of Clubland," while in contrast, "the workingmen throughout the country, *instructed by Bright* [italics mine], saw in the Southern Confederacy the men who would degrade labour to a chattel of the capitalist, and in the great Northern Republic the central force of democracy." [11]

9. *Education*, p. 189.
10. Herman Ausubel, *John Bright* (New York, 1966), pp. 117–18, 121–22, 129.
11. G. M. Trevelyan, *Life of John Bright* (Boston and New York, 1913), pp. 304–5, 308–9. For the U.S. side, Trevelyan drew heavily on James Ford Rhodes.

Such rhetoric confuses the judgment of the historian with the political speeches of his hero; and a few pages later comes Trevelyan's statement of the myth of the suffering, pro-Union workers—one of the completest statements I have found, and one that Bright himself might well have written.

Wherever one turns in seeking to locate the origin and explain the strength of this myth, John Bright appears. Together with his famous colleague Richard Cobden, Bright had great influence in Washington. Cobden, however, was for some time wary of coming out fully for the Union. Like many English observers he did not fully appreciate Lincoln's dilemma over winning the border states to the North, his need to tread softly on the slavery issue. Cobden was nonplussed by Lincoln's claim that the war was being fought to maintain the union—nonplussed even though he admitted himself in 1861 that, if given the difficult choice of maintaining black slavery or causing countless white deaths, he would have chosen the former. Cobden, like others, needed clear leadership on this issue. Yet when the preliminary Emancipation Proclamation appeared, he again shared the doubts of other Englishmen about its purpose. Was it not political? Would it foment a bloody slave uprising? He did not go as far as the venomous London *Times* editorial of 7 October 1862 that attacked Lincoln in sex-charged language: "He will appeal to the black blood of the African, he will whisper of the pleasures of spoil and of the gratification of yet fiercer instincts; and when blood begins to flow and shrieks come piercing through the darkness, Mr. Lincoln will wait till the rising flames tell that all is consummated." [12] Such political pornography was the special delight of the conservative press. Gradually, with Bright's pressure and the flow of events favoring the North, Cobden came round more fully to the Union position.

Together Cobden and Bright exerted special influence through steady political correspondence, often a vital element in nineteenth-century affairs. Occasionally their ideas filtered up to Lincoln, through their chief correspondent, Charles Sumner, chairman of the Senate Foreign Relations Committee. Also, news of their propaganda activities in Britain reached the United States. The historian of their partnership, Donald Read, has pointed out that at this time their power was probably greater

12. London *Times,* 7 October 1862, quoted in Franklin, *The Emancipation Proclamation,* p. 73.

in Washington than in London.[13] What is important from the viewpoint of this investigation is that wherever their influence was felt, the myth was part of it, as was the exaggeration of their position as true spokesmen for a large segment of British society. It is simply inaccurate to claim, as did Trevelyan and later historians, that Bright managed to rally the working classes to his banner over the issue of the American Civil War.

If Bright was a major creator of the myth, Gladstone, in one dramatic gesture in 1866, sent the myth spinning into the future. His support for the Confederacy until the war was almost over and won by the North, his later personal attack of remorse, and his public confession of guilt in 1866 and blessing of the workers for their alleged superior moral and political judgment in choosing the right side, are all well-known events to students of British history. Like Acton, Gladstone felt for the Confederacy's rights of self-determination. What he took to be the attitude of the Lancashire workers had a decided impact upon his ideas. Always a man slow to change, Gladstone nevertheless, managed to create a dramatic moment when he finally announced each major political decision of his life. One afternoon in May 1864 Gladstone let loose, in the words of his biographer, John Morley, a "thunderbolt of a sentence" in an otherwise quiet debate, declaring every man's *moral title* to the franchise. The "passive fortitude" of the textile workers in their distress had helped to bring him to this stage in his political evolution. "What are the questions that fit a man for the exercise of a privilege such as the franchise?" he had asked earlier. "Self-command, self-control, respect for order, patience under suffering, confidence in the law, regard for superiors; and when . . . were all these great qualities exhibited in a manner more signal, even more illustrious, than in the conduct of the general body of the operatives of Lancashire under the profound affliction of the winter of 1862?"[14]

By 1866 not only the workers' fortitude impressed him, but their moral and political acumen. He was by now quite aware that he had backed the wrong side in the war. Moreover he was determined to pass a reform bill to extend the franchise and would himself use the outcome of

13. Donald Read, *Cobden and Bright* (New York, 1968), pp. 218–29. Dr. Read explains the restraint of the workers by their understanding that their own government was not responsible for the cotton famine. In view of their demands, as revealed by Dr. Ellison, I feel this explanation is inadequate.

14. John Morley, *Life of Gladstone*, 3 vols. (London, 1903), 2:124–26. For some reason Morley fails to mention Gladstone's famous speech of 1866.

the Civil War as a direct political argument in favor of extending the vote. So a combination of moral self-searching, courage, supreme arrogance, and politics brought him to the famous speech of 27 April 1866, in which he made the direct and overt connection between the American Civil War and the English reform struggle. This speech, which he made as chancellor of the exchequer in the Whig government, is worth examining.

The debate on the Reform Bill had been continuing for eight days and nights. Gladstone rose at about one in the morning to reply to Disraeli's objection to the proposed measure, namely, that it threatened to "re-construct the Constitution on American principles." Towards the end of his reply he asked the members to consider "the enormous and silent changes" that had been happening among the British workers, "a steady movement . . . a movement onwards and upwards . . . unobservable in detail, but as solid and undeniable as it is resistless in its essential character." He hinted that Disraeli was unsympathetic to such a movement—"Has my right honorable Friend, in whom mistrust rises to its utmost height, ever really considered the astonishing phenomenon connected with some portion of the labouring classes, especially in the Lancashire distress? . . . what an act of self-denial was exhibited by these men?" It was, of course, Disraeli's government that eventually enacted a reform bill the following year; such is the course of politics. Gladstone's speech went on, however, to plant the myth of the noble pro-Union worker in the British public mind for years to come:

> They knew that the source of their distress lay in the war, yet they never uttered or entertained the wish that any effort should be made to put an end to it, as they held it to be a war for justice, and for freedom. Could any man have believed that a conviction so still, so calm, so energetic, could have planted itself in the minds of a population without becoming a known patent fact throughout the whole country? But we knew nothing of it.

We, apparently, meant Gladstone and his associates. Remorse and politics drove him on: "when the day of trial came we saw that noble sympathy on their part with the people of the North. On one side there was a magnificent moral spectacle; on the other side was there not also a great lesson to us all, to teach us that in those little tutored, but yet reflective minds, by a process of quiet instillation, opinions and sentiments gradually form themselves of which we for a long time remain unaware, but which, when at last they make their appearance, are found to be deep-rooted, mature and ineradicable?" [15]

The totally unself-conscious arrogance of this peroration, its treatment of the Lancashire workers as an alien subculture, is matched only by what we now know to be its complete inaccuracy.

After Gladstone's unwitting service on behalf of the myth, little more was needed for many years. Its fate was now left to the historians, whose work was so effective that as late as the 1960s the myth was still standard textbook fare. Certain inroads had been made, as we shall see. The *Harvard Guide to American History,* in 1963, made factual subheads of the myth: "Confederate sympathies of the governing class and English colonies; Union sympathies of the working class." [16] A fine and long-lived textbook, Morison and Commager, in its sixth edition of 1969 still found French and British opinion on the Civil War to divide "on the whole along class lines." The "plain people of Europe" stood for the Union; the "ruling classes" for the South. It was added that some liberals favored the Confederacy and doubted the North's motives. The interpretation followed closely that of the first edition of 1930, and made use of the same telling quote from Montalembert: "An involuntary instinct, all-powerful and unquenchable, at once arrayed on the side of the pro-slavery people all the open or secret partisans of the fanaticism and absolutism of Europe." [17] With this powerful sentence the myth is buttressed by psychological drives, and the Union cause contrasted with the traditional American view of a decadent Europe.

Less sophisticated and more elementary textbooks split Britain in half, "aristocrats" versus "workers." The middle classes do not appear at all; the 1832 Reform Act and the host of bourgeois reforms that followed it never seem to have happened. D. S. Muzzey, H. U. Faulkner, J. D. Hicks, all repeat with differing degrees of understanding and detail the essential tale of a Tory aristocracy that feels kinship with the Southern planters and hatred for the Yankee peddlers. For Muzzey, in fact, Britain in the 1860s was "still governed by an aristocracy which had not changed

15. *Hansard Parliamentary Debates,* 3d ser., 183 (1866):113–48.
16. *Harvard Guide to American History,* 4th printing (Cambridge, Mass., 1963), p. 396.
17. Morison and Commager, *Growth of the American Republic,* 1st ed. (New York, 1930), p. 589; 6th ed., rev. W. Leuchtenburg, 2 vols. (New York, 1969), 1:646.

essentially since the eighteenth century." [18] In this view, British history conveniently stands still for a while, somewhere about the time of the War of Independence, while the United States surges ahead. These textbooks of U.S. history were best-sellers in the 1930s, 40s, and 50s; Muzzey was first published in 1922. They all flatter the United States by contrast with Europe.

Textbooks of British history presumably deal with matters closer to the original source materials for the myth; yet they also had little reason to change the story fundamentally. As late as 1964 a new social history textbook, *The Rise of Industrial Society in England,* by a leading scholar, claimed quite flatly that the English "upper class" supported the "slave-owning South"—implying that they supported slavery as an institution. In contrast, "the workers, in spite of the sufferings of the cotton famine, largely supported the North." [19] R. K. Webb's more thoughtful treatment (*Modern England,* 1968), adopts Gladstone's view, that the "seriousness and responsibility" of the workers during the famine impressed middle-class radicals with their worthiness for the franchise; but Professor Webb goes on to point out that the relative calm of the Lancashire workers can be attributed in part to a successful public works and relief program. [20] This judgment is in line with Dr. Ellison's findings, that the only approach to violence the textile workers ever made was over the relief program itself. The earlier English history textbooks are naturally strongly influenced by the Gladstone version, G. M. Trevelyan's texts throwing in the Nonconformist conscience for good measure.

What of the older historians, whose works formed the bases for later distillations? James Ford Rhodes was in many ways more sophisticated, not less. He found "the main body of the aristocracy *and the middle class*" (italics mine) of England longing for the Civil War to end, but doubting that the North could ever conquer and subjugate the Confederacy. What kind of a United States would it be after such a war? While Rhodes did lean heavily on John Bright and chastized the antidemocratic fears of the

18. D. S. Muzzey, *The United States,* 2 vols. (New York, 1933, first pub. 1922), 1:614; H. U. Faulkner, *American Political and Social History* (New York, 1947, first pub. 1937), p. 368; J. D. Hicks, *The Federal Union* (Boston, 1937), pp. 672–73.

19. S. G. Checkland, *The Rise of Industrial Society in England* (New York, 1964), p. 287.

20. R. K. Webb, *Modern England* (New York and Toronto, 1968), pp. 318–19.

English aristocrats, it is clear that for him the crucial matter was a more pragmatic one: military success or failure. In his earlier lectures of 1912 to students at Oxford, as in his fuller study of the Civil War in 1917, Rhodes emphasizes the importance of the first Southern victory at Bull Run in setting the tone for British opinion on the war. Indeed, he thought that an early sympathy on the part of most Englishmen for the Union side was dissipated by that Confederate victory.[21] Englishmen of all classes wanted to back a winner.

The volume by J. K. Hosmer, published in 1907 in the American Nation series, also recognizes that England had a viable middle class in the 1860s. Hosmer uses Henry Adams as his direct source for the love English aristocrats bore for the Confederacy; yet he does admit that *"even the masses"* had doubts about supporting the Union at first.[22] The more famous Edward Channing, in his sixth volume of the narrative history of the United States, describes the myth in classic form (upper class hostility, workers' mass meetings for the Union), in heavily economic terms. Channing's special strength was in details, however; his economic approach is more muted than the verities of Charles Beard, who repeats the myth with much added pathos.[23]

Three major studies dealt directly with the problem of British reactions to the Civil War. In 1925 E. D. Adams' two-volume *Great Britain and the Civil War* brought out fully the intimate connection between events in the United States and British internal political history, doing so by use of much contemporary evidence. This study makes it obvious that *at the time* many Americans and Englishmen alike believed in the upper class-lower class dichotomy that we now find too simple. Much of the evidence used by Adams, however, is heavily partisan.[24] D. Jordan and E. J. Pratt's

21. James Ford Rhodes, *Lectures on the Civil War* (New York, 1913), pp. 154–55; idem, *History of the Civil War, 1861–65* (New York, 1917), p. 66; idem, *History of the United States from the Compromise of 1850*, vols. 1–5 (New York, 1907), abridged and ed. A. Nevins (Chicago, 1966), pp. 392, 396. Rhodes' emphasis on the winning side is echoed fifty years later by Sheldon Van Auken, "English Sympathy for the Southern Confederacy" (B. Litt thesis, Oxford, 1957).

22. J. K. Hosmer, *The Appeal to Arms, 1861–63,* American Nation series (New York, 1907), pp. 306–8.

23. Edward Channing, *History of the United States* (New York, 1926), 6:338, 342–43, 384–85; Charles and Mary Beard, *Rise of American Civilization,* 2 vols. (New York, 1927), 2:82; idem, *Beards' Basic History of the United States* (New York, 1944), p. 274.

24. E. D. Adams, *Britain and the Civil War,* 2:274, 288–89, 299.

broader *Europe and the American Civil War* (1931) is more complex in interpretation and had E. D. Adams's work on which to build. Like Adams, Jordan and Pratt follow basically the lines of the myth laid down by Henry Adams, John Bright, and Gladstone. They devote an entire chapter to "The Gentlemen and the Masses: The Keynote of British Opinion," although they understand that the English upper classes were "far more definitely anti-Northern than pro-Southern." For me the most interesting parts of their work are their approach to the nagging question of how influential was working-class opinion and their emphasis (following Rhodes) on the role of military events in determining British attitudes.

"The winning side in America," they make clear, "would undoubtedly be treated with great courtesy by English opinion." Lord Robert Cecil is quoted, very effectively, telling a Union supporter: "There is one way to convert us all—win the battles, and we shall come round at once." It is a pity the authors did not develop this point more fully. Instead, like many of their predecessors, they fall back on the "Nonconformist conscience" and other basic elements of the myth. Did it really matter what the workers thought anyway? Dr. Ellison puts the case strongly for the impotence of the workers, their total exclusion from political consideration by the governing classes. Jordan and Pratt take a different position: certainly laboring-men had little clear political power, but they had much political *influence*—"their dead weight was great." This negative influence meant that it was "very difficult to initiate any large policy of which the working classes disapproved." [25] What Jordan and Pratt had in mind here was that the "dead weight" of working-class opinion prevented the pro-Confederate government from outright recognition of the South and lifting of the blockade. Dr. Ellison's new research shows that their "dead weight" would have had the very opposite effect, since they *demanded* Southern recognition and removal of the blockade. However, she does not believe in the efficacy of workers' opinions anyway, and uses this political ineffectiveness to explain the comparative restraint of the official policy towards the Union, despite worker pressure for a more pro-Southern approach. It may be ungallant of me to disagree slightly here with Dr. Ellison, but I find this view unconvincing because the weight of worker opinions, dead or otherwise, had already been felt in British history several

25. D. Jordan and E. J. Pratt, *Europe and the American Civil War* (Cambridge, Mass., 1931), pp. 17, 48, 87, 145–47.

times at least since the late eighteenth century; and both political parties were acutely aware of the growing need, sooner or later, to begin to cater more to lower-class needs. The Reform Act of 1867 that enfranchised the town workers was jockeyed between the parties and subsequently passed by Disraeli as a political coup.[26]

The third direct specialist study of note was F. L. Owsley's *King Cotton Diplomacy* (1931), essentially a volume in Confederate history, with the added advantage, therefore, of taking a very different angle of vision. Since he is not concerned with justifying the North and its victory, it is not surprising that Owsley, as early as 1931, rejects much of the myth of suffering workers defending the Union and ignoble English aristocrats jeering at every Northern defeat. This "older school" of interpretation, in Owsley's words, used "a high and idealistic basis" which was simply "too good to be true." The myth school ignored pro-Confederate mass meetings and declarations, and grossly exaggerated the "spontaneous" nature of all such meetings, "drummed up by well-subsidized leaders."

Owsley takes a very bleak view of the workers, reminiscent of Henry Adams's immediate reactions on seeing the Manchester operatives. "The population of Lancashire and of all industrial England," he claimed, "was politically apathetic, sodden, ignorant, and docile, with the exception of a few intelligent and earnest leaders." Such people were not aware of world events; not worked up about slavery and the preservation of American democracy. On the contrary: "They wanted bread, they wanted clothes, they needed medicines to give to their sick children and aged parents, they wanted pretty clothing for their daughters and sisters who were being forced into prostitution." [27] Sick children, aged parents, and innocent prostitutes—Owsley manages to drag in several battered clichés; it is clear that in this section he has himself swallowed the well-known Southern "wage-slavery" argument and applied it to the English rather than to the Yankees. Meanwhile, his sharp rejection of the myth we are tracing seems to have had little impact on its continued acceptance.

Not until the 1950s did fresh historical research add fuel to the arguments of Owsley against the myth. In 1953, W. D. Jones, having read in

26. See Gertrude Himmelfarb, *Victorian Minds* (New York, 1968), chap. 13, for a revisionist view of the passing of the Act of 1867. The Tories passed the measure, confident that it would not bring any revolutionary alteration of the power structure.

27. F. L. Owsley, *King Cotton Diplomacy*, rev. ed. (Chicago, 1959, first pub. 1931), pp. 544–46; Owsley's use of allegedly Confederate evidence is criticized in H. M. Pelling, *America and the British Left* (London, 1956), p. 8, n. 2.

the Disraeli papers the letters of leading Conservatives, concluded that the alleged affinity of British Conservatives for the Southern plantocracy was very thin indeed—"a detached, innocuous sympathy which was quickly lost amid practical concerns." The United States was very far away; Poland and Denmark were nearer.[28] This certainly tallies with still more recent conclusions drawn by J. M. Hernon, Jr., namely that Lord Palmerston himself, after deciding that England should stay out of the American struggle in October 1862 (at least "till the war shall have taken a more decisive turn"), rapidly became involved in the closer problems of Bismarck and Sleswig-Holstein.[29] The upper classes were not all that interested in American affairs.

In his subtle history of Anglo-American relations written in 1954, Professor H. C. Allen also threw cold water on the aristocratic affinity theory, and tried to show how the English government had genuine problems with regard to the American situation—how to recognize the fact that a war was in progress, yet without alienating the South (which might after all win, and become a new nation) or the North (which already was a nation, and very suspicious of Britain anyway). Such problems were left mainly to four men: Lincoln and Seward, and Palmerston and Russell.[30] How they coped is the true story. In Allen's book England is of course a far more complex place than the myth allows.

Further hints were soon to appear. The labor side of the myth came under attack in 1955 from an Edinburgh Ph.D. thesis by R. Botsford, which found Scots labor leaders supporting the Confederacy. In two articles of 1957 and 1961 Royden Harrison disclosed that the anti-capitalist workers had anti-Yankee and therefore pro-Southern views, whatever they thought about slavery itself. The myth of workers' support for the Union was created only in the minds of "middle class observers, many of whom were eager to persuade themselves."[31]

28. W. D. Jones, "British Conservatives and the American Civil War," *American Historical Review* 58, no. 3 (April 1953): 527–43.

29. J. M. Hernon, Jr., "British Sympathies in the American Civil War," *Journal of Southern History* 33 (August 1967): 356–67.

30. H. C. Allen, *Great Britain and the United States: A History of Anglo-American Relations* (London, 1954), p. 452.

31. Royden Harrison, "British Labour and the Confederacy," *International Review of Social History* 2 (1959): 78–105; idem, "British Labour and American Slavery," *Science and Society* 25 (1961: 291–319; J. M. Hernon, Jr., *Celts, Catholics and Copperheads: Ireland Views the American Civil War* (Columbus, Ohio, 1968), finds no Irish labor support for the Union either; the Irish did not favor emancipation.

Another English scholar, J. R. Pole, suggested in a pamphlet on Lincoln in 1959 that the older English labor leaders controlled the labor press; the younger men, who favored the Union more, were effectively excluded.[32] One finds this idea also much earlier in the correspondence of Karl Marx, as we shall see. That same year Frank Thistlethwaite's *Anglo-American Connection* rejected the affinity theory, suggested a certain degree of English middle-class and worker support for the Confederacy, but in the end, after this tentative revision, fell back on the Nonconformist conscience and the idea that the Lancashire textile hands took the lead in upholding the blockade. A few steps forward, and a few steps backwards—in 1955 G. D. Lillibridge's *Beacon of Freedom* had appeared, a book which appeared to place on a firm, scholarly basis the essence of the myth: the European social class-differentiated reactions to things American. Lillibridge's study was much more knowledgeable about European institutions and developments, much more astute than many earlier works; yet so far as this particular myth was concerned we see no advance. The Civil War, he wrote, "brought to a head a long-standing conflict between those who clung to the lure of American democracy, and those who detested and feared the American influence." British opinion is divided into Conservative, Middleclass, and Radical. The titles are perhaps not quite commensurate, yet the inclusion of the middle class is some sort of step forward in analysis. Unfortunately, for the "Radicals" Lillibridge chose to use as a source *Reynold's Weekly*—attacked by Marx in the 1860s for having sold out to the Confederacy. He made no use of Marx. Naturally Lillibridge found that the "solidarity of working class support for the Northern cause" was to be explained by "the strength of the long tradition of American democratic leadership." Marx himself subscribed to this view.[33]

Direct evidence that Lancashire workers in particular backed the Confederacy came with a brief article by Michael Brook in 1965; his work was based on the cotton weaving towns of Northeast Lancashire, mainly Burnley.[34] And in 1967 J. M. Hernon, Jr. could conclude that "possibly a

32. J. R. Pole, *Abraham Lincoln.*
33. Frank Thistlethwaite, *The Anglo-American Connection in the Early Nineteenth Century* (Philadelphia, 1959), pp. 119–20; G. D. Lillibridge, *Beacon of Freedom: The Impact of American Democracy upon Great Britain, 1830–1870* (Philadelphia, 1955), pp. 107, 109, 119.
34. Michael Brook, "Confederate Sympathies in North East Lancashire, 1862–1864," *Transactions of the Lancashire and Cheshire Antiquarian Society*, vols. 75–76 (1965–66): 211–17.

majority" of British workers supported Gladstone's pro-Confederate statements.[35] Meanwhile, the late Allan Nevins, with customary brilliance, had swept together into a couple of pages the many elements of the myth and rejected the "fallacious" view of the English social structure on which it was built. In 1960 Nevins had little reason, despite his own voluminous research, to doubt that the Lancashiremen had in fact sided with Lincoln. But his demolition of the remainder of the myth is masterly. He rejects its distortion of the role of the English middle classes; its overstatement of the role of the workers; its overemphasis on the impact of the Emancipation Proclamation;[36] its failure to face up to the legitimate British policy problems caused by the war; and its injustice to Russell and Palmerston. There was very little that escaped the attention of Allan Nevins.[37]

Now, as the most recent of a long line of scholars, Dr. Mary Ellison has completed the story for us in a remarkable fashion. The men and women of Lancashire did not, in fact, suffer for the Union. Even the great Karl Marx himself, very much alive and active at the time, was wrong. Marx and Engels believed that the British workers accepted their deprivations because they yearned for American democracy. Moreover, could not the solidarity of the British textile workers with the black American slave be hailed as a startling example of Marxian class-consciousness, cutting across barriers of space, nationality, and race, running roughshod over narrow personal economic self-interest and *"false* materialism"?

On the other side, one may wonder why Marx and Engels, with their immense reading in the European press, and their North-of-England connections, missed altogether the sort of local evidence used by Dr. Ellison for her book. We know from their extraordinary correspondence and from Engels' military study and Marx's articles in the *New York Tribune* and the Vienna *Die Presse,* that the two men made an intense study of the war as it was going on. Writing to Marx as late as September 1862, Engels doubted that the North could win.[38] He was not alone in this. Marx, in a *Tribune* article in December 1861, also was not alone in getting the English political side of the story all wrong, blaming Palmerston for being recal-

---

35. J. M. Hernon, Jr., "British Sympathies."
36. The real importance of the Emancipation Proclamation in changing British opinion has been questioned by J. M. Hernon, Jr., in "British Sympathies."
37. A. Nevins, *The War for the Union* (New York, 1960), 2:242–43, 264–65.
38. Karl Marx and F. Engles, *The Civil War in the United States,* collected papers (New York, 1961), p. 253.

citrant and thinking that Gladstone was a moderating influence opposed to intervention, when the opposite was the case.[39]

"It ought never to be forgotten in the United States," Marx wrote in January 1862, "that at least the *working classes* of England, from the commencement to the termination of the difficulty, have never forsaken them." Why do the British workers choose the North? Marx's explanation, in another *Tribune* article for February 1862, is not too far behind Lillibridge's *Beacon of Freedom:* "the conduct of the British workingmen might have been anticipated from the natural sympathy the popular classes all over the world ought to feel for the only popular government in the world." The operatives exceeded themselves in their noble sufferings, and "simple justice requires to pay a tribute to the sound attitude of the British working classes, the more so when contrasted with the hypocritical, cowardly and stupid conduct of the official and well-to-do John Bull." [40]

In the same article he accuses several leading working-class newspapers of being turncoats. *Reynold's Weekly* "has sold itself to Messrs. Yancey and Mann [the Confederate diplomats], and week after week exhausts its horsepower of foul language in appeals to the working classes to urge the government, for their own interests, to war with the Union." [41] False materialism is at work. The restraint of the mass of the workers, in face of incredible misery, is remarkable, Marx tells the readers of *Die Presse* in February 1862. While the government circles and bourgeois press push for British official intervention in the Civil War in favor of the Confederacy, the workers resist; they refuse to make trouble and thus give their government the excuse it is looking for to enter the war. "The working class is accordingly fully conscious that the government is only waiting for the intervention cry from below, the *pressure from without,* to put an end to the American blockade and English misery." The silence of the heroic workers is a "new, brilliant proof of the indestructible excellence of the English popular masses, of that excellence which is the secret of England's greatness." [42]

What a change in Marx by the end of 1862! By November he was having second thoughts about the whole theory; what did this "restraint"

39. Ibid., p. 45.
40. Ibid., pp. 47–49.
41. Ibid., p. 49.
42. Ibid., pp. 139–43.

really mean? He began to doubt his own propaganda; the workers' silence was getting him down. In an angry letter to Engels he wrote: "much more injurious in my view [than French attempts to organize official intervention] is the sheep's attitude of the workers in Lancashire. Such a thing has never been heard of in the world." Perhaps Marx did not understand how effective the poor relief program was in the county. Anyway, that "indestructible excellence" of the English worker noted in February had become a sheepish servility by November. "During this recent period England has disgraced herself more than any other country, the workers by their christian slave nature, the bourgeois and aristocrats by their enthusiasm for slavery." [43] So much for England's greatness. For a painful moment Marx was caught on the prongs of his own ideology.

Writing again to Engels in the New Year, after the Emancipation Proclamation, his spirits rose once more, and he thought a little better of the workers.[44] Were the workers noble, suffering silently in a great cause, or were they servile sheep? Marx found his view fluctuating, and we can sympathize with his dilemma, having now traced the history of the myth. For the workers did not resort to any sort of revolutionary activity or violence, even though they did not suffer silently for Lincoln and the black slaves. Dr. Ellison wants to point out that nonviolence is not the same thing as passivity or silence; but it seems to me to be a remarkable matter all the same. Her study destroys the notion that the workers supported the Union. She describes their real activities and their genuine demands. But the question of the nonviolent nature of the British working class remains to be investigated; it bothers us as it irritated Marx.

As I suggested at the outset, the myth was born in propaganda and was sustained because it suited the purposes and self-images of those who sustained it. Marx, despite his problems with it, found it useful as an example of class solidarity. (He does not seem to have developed the idea, as Royden Harrison did years later, that the workers' anticapitalism could logically lead them to support the South and oppose the Yankee). The British Radical, Whig-Liberal parliamentary reformers exploited the myth as an argument in the struggle for extending the vote—Gladstone only after a public change of heart, characteristic of the man. As Jordan and Pratt explained in 1931: "America was for Englishmen but a part of

43. Ibid., pp. 261–62.
44. Ibid., p. 264.

an endless political campaign within England itself." [45] Conversely, Americans maintained a certain self-flattering image of Europe which suited them and into which the myth could fit very snugly. Their vision of upper- and lower-class Europeans, fearing and admiring American institutions respectively, went back in time at least to the American Revolution itself. Based on a superficial view of European social structure, this vision was nonetheless effective. In vain, as late as February 1865, did the London *Economist* plead that Britain had supplied far more war materiel over the years to the North than ever managed to reach the Confederacy;[46] American irritation would not be so assuaged. The Civil War was yet another occasion to point a finger at those English "aristocrats." What the aristocrats had done in favoring the Confederacy, was only what Henry Adams had expected them to do before he ever reached England. The myth of the anti-American aristocrat was one side of the coin; the myth of the noble worker during the Civil War was the other side. This latter half of the illusion, necessary alike to the Marxist and American world views, is now evaporated.

I suppose, as a coda, it is only to be expected that in this whole long international debate the black American appears mainly as an abstraction, a slave to be emancipated or a figure to be dreaded in a servile uprising. Negroes scarcely feature in the British side of the story, certainly not as individual human beings. British views of the black man in the 1860s can hardly be supposed to be less racist than American views. So it is interesting to note that those blacks who took the lead in the emancipation struggle shared many of the doubts and suspicions felt by British observers over Lincoln's policies—his statement that the war was being fought to save the Union; his Negro colonization schemes that filled Frederick Douglass with despair; his revocation of abolitionist decrees in captured territories. What was this war about? Henry Adams and other white Union patriots were furious at British caution and suspicion of the Union. But black leaders would have found themselves more in agreement with the British at the time—at least until the Emancipation Proclamation. Disgusted with Union policy, Frederick Douglass declared in a July 1862 editorial: "Abraham Lincoln is no more fit for the place he holds than

45. Jordan and Pratt, *Europe and the Civil War,* p. 52.
46. D. R. Adler, *British Investments in American Railways, 1834–98* (Charlottesville, Virginia, 1970), p. 73.

was James Buchanan." And Harriet Tubman feared a Northern victory
before Lincoln had been pushed to the point of proclaiming the slaves lib-
erated. "God won't let Massa Linkum beat de South till he do the right
ting," she prayed hopefully in 1861. Once Lincoln moved towards emancipation, their feelings altered. From the date of the preliminary proclamation on—22 September 1862—said Frederick Douglass, the war was
changed into a moral crusade, "invested with sanctity." He wrote a *Slaves'*
Appeal to Great Britain urging the point that England was now "morally
bound to hold aloof from the Confederacy." [47] Whether his appeal was
heard I do not know; but he was as right as Gladstone's illusory textile
workers would have been, if they had indeed stood by the Union in their
hour of misery.

47. Franklin, *The Emancipation Proclamation,* p. 61; J. M. McPherson, *The Negro's Civil
War* (New York, 1967), pp. 43, 47.

APPENDIX

TABLE 1
Members of Parliament for Lancashire 1861–65 (North/South Allegiance Denoted by N or S Where Known)

Area	Liberal	Conservative
Northeast		
Preston	C. P. Grenfell (S)	Richard Assheton Cross, '62
		Frederick Arthur Stanley,
		'62–65 (N)
Blackburn		W. H. Hornby (S)
		Joseph Cook, '62
		James Pilkington, '62–65
Clitheroe	John Turner Hopwood (S)	
Southeast		
Ashton-under-		
Lyne	Thomas Milner Gibson (N)	
	John Morgan Cobbett (S)	
Oldham	W. Johnson Fox, '62	
	John Tomlinson Hibbert,	
	'60–65 (S)	
Bolton	Thomas Barnes (N)	Col. William Gray
Bury	Rt. Hon. Frederick Peel (S)	
	Richard Cobden (N)	
Wigan	Henry Woods	Major General James Lindsay
Salford	William Nathaniel Massey (S)	
Manchester	Thomas Bazley	
	J. Aspinall Turner (S)	
Lancaster	E. M. Fenwick	
	S. Gregson	
Liverpool		Thomas Berry Horsfall (S)
		John C. Ewart (S)
Warrington		Gilbert Greenall
N. Lancashire	Spencer Compton Cavendish,	Colonel John Wilson Patten
	Marquis of Hartington (S)	
S. Lancashire		Hon. Algernon F. Egerton (S)
		William John Legh
		Charles Turner (S)

TABLE 2
Poor Law Relief in Distressed Lancashire Unions during the Cotton Famine

	Population 1861	Total Expenditure for Relief to the Poor, Half-Years Ended Michaelmas		No. of Paupers, 4th week November 1862	No. of Paupers, 4th week November 1864
		1862	1863		
Ashton-under-Lyne	134,753	£17,980	£40,609	34,541	12,577
Barton-upon-Irwell	39,038	3,844	4,350	1,816	1,181
Blackburn	119,942	21,258	22,401	24,019	7,650
Bolton	130,269	13,692	16,993	8,685	5,330
Burnley	75,595	9,345	9,224	8,463	4,064
Bury	101,135	11,283	15,210	11,883	7,550
Chorley	41,678	4,406	7,221	4,249	2,059
Chorlton	169,579	15,647	31,157	15,310	6,039
Clitheroe	20,476	2,828	3,079	1,477	1,070
Haslingden	69,781	5,441	9,265	11,504	4,600
Liverpool (Parish)	269,742	55,257	53,638	18,021	15,557
Manchester (Township)	185,410	48,591	63,776	39,023	11,743
Oldham	111,276	8,598	17,021	15,767	4,517
Preston	110,523	27,776	37,360	23,180	8,788
Rochdale	91,754	12,788	17,883	13,975	4,547
Salford	105,335	12,987	17,005	11,479	3,741
Warrington	43,875	5,281	5,875	2,324	1,791
Wigan	94,561	9,769	15,462	5,512	4,776

TABLE 3
Number of Cotton Operatives in the Three Types of Factories in 1841

Southeast		
Spinning	53,000	
Mixed	65,000	
Weaving	4,000	
Northeast		
Spinning	8,000	
Mixed	32,654	
Weaving	3,000	

NOTE: Based on Horner's *Report.* Rochdale is taken as the dividing line between southeast and northeast.

TABLE 4
Occupations of Adults over 20 in Lancashire in 1861

	Total Adults	Professional	Domestic	Commercial	Agricultural	Industrial	Indefinite & Non-productive	Cotton Manufacture Males	Cotton Manufacture Females	Coal Mining
Liverpool	156,537	3,710	63,890	29,874	1,451	47,043	10,569	330	274	–
West Derby	122,864	4,977	54,765	15,447	4,330	35,253	8,092	–	–	–
Prescot	37,478	704	14,927	1,319	4,165	13,590	2,773	–	–	2,315
Ormskirk	24,539	609	8,683	952	8,202	5,330	763	–	–	224
Wigan	48,654	651	16,832	1,340	3,901	24,458	1,472	222	3,700	9,085
Warrington	22,987	462	8,401	999	3,002	8,499	1,624	239	325	619
Leigh	20,262	265	4,394	513	2,229	12,348	513	1,627	1,950	1,323
Bolton	69,298	896	22,359	1,932	3,625	38,665	1,821	8,395	9,105	3,216
Bury	54,873	715	16,406	1,498	3,043	30,931	2,280	7,341	8,402	952
Barton-upon-Irwell	21,263	477	7,565	1,017	2,509	8,876	819	1,151	1,581	1,034
Chorlton	94,964	3,627	37,123	8,411	1,980	38,725	5,098	2,577	7,145	–
Salford	58,528	2,161	21,286	3,880	1,119	27,637	2,445	2,110	3,821	660
Manchester	137,351	2,662	44,723	9,564	2,167	71,868	6,367	7,049	10,983	319
Ashton	74,390	898	20,565	1,957	2,356	45,924	2,690	11,774	15,373	1,931
Oldham	60,816	670	16,874	1,529	1,970	38,088	1,685	8,233	8,448	1,815
Rochdale	50,428	600	15,080	1,608	2,332	29,159	1,649	5,467	6,117	1,100
Haslingden	37,093	432	11,258	837	1,974	21,251	1,341	6,640	5,700	429
Burnley	39,978	550	11,462	674	3,095	22,674	1,523	7,943	6,384	1,438
Clitheroe	11,302	274	2,937	115	3,391	4,294	291	957	1,158	–
Blackburn	62,612	791	16,709	777	3,349	37,976	3,010	12,647	12,713	924
Chorley	21,710	305	6,038	348	3,977	10,515	527	2,993	3,173	668
Preston	60,193	1,828	16,572	1,758	5,413	31,647	2,975	8,284	10,995	–
Fylde	13,690	439	5,125	696	3,672	3,236	522	226	243	–
Garstang	6,583	108	1,789	68	3,296	1,170	152	–	–	–
Lancaster	19,181	631	6,578	715	4,626	5,516	1,115	357	534	–
Ulverston	18,629	451	6,759	595	4,161	5,817	846	–	–	–

Source: 1861 Census.

TABLE 5
Cotton Imports and Exports, 1859–67

		1859	1860	1861	1862	1863	1864	1865	1866	1867
Yarn Exports										
Quantity	lb.	192,206	197,343	177,848	93,225	74,398	75,677	103,533	138,804	199,096
Value	£	9,458	9,871	9,293	6,202	8,063	9,083	10,343	13,686	14,871
Piece Good Exports										
Quantity	yards	2,562,545	2,562,545	2,563,218	1,681,394	1,710,962	1,751,989	2,014,303	2,575,698	2,832,023
Value	£	37,038	40,346	36,124	28,562	37,633	43,917	44,876	57,903	53,128
Hosiery, Lace, &c., Exports										
Value	£	1,706	1,795	1,455	1,986	1,891	1,882	2,047	3,024	2,837
Total Value, all Exports	£	48,202	52,012	46,872	36,750	47,587	54,882	57,266	74,613	70,836
Cotton Imports										
United States	lb.	961,707	1,115,891	819,501	16,656	25,672	39,738	172,497	520,414	528,170
Brazil	lb.	22,479	17,287	17,290	23,339	22,603	38,018	55,403	68,524	70,430
Mediterranean	lb.	38,106	44,037	41,479	65,238	107,359	147,249	204,077	129,772	133,066
East Indies, &c.	lb.	192,331	204,145	369,040	394,421	465,988	602,089	484,787	621,186	498,844
British West Indies	lb.	592	465	486	5,563	25,182	26,738	16,537	3,600	4,810
Other Countries	lb.	10,774	9,114	9,189	18,756	23,280	40,270	45,201	34,018	27,566
Total	lb.	1,225,989	1,390,939	1,256,985	523,973	670,084	894,102	978,502	1,377,514	1,262,886
Cotton Exports										
Total	lb.	175,143	250,339	298,288	214,715	241,352	244,702	302,909	388,982	350,636

TABLE 6

English Emigration to the United States and the British Colonies, 1860–65

Year	United States	British Colonies
1860	13,600	12,700
1861	8,700	13,200
1862	14,200	21,200
1863	32,600	28,300
1864	30,000	27,700
1865	15,000	18,900

Sources: "Returns Relating to Emigration," *P.P.*, XXXVIII (1863), p. 19; "Returns Relating to Emigration," *P.P.*, L (1868–69), p. 489; "Twenty-Third General Report of the Emigration Commissioners," *P.P.*, XV (1863), p. 11; *Historical Statistics of the United States. Colonial Times to 1957*, prepared by the Bureau of the Census with the cooperation of the Social Science Council (Washington, 1960), p. 57; Stanley C. Johnson, *A History of Emigration from the United Kingdom to North America 1763–1912* (London, 1913), p. 344; "Distribution of Immigrants 1850–1900," in *Statistical Review of Immigration*, Senate Documents, vol. 20 (Washington, 1911), pp. 28–29.
Note: Figures taken to nearest round figures as varied sources were used.

TABLE 7

Main Exports to U.S.A. from U.K., Produce and Manufactures, 1856–67

	Average Annual Declared Value (in millions of £s)								
	1859	1860	1861	1862	1863	1864	1865	1866	1867
Cotton manufactures and yarn	4.6	4.5	1.5	2.4	2.2	2.1	3.6	4.4	3.2
Woolen manufactures and yarn	4.4	4.1	2.0	2.7	3.5	3.6	5.1	5.6	3.7
Iron and steel, wrought and unwrought	3.0	3.1	1.0	1.4	2.1	2.8	1.6	3.2	3.3
Linen manufactures and yarn	2.1	2.1	0.7	1.9	2.3	2.7	3.8	4.4	2.9
Clothing, etc.	1.6	1.4	0.7	0.7	0.8	0.9	1.0	1.3	1.0
Hardwares and cutlery	1.2	1.0	0.7	0.4	0.3	0.4	0.5	1.0	0.7
Arms and ammunition				1.0	0.4				
Tin and pewter wares, unwrought tin and tinplate	1.1	1.0	0.4	0.8	0.8	0.7	1.2	1.5	1.5
Earthenware	0.6	0.7	0.2	0.3	0.4	0.4	0.5	0.8	0.7
Silk manufactures	0.6	0.5	0.2	0.2	0.2	0.2	0.3	0.4	0.2
Machinery						0.1	0.1	0.3	0.3
Glass manufactures	0.1	0.1						0.1	0.1
Other items	3.1		1.7	2.5	2.4	2.8	3.4	4.9	4.2
Totals	22.6	21.7	9.1	14.3	15.3	16.7	21.2	28.4	21.8

Source: British Board of Trade annual returns.

TABLE 8
Wheat Imports and Total Imports From U.S. to U.K., 1860–66

| | Average Annual Declared Value (in millions of £s) | | |
	Grain	Wheatmeal and Flour	Total Imports
1860	2.0	2.1	44.7
1861	4.3	3.6	49.4
1862	9.3	3.2	27.7
1863	4.4	1.6	19.6
1864	3.7	1.0	17.9
1865	0.6	0.2	21.7
1866	0.4	0.2	46.9

SOURCE: British Board of Trade annual returns.

TABLE 9
Neutrality, Mediation, Recognition in the Cotton Districts

	Neutrality			Mediation			Recognition		
	M*	R	P	M	R	P	M	R	P
Northeast									
BLACKBURN	1	1		(2) 1(June 1862)	1	1	1(3)	1(2)	1
Darwen				1			1	1	
Great Harwood				1				1	1
BURNLEY	1(2)	1(2)	3(4)	2	2	2	1	1	1
Brierfield	1	1	1		2	2			
HASLINGDEN	(2)	(2)		(3) 3	(3)	(2)	(2) 1	(1) 1	
Accrington		1		1	1	1	1	1	
Bacup		1		1	1	1			
Rawtenstall				1	1		1		
Rossendale				1	1	1			

				3 (1 in Feb. 1862)					
PRESTON									
Total	5(8)	5(8)	4(5)	10(16)	9(12)	8(10)	9(10)	6(8)	3
Southeast									
ASHTON	3			2(4)	1(3)	1(4)	5(14)	4(11)	2(6)
Dukinfield		1		1	1	1		2	1
Lees			1	1	1		3	5	1
Mossley		1		3	3		6		3
BOLTON	3(4)	1(2)		3	1(3)		1(2)	1(2)	1(2)
Edgeworth	1	1			1		1	1	1
Farnworth					1				
Kearsley					1				
BURY	5	1		1	1		2(4)	1(2)	1(2)
Heywood					1		1	1	1
Ramsbottom					1		1	1	
OLDHAM				1			5(8)	3(6)	2(3)
Cowhill							1	1	1
Crompton							1	1	
Royton							1	1	
Waterhead							1	1	
ROCHDALE	8		1	1			1(2)		
WIGAN	2		1	2	1		1		
Hindley									
Total	22(23)	4(5)	2(9)	12(14)	8(10)	8(13)	31(47)	21(34)	9(14)
Grand total	27(34)	9(13)	8(7)	22(29)	17(22)	16(23)	40(60)	27(44)	12(17)

NOTE: * M = Meetings, R = Resolutions, P = Petitions. Only petitions with a substantial number of signatures or those based on resolutions of a public meeting are included.

Towns in capitals are also "unions," and figures in brackets are totals for each whole union where this is more than the total for the town.

BIBLIOGRAPHY

PRIMARY SOURCES

Manuscripts

Adams Papers (microfilm), Rhodes House, Oxford
Antislavery Papers, Rhodes House, Oxford
Bright Papers, British Museum
Bright Papers, University College Library, London
Brougham Papers, University College Library, London
George Alex Brown Diaries, Liverpool Record Office, Brown Library
Cobden Papers, British Museum
Cross Papers, British Museum
Devonshire Papers (7th Duke, Marquis of Hartington), Chatsworth
    Settlement Library
Disraeli Papers, Disraeli Collection, Hughenden
Gladstone Papers, British Museum
Gordon Papers, Unitarian College Library, Manchester
Moses Heap Diary, Rawtenstall Central Library
Holyoake Papers, The Co-operative Society Library, Manchester
George Howell Collection, Bishopsgate Institute
Leary, Frederick, "History of the Manchester Periodical Press," 1897
    (handwritten), Manchester Central Library
Liverpool Town Books, 1860–65, Liverpool Record Office, Brown Library
Mason Papers (microfilm), Library of Congress
Melly Papers, Liverpool Record Office, Brown Library
Miscellaneous relief fund documents, 1862–65, Bury Public Library
Miscellaneous relief fund documents, Preston Public Library
Proceedings of the Cotton Brokers Association of Liverpool, 1860–64,
    Liverpool Cotton Association
Proceedings of the Manchester Chamber of Commerce, Manchester Cen-
    tral Library
Rathbone Papers, University of Liverpool Library
Rawson Collection, English Manuscripts 741–43, John Rylands Library,
    Manchester
Religious Returns, 1851, H. O. 129, Lancashire: 461–86, Public Record
    Office
Russell Papers, Public Record Office
Smith Papers, Manchester Central Library

Wardle, Arthur C., "Blockade Runners Built on Merseyside and Registered at the Port of Liverpool During the American Civil War,
1861–65," 23 November 1861 (typed manuscript), Liverpool Record Office, Brown Library
Wilson Papers, Manchester Central Library

Printed Works

Government Publications

Hansard Parliamentary Debates, third series, commencing with accession of
William IV
Parliamentary Papers

  1835   XIII, "Report from the Select Committee on Handloom
          Weaver's Petitions"
  1842   XXII, "Reports of Factory Inspectors"
  1843   XIV, "Report by John Kennedy on the Employment of
          Children"
  1847–48 IX, "Report from the Select Committee on the Growth of
          Cotton in India"
  1852–53 LXXXIX, "Census of Religious Worship" XXVIII, "Re-
          turns Relating to Dissenters, Places of Worship"
  1861   LXII, "Miscellaneous Statistics of the United Kingdom"
          LXV, "Correspondence with the United States Govern-
          ment Respecting Blockade"
          XXVIII, "Annual Reports of the Poor Law Board"
          XVI, "Annual Reports on the State of Public Health"
          XXII, "Reports of the Factory Inspectors"
          XLVII, "Progress and Condition of India, 1859–60"
  1862   XXII, "Report of the Factory Inspectors"
          XLIX, "Reports by Mr. Farnell to the Poor Law Commis-
          sioners. Cost of Relief"
          LXII, "Correspondence Relating to the Civil War in the
          United States of America"
  1863   XVIII, "Reports of the Factory Inspectors"
          XXXVIII, "Papers Relating to Emigration"
          LII, "Papers Relating to Poor Relief. Reports by Rawlin-
          son and Farnell"
          LXXII, "Correspondence Relating to the Civil War in the

United States of America"
LIII, "Population and Occupations of Lancashire
Boroughs and Unions"
1864   XXII, "Reports of the Factory Inspectors"
LII, "Reports by Farnell to Poor Law Commissioners"
1865   XXII, "Annual Report of the Poor Law Board"
XVIII, "Papers Relating to Emigration"
1868–69 L, "Returns Relating to Emigration" "Reports on the
Committee on Public Petitions," 1861–65
Senate Documents (U.S.A.), vol. 20, Washington, 1911

Newspapers and Periodicals

In Lancashire

Advertiser
Albion (Liverpool)
Ashton and Stalybridge Reporter
Ashton Standard
Barrow Herald Furness
Blackburn Patriot
Blackburn Standard
Blackburn Times
Bolton Chronicle
Burnley Advertiser
Burnley Free Press
Bury Free Press
Bury Times
Co-operator (Manchester)
Cotton Supply Reporter (Manchester)
Daily Courier (Liverpool)
Fleetwood Chronicle
Gore's General Advertiser (Liverpool)
Heywood Advertiser
Lancaster Gazette
Lancaster Guardian
Leigh Chronicle
Liverpool Daily Post
Liverpool Mail
Liverpool Mercury

Liverpool Weekly Mercury
Manchester Alliance Weekly News
Manchester Courier
Manchester Examiner and Times
Manchester Guardian
Manchester Review of Politics and
   Literature
Manchester Weekly Express & Review
Manchester Weekly Penny Budget
Manchester Weekly Times
Middleton Albion
Oldham Chronicle
Oldham Standard
Oldham Times
Porcupine (Liverpool)
Preston Chronicle
Preston Guardian
Preston Mercury
Preston Pilot
Rochdale Observer
Rochdale Pilot
Rochdale Spectator
Salford Weekly News
Southport Independent
Todmorden Times

Ulverston Mirror
Warrington Advertiser
Warrington Guardian

Warrington Standard and Times
Wigan Examiner
Wigan Observer

In London
Bee Hive
Economist
Index
Inquirer

Journal of the Royal Agricultural Society,
     1849
Journal of the Statistical Society of
     London, 1860–90
The Times

Pamphlets

Anon. *A Concise History of the Four Years' Civil War in America.*
     Manchester, 1865.

———. *A Few Words to All on the Present Distress in Lancashire.* London, 1862.

———.*English Neutrality. Is the Alabama a British Pirate?* New York, 1865.

———.*A Few Words to All on the Present Distress of Our Brethren in Lancashire.*
     London, 1862.

———.*The Fallacies of Freemen and Foes of Liberty: A Reply to "The American
     War: The Whole Question Explained."* Manchester, 1863.

———.*Mursell's Latest Folly. A Free Examination of the Lax Principle Propounded
     in His Lecture "No Smoking!"* Manchester, 186?.

———.*The Negro, or the Crimes and the Recompence of the North and South.* Man-
     chester, 1863.

———.*What the South Is Fighting For.* Tracts on Slavery in America, no. 1.
     London, 1862.

Balme, Joshua R. *The American War Crusade.* London, 1863.

———. *Letters on the American Republic, or, Common Fallacies and Monstrous Er-
     rors Refuted and Exposed.* London, 1863.

Banks, Thomas. *A Short Sketch of the Cotton Trade of Preston for the Last 67
     Years.* Preston, 1888.

Bayley, Mrs. M. *Lancashire Homilies.* London, 1863.

Beecher, Henry Ward. *American Rebellion.* Report of speeches, etc. delivered
     at public meetings in Manchester, Glasgow, Edinburgh, Liverpool,
     etc. Manchester, 1864.

Bellows, N.W. *The War to End Only When the Rebellion Ceases.* New York,
     1863.

Belmont, August. *A Few Letters and Speeches of the Late Civil War.* New York,
     1870.

Beresford Hope, A.J.B. *The Social and Political Bearings of the American Disruption.* London, 1863.

Bourne, John. *The Cotton Crisis and How to Avert It.* London, 1861.

Bright, John. *Speech in the Town Hall.* Birmingham, 1862.

Cairnes, J. E. *The Revolution in America,* n.d.

Central Executive Relief Committee. *Report on Fund for Relief of Distress in the Manufacturing Districts.* Manchester, 1862.

Channing, William H. *The Civil War in America; or, the Slaveholders' Conspiracy.* Manchester, 1861?

Cobbett, James Paul. *Causes of the Civil War in the United States.* Manchester, 1861.

A Cotton Manufacturer. *An Inquiry into the Causes of the Present Long-continued Depression in the Cotton Trade. With Suggestions for Its Improvement.* Bury, 1869.

Colyer, Vincent. *Report of the Committee of Merchants for the Relief of Coloured People, Suffering from the Late Riots in the City of New York.* New York, 1863.

———. *Report of the Services Rendered by the Freed People to the United States Army in North Carolina in the Spring of 1862, after the Battle of Newbern.* New York, 1864.

Cooper, Peter. *Letter on Slave Emancipation.* New York, 1862.

Cordner, John. *Canada and the United States.* Manchester, 1865.

Cossham, Handel. *The American War: Facts and Fallacies.* Manchester, 1864.

Darling, Rev. Henry. *Slavery and the War.* Philadelphia, 1863.

Derby, Earl of. *Distress in Lancashire.* Manchester, 1862.

Dudley, Thomas H. *Three Critical Periods in Our Diplomatic Relations with England During the Late War.* Reprinted from *Pennsylvania Magazine of History and Biography.* April, 1893.

Estcourt, J. H. *Rebellion and Recognition. Slavery, Sovereignty, Secession, and Recognition Considered.* Manchester, 1863.

Executive Committee of the Union and Emancipation Society, Manchester. *Earl Russell and the Slave Power.* Manchester, 1863.

Fairbanks, Charles. *The American Conflict as Seen from a European Point of View.* Boston, 1863.

Forster, W. E. *Speech on the Slaveholders' Rebellion, and Professor Goldwin Smith's Letter on the Morality of the Emancipation Proclamation.* Manchester, 1863.

Gladstone, W. E. *The Working Classes and the Cotton Crisis.* London, 1863.

Gow, Dan. *Civil War in America: A Lecture Delivered in Aid of the Lancashire Relief Fund.* Manchester and London, 1863.

Guthrie, Thomas. *An Address on Practical Sympathy and Prompt Beneficience.* London, 1863.

Hare, Mrs. Augustus. *A True and Sad Story of 1862.* London, 1862.

Hoyle, William. *An Inquiry into the Causes of the Present Long-continued Depression in the Cotton Trade.* London and Manchester, 1869.

Jones, Ernest. *Oration on the American Rebellion.* Rochdale, 1864.

———. *The Slaveholder's War.* Ashton, 1863.

Kershaw, Thomas Bentley. *The Truth of the American Question: Being a Reply to the Prize Essay of Mr. Rowan.* Manchester, 1864.

Lincoln, Abraham. *The Letters of President Lincoln on Questions of National Policy.* New York, 1863.

Lowry, Grosvenor P. *English Neutrality.* Philadelphia, 1863.

Ludlow, J. M. *The Southern Minister and His Slave Convert.* Manchester, 186?.

MacHenry, George. *Annals of Industry and Genius.* London, 1863.

MacHenry, George (Philadelphia). *The African Race in America.* London, 1861.

———. (P). *The Cotton Question.* London, 1864.

———. (P). *The Cotton Trade: Its Bearing upon the Prosperity of Great Britain and Commerce of the American Republics Considered in Connection with the System of Negro Slavery in the Confederate States.* London, 1863.

———. (P). *A Familiar Epistle to Robert J. Walker, Formerly of Pennsylvania, from an Old Acquaintance.* London, 1863.

———. (P). *A Paper Presenting Some Remarks in Reference to Duties upon Exports.* Richmond, 1865.

McKaye, James. *Mastership and Its Fruits: The Emancipated Slave Face to Face with His Old Master.* New York, 1864.

Manchester Southern Independence Association. *Ought England to Acknowledge the Independence of the Confederate States?* Occasional Paper no. 5. Manchester, 1863.

———.Papers for the People. No. 2, *The Right of Southern Secession;* no. 5, *The Principles and Policy of President Lincoln;* no. 6, *Notes on Slavery;* no. 7, *The American Tariff;* no. 8, *The Negro in the North.* Manchester, 1864.

Manchester Union and Emancipation Society. *Report of the Proceedings of a*

Conversazione Held in the Manchester Atheneum, on Monday Evening, February 7, 1864, to Receive the Report of the Rev. Dr. Massie, Respecting His Anti-Slavery Mission to the American Clergy and Churches. Manchester, 1864.

Miller, Marmaduke. *Slavery and the American War.* Manchester, 1863.

Newman, F. W. *Character of the Southern States of America.* Manchester, 1863.

"One of the Ruck." *The Cotton Famine: An Attempt to Discover Its Cause, with Suggestions for Its Future Prevention.* Manchester, 186?.

Parker, Joseph. *American War and American Slavery.* Manchester, 1863.

―――. *For Peace in America. A Report from Joseph Parker of Manchester to Sir Henry de Hoghton, Bart., on His Mission as Bearer of the Peace Address from the People of Great Britain and Ireland to the People of the United States of America.* Manchester, 1865.

"Peter the Hermit." *Secession, Slavery and War.* Warrington, 1864.

"A Poor Peacemaker." *The Slavery Quarrel, with Plans and Prospects of Reconciliation.* London, 1863.

Pope, Samuel. *The American War: Secession and Slavery.* Reprinted from *Staffordshire Sentinel.* Manchester, 1863.

―――. *Legal View of the "Alabama" Case, and Ship Building for the Confederates.* Manchester, 1863.

Robbins, E.Y. *The War in America and What England or the People of England May Do to Restore Peace.* New York, 1863.

Seward, W. *Speech at Auburn, New York, November 7, 1864.* New York, 1864.

Shaw, A. N. *The Cotton Crisis and How to Avoid It.* London and Manchester, 1857.

Smith, Goldwin. *Does the Bible Sanction American Slavery?* Oxford, 1863.

―――. *England and America: A Lecture Delivered before the Boston Fraternity, During His Recent Visit to the United States.* Manchester, 1865.

Spence, James. *On the Recognition of the Southern Confederacy.* London, 1862.

―――. *Southern Independence.* London, 1863.

Steinthal, S. Alfred. *Address on the Assassination of Abraham Lincoln.* London and Manchester, 1865.

Stowe, Harriet Beecher. *On the American War and Slavery, in Reply to the Ladies of England.* London, 1863.

Sturvetant, J. M. *English Institutions and the American Rebellion.* Manchester, 1864.

———.*Three Months in Great Britain: A Lecture on the Present Attitude of England Towards the United States, as Determined by Personal Observation.* Chicago, 1864.

Sumner, Charles. *Our Foreign Relations.* New York, 1863.

———. *Slavery and the Rebellion, One and Inseparable.* New York, 1864.

J. G. T. *The Cotton Famine.* London, 1863.

Taylor, William. *Causes and Probable Results of the Civil War in America: Facts for the People of Great Britain.* London, 1862.

Torrens, W. T. M. *Lancashire's Lesson.* London, 1864.

Trimble, Robert. *Popular Fallacies Relating to the American Question.* Manchester, 1863.

———. *The Present Crisis in America.* Manchester, 1865.

———. *A Review of the American Struggle in Its Military and Political Aspects, from 1861 till 1864.* Manchester, 1864.

War Ships for the Southern Confederacy. Report of Public Meeting in the Free-Trade Hall, Manchester; with Letter from Professor Goldwin Smith to the "Daily News." Manchester, 1863.

Watts, John. *The Power and Influence of Co-operative Efforts.* London, 1872.

Whiting, William. *The War Powers of the President and the Legislative Powers of Congress in Relation to Rebellion, Treason and Slavery.* Boston, 1862.

Wilson, George B. "Lancashire's Finest Hour." Wilson Papers. Printed but not published, n.d.

Printed Books (Reports, Annuals, Directories, etc.)

Abram, William Alexander. *Blackburn Characters of a Past Generation.* Blackburn, 1894.

———.*A History of Blackburn.* Blackburn, 1877.

Adams, Henry. "Diary of a Visit to Manchester." Edited by Arthur W. Silver. *American Historical Review,* vol. 51 (October 1945).

Annual Register. 1861–65.

Arnold, Robert Arthur. *The History of the Cotton Famine.* London, 1865.

Ashworth, T. C. *A Fragment of Todmorden History.* Todmorden, 1901.

Axon, William E. A., ed. *The Annals of Manchester: A Chronological Record from the Earliest Times to the End of 1855.* Manchester and London, 1885.

Baines, Edward. *The History of the County Palatine and Duchy of Lancaster.* Revised and edited by James Croston. Manchester and London, 1889.

Barker, John Thomas, ed. *The Life of Joseph Barker.* London, 1880.

Barton, B. T., ed. *Historical Gleanings of Bolton and District.* Bolton, 1883.

———.*History of the Borough of Bury and Neighbourhood in the County of Lancaster.* Bury, 1874.

Beaman, Charles C., Jr. *The National and Private "Alabama Claims" and Their "Final and Amicable Settlement."* Washington, 1871.

Bernard, Montague. *A Historical Account of the Neutrality of Great Britain During the American Civil War.* London, 1870.

Blanc, Louis. *Letters on England.* Translated by J. Hutton and L. J. Trotter. 2 vols. London, 1867.

Bland, C. *Annals of Southport. A Chronological History of North Meols A.D. 1086 to 1886.* Southport, 1888.

Bright, John. *The Diaries of John Bright.* Foreword by Philip Bright. Edited by R. A. J. Walling. London, 1930.

———. *Speeches of John Bright, M. P., on the American Question.* Edited by F. Moore. Boston, 1865.

———.*Speeches on Questions of Public Policy.* Edited by J. C. Thorold Rogers. London, 1868.

British Almanac of the Society for the Diffusion of Useful Knowledge. 1860–65.

Bulloch, James D. *The Secret Service of the Confederate States in Europe, or, How the Confederate Cruisers Were Equipped.* 2 vols. London, 1959.

The Case of the United States, to Be Laid before the Tribunal of Arbitration, to Be Convened at Geneva under the Provisions of the Treaty between the United States of America and Her Majesty the Queen of Great Britain, Concluded at Washington, May 8, 1871. Washington, 1871.

Cobden, Richard. *American Diaries.* Edited by Elizabeth Hoon Cawley. Princeton, 1952.

———. *Political Writings.* 2 vols. London, 1867.

———. *Speeches on Questions of Public Policy.* Edited by John Bright and J. C. Thorold Rogers. London, 1903.

Cotton Circulars of Hall and Mellor, Holt, R. C. Hall, Ellison and Haywood, Buchanan & Co., Dubany, T. and H. Littledale, Neill Bros., W. P. Wright.

Davis, Jefferson. *The Rise and Fall of the Confederate Government.* New York, 1881.

Defoe, Daniel. *A Tour through England and Wales.* 2 vols. London, 1927.

Dickson, R. W. *General View of the Agriculture of Lancashire with Observations on the Means of Its Improvement. Drawn up for the Consideration of the Board of Agriculture and Internal Improvement.* Revised and prepared for the press by W. Stevenson. London, 1815.

Ellison, Thomas. *The Cotton Trade of Great Britain, Including a History of the Liverpool Cotton Market and of the Liverpool Cotton Brokers Association.* London, 1886.

———. *Slavery and Secession in America, Historical and Economical.* 2d ed. London, 1862.

Espinasse, F. *Lancashire Worthies.* London, 1874.

Fishwick, H. *A History of the Parish of Rochdale.* Rochdale, 1889.

Folkard, H. T. *Industries of Wigan.* Wigan, 1889.

Ford, Worthington Chaunery, ed. *A Cycle of Adams Letters.* 2 vols. London, 1921.

Forwood, Sir William B. *Some Recollections of a Busy Life.* Liverpool, 1910.

Garrison, F. J. and W. P. *Willaim Lloyd Garrison, 1805–79. The Story of His Life Told by His Children.* 4 vols. New York and London, 1884.

(Gibbs) H.S.G. *Autobiography of a Manchester Cotton Manufacturer; or, Thirty Years Experience of Manchester.* Manchester and London, 1887.

Gillet, George A. *Commercial and General Directory of Preston.* Preston, 1869.

Gladstone and Palmerston, Being the Correspondence of Lord Palmerston with Mr. Gladstone, 1851–65. Edited with an introduction and commentary by Philip Guedella. London, 1928.

Gould, B. A. *Investigations in the Military and Anthropological Statistics of American Soldiers.* New York, 1867.

Grant, J. *The Newspaper Press.* London, 1871.

Greeley, Horace. *The American Conflict: A History of the Great Rebellion in the United States of America, 1860–65.* Hartford, Conn., 1866.

Hammond, M. B. *The Cotton Industry.* Saratoga, 1897.

Harland, John, ed. *Ballads and Songs of Lancashire, Ancient and Modern.* Collected, compiled, and edited, with some notes, by John Harland. 2d ed. corrected, revised, and enlarged by T. T. Wilkinson. London, 1875.

Hewitson, Anthony. *History (from A.D. 705 to 1883) of Preston, in the County of Lancaster.* Preston, 1883.

Heywood, T. T. *New Annals of Rochdale. A Short History since 1899, and A*

Chronological Review from the Earliest Times to the End of the Year 1930. Rochdale, 1931.

Historical Statistics of the United States, Colonial Times to 1957. Washington, 1960.

Holt, John. *General View of the Agriculture of the County of Lancaster.* London, 1795.

Holyoake, G. J. *The History of the Rochdale Pioneers.* London, 1867.

Hunt, William. *Then and Now, or, Fifty Years of Newspaper Work.* London, 1887.

Jessop, William. *An Account of Methodism in Rossendale and the Neighbourhood.* Manchester, 1880.

Lincoln, Abraham. *Complete Works, Comprising the Speeches, Letters, State Papers and Miscellaneous Writings.* New York, 1920.

Livesay, Joseph. *Life of Joseph Livesay.* Blackburn, 1885.

Lodge, Edmund, *The Peerage and Baronetage of the British Empire as at Present Existing. Arranged and Printed from the Personal Communications of the Queen's Most Excellent Majesty.* London, 1888.

Ludlow, J. M., and Jones, Lloyd. *Progress of the Working Class, 1832–1867.* London, 1867.

Malmesbury, Lord. *Memoirs of an Ex-Minister.* 3 vols. London, 1884.

Mann, J. A. *The Cotton Trade of Great Britain.* Manchester, 1860.

Marx, Karl, and Engels, Frederick. *The Civil War in the United States.* London, 1938.

Mason, James M. *The Public Life and Diplomatic Correspondence, with Some Personal History by Virginia Mason.* New York and Washington, 1906.

McPherson, Edward. *The Political History of the United States of America During the Great Rebellion.* Washington, 1865.

Morley, John. *The Life of Richard Cobden.* 1-vol. ed. London, 1903.

———. The Life of William Ewart Gladstone. 3 vols. London, 1903.

Mortimer, John. *Industrial Lancashire.* Manchester, 1897.

———. *Mercantile Manchester.* Manchester, 1896.

———. *Spinning, the Story of Spindle.* Manchester, 1895.

Newbigging, Thomas. *History of the Forest of Rossendale.* With a chapter on the geology of Rossendale by Captain Aitken, M. P. London and Bacup, 1868.

————. *Lancashire Characters and Places.* London and Bacup, 1891.

The Newspaper Press Directory, 1860–1865.

Nichols, S. A. *Darwen and the Cotton Famine.* Rawtenstall, 1893.

Nightingale, Rev. B. *Lancashire Nonconformity.* 5 vols. Manchester and London, 1893.

Pierce, Edward L. *Memoir and Letters of Charles Sumner, Period 1860 to Death.* London, 1893.

Pinnock's County History. *History and Topography of Lancashire.* London, 1820.

Place, Francis. *G. J. Holyoake's Life of J. R. Stephens.* London, 1881.

Poole, Benjamin. *Coventry, Its History and Antiquities.* London, 1870.

Preston Relief Committee. *Fourth Report of Proceedings.* May, 1865.

Ramsdell, Charles W., ed. *Laws and Joint Resolutions of the Last Session of the Confederate Congress Together with the Secret Acts of the Previous Congresses.* Durham, N.C., 1941.

Robertson, William. *Life and Times of the Right Honourable John Bright, M.P.* London, 1883.

————. *Rochdale, Past and Present.* Rochdale and London, 1875.

Roebuck, John Arthur. *Life and Letters.* Edited by Robert E. Leader. London, 1897.

Russell, William Howard. *My Civil War Diary.* Edited by Fletcher Pratt. London, 1954.

Saintsbury, G. *Manchester.* London, 1887.

Schulze-Gaevernitz, G. von. *The Cotton Trade in England and the Continent.* London, 1895.

Semmes, Admiral Raphael. *Memories of a Service Afloat, During the War between the States.* Baltimore, 1869.

Seward, Frederick W. *Seward at Washington as Senator and Secretary of State. A Memoir of His Life, with Selections from His Letters, 1861–1872.* New York, 1891.

Seward, William H. *Works.* Edited by George C. Baker. Vol. 5, *The Diplomatic History of the War for the Union.* Washington, 1883.

Slater's General and Classified Directory and Street Register of Manchester and Salford, with Their Vicinities. . . . 1859.

Smith, Gustavus W., ed. *Confederate War Papers.* New York, 1884.

Society of Coachmakers, England, Ireland and Scotland. *Fifty-sixth Quarterly Report of the United Kingdom.*

Soley, James Russell. *The Navy in the Civil War.* London, 1898.

Spackman, Wm. Frederick. *An Analysis of the Occupations of the People, Showing the Relative Importance of the Agricultural, Manufacturing, Shipping, Colonial, Commercial and Mining Interests of the United Kingdom of Great Britain and Its Dependencies. . . .* Complied from the Census of 1851 and other official returns. London, 1847.

Spence, James. *The American Union, Its Effect on National Character and Policy with an Inquiry into Secession as a Constitutional Right, and the Causes of Disruption.* 4th ed. London, 1862.

Taylor, Richard. *Destruction and Reconstruction: Experiences of the Late War.* New York, 1879.

Taylor, Thomas E. *Running the Blockade: A Personal Narrative of Adventure, Risks, and Escapes During the American Civil War.* London, 1896.

Taylor, Dr. W. C., and Beard, Dr. *An Illustrated Itinerary of the County of Lancaster.* London, 1842.

Ure, Andrew. *The Cotton Manufacture of Great Britain with Supplement by P. L. Simmonds.* 2 vols. London, 1861.

Warneford, R. *Running the Blockade.* London, 1863.

Watson, William. *The Adventures of a Blockade Runner, or, Trade in Time of War.* London, 1892.

Watters, J. Cuming. *Lancashire: Its Chief Resources and Characteristics.* Issued under the auspices of the Governing Councils in Lancashire. Burrows County Guides, 18?.

Watts, John. *The Facts of the Cotton Famine.* London and Manchester, 1866.

Waugh, Edwin. *Home Life of the Lancashire Factory Folk During the Cotton Famine.* London, 1867.

Wilkinson, J. *The Narrative of a Blockade-Runner.* New York, 1877.

Williams, James. *The South Vindicated, Being a Series of Letters Written for the American Press During the Canvas for the Presidency in 1860.* London, 1862.

Workpeople of Hurst Mills. "Testimonial to John Whittaker as a Token of Respect and Esteem for His Generous and Munificent Conduct During the Period of the Cotton Famine, Caused by the War in America." Printed but not published. December 1862.

Young, Edward. *Special Report on Immigration Accompanying Information to Immigrants.* Washington, 1871.

Broadsheets of the Manchester Union and Emancipation Society; the

Southern Independence Association of Manchester.

SECONDARY SOURCES

Books

Adams, Charles Francis, Jr. *Charles Francis Adams.* London, 1900.

Adams, Ephriam D. *Great Britain and the American Civil War.* 2 vols. New York, 1900.

Allen, H. C. *Great Britain and the United States.* London, 1954.

Armytage, W. H. G. *Heavens Below, Utopian experiments in England, 1560–1960.* London, 1961.

Ausubel, Herman. *John Bright, Victorian Reformer.* New York, 1966.

Bagley, J. J. *History of Lancashire.* Liverpool, 1956.

Bateson, Hartley, *A Centenary History of Oldham.* Oldham, 1949.

Batten, R. *Communities and Their Development.* London, 1951.

Bell, H. C. F. *Lord Palmerston.* 2 vols. London, 1936.

Benet, Stephen Vincent. *John Brown's Body.* New York, 1928.

Bennet, W. *The History of Burnley from 1850.* Burnley, 1951.

Berthoff, Rowland T. *British Immigrants in Industrial America, 1790–1950.* Cambridge, Mass., 1953.

Boase, Frederick. *Modern English Biography.* 4 vols., 4 supplements. London, 1965.

Bourne, Kenneth. *Britain and the Balance of Power in North America, 1815–1908.* London, 1967.

Bowman, Winifred. *England in Ashton-under-Lyne, Being the History of the Ancient Manor and Parish. . . .* Ashton-under-Lyne, 1960.

Briggs, Asa. *Victorian Cities.* London, 1963.

———. *Victorian People.* London, 1945.

Callahan, James Morton. *The Diplomatic History of the Southern Confederacy.* Baltimore, 1901.

Cash, W. J. *The Mind of the South.* New York, 1960.

Chandler, George. *Liverpool Shipping. A Short History.* London, 1960.

Chapman, S. J. *The Lancashire Cotton Industry.* London, 1904.

Chorley, Katherine. *Manchester Made Them.* London, 1951.

Cochran, Hamilton. *The Blockade Runners of the Confederacy.* New York, 1958.

Court, W. H. B. *A Concise Economic History of Britain from 1750 to Recent Times.* Cambridge, 1962.

Cowling, Marucie. 1867: *Disraeli, Gladstone and Resolution. The Passing of the Second Reform Bill.* Cambridge, 1967.

Craven, Avery O. *The Growth of Southern Nationalism, 1848–1861.* Baton Rouge, 1953.

Creighton, Donald. *Dominion of the North. A History of Canada.* Toronto, 1966.

Crook, David Paul. *American Democracy in English Politics.* Oxford, 1965.

Daniels, G. W. *The Early English Cotton Industry.* Manchester, 1920.

Dawson, William Harbutt. *Richard Cobden and Foreign Policy. A Critical Exposition, with Special Reference to Our Day and Its Problems.* London, 1926.

Derry, John W. *The Radical Tradition: Tom Paine to Lloyd George.* London, 1967.

Dumond, Dwight L. *Anti-Slavery Origins of the Civil War in the United States.* Ann Arbor, 1939.

Edwards, Michael M. *The Growth of the British Cotton Trade, 1780–1815.* Manchester, 1967.

Ellison, William. *Marginal Land in Britain.* London, 1953.

Fay, C. R. *Round about Industrial Britain, 1830–1860.* Toronto, 1952.

Frangopulo, N. J. *Rich Inheritance. A Guide to the History of Manchester.* Manchester, 1963.

Garfinkle, Norton, ed. *Lincoln and the Coming of the Civil War.* Boston, 1959.

Gilchrist, D., and Lewis, D., eds. *Economic Change in the Civil War Era.* Charlottesville, N.C., 1965.

Gillespie, Frances Emma. *Labour and Politics in England, 1850–1867.* Durham, North Carolina, 1927.

Gosden, P. H. J. *The Friendly Societies in England, 1815–1875.* Manchester, 1961.

Greswell, R. Kay, and Laughton, R. *Merseyside.* Sheffield, 1964.

Habakkuk, H. J. *American and British Technology in the Nineteenth Century. The Search for Labour Saving Inventions.* Cambridge, 1962.

Hacker, L. M. *England and America. The Ties That Bind.* Oxford, 1948.

Hanham, H. J. *Elections and Party Management. Politics in the Time of Disraeli and Gladstone.* London, 1959.

Harrison, Royden. *Before the Socialists.* London, 1965.

Henderson, W. O. *The Lancashire Cotton Famine, 1861–1865.* Manchester, 1934.

Hernon, Joseph M., Jr. *Celts, Catholics and Copperheads: Ireland Views the American Civil War.* Columbus, Ohio, 1968.

Hertz, G. B. *The Manchester Politician.* Manchester, 1912.

Higham, John, ed. *The Reconstruction of American History.* London, 1962.

Hobshawn, Eric. *Industry and Empire: An Economic History of Britain since 1750.* London, 1968.

———. *Labouring Men.* London, 1964.

Houghton, Walter C. *The Victorian Frame of Mind.* New Haven, Conn., 1957.

Hovell, Mark. *The Chartist Movement.* London, 1925.

Hulbert, Henry L. P. *Sir Francis Sharp Powell.* Leeds, 1914.

Hyde, Francis E. *Blue Funnel: A History of Alfred Holt and Company of Liverpool from 1865 to 1914.* Liverpool, 1956.

Hyman, Harold, ed. *Heard around the World: The Impact of the American Civil War Abroad.* New York, 1969.

Jewkes, J., and Gray, E. M. *Wages and Labour in the Lancashire Cotton Industry.* 1935.

Johnson, L. G. *The Social Evolution of Industrial Britain.* Liverpool, 1959.

Johnson, Stanley C. *A History of Emigration from the United Kingdom to North America, 1763–1912.* London, 1913.

Jones, Wilbur Devereux. *Lord Derby and Victorian Conservatism.* Oxford, 1956.

Jordon, D., and Pratt, E. J. *Europe and the American Civil War.* Cambridge, 1931.

Lillibridge, G. D. *Beacon of Freedom.* Philadelphia, 1955.

Lonn, Ella. *Foreigners in the Confederacy.* Chapel Hill, 1940.

———. *Foreigners in the Union Army and Navy.* Baton Rouge, 1951.

McConnel, John W. *A Century of Fine Cotton Spinning.* Manchester, 1913.

Macoby, S. *English Radicalism, 1853–1886.* London, 1938.

Magnus, Philip. *Gladstone.* London, 1954.

Marriner, Sheila. *The Rathbones of Liverpool, 1845–1873.* Liverpool, 1961.

Miller, G. C. *Blackburn: Evolution of a Cotton Town.* Blackburn, 1951.

Millward, R. *Lancashire.* London, 1955.

Mountfield, Stuart. *Western Gateway. A History of the Mersey Docks and harbour Board.* Liverpool, 1965.

National Dictionary of Biography.

Nevins, Allan. *America through British Eyes.* New York, 1948.

———. *American Social History as Recorded by British Travellers.* New York, 1923.

———. *The Emergence of Lincoln.* New York, 1950.

Nichols, Roy F. *The Stakes of Power, 1845–1877.* London, 1965.

Owsley, Frank L. *King Cotton Diplomacy.* Chicago, 1959.

Pelling, Henry. *American and the British Left.* London, 1956.

———. *Social Geography of British Elections, 1885–1910.* London, 1967.

Pole, J. R. *Abraham Lincoln and the Working Classes of Britain.* Pamphlet. London, 1959.

Presnell, L., ed. *Studies in the Industrial Revolution.* Presented to T. S. Ashton. London, 1960.

Randall, J. G., and Donald, D. *The Civil War and Reconstruction.* Boston, 1961.

Redford, Arthur. *The History of Local Government in Manchester,* vol. 2. Manchester, 1956.

———. *Labour Migration in England, 1800–1850.* Manchester, 1926.

———. *Manchester Merchants and Foreign Trade.* Vol. 2, *1850–1939.* Manchester, 1956.

Robson, Robert, ed. *Ideas and Institutions of Victorian Britain. Essays in Honour of George Kitson Clark.* London, 1967.

Roebuck, Arthur. *The Roebuck Story.* Ontario, 1963.

Rostow, W. W. British *Economy of the Nineteenth Century.* Oxford, 1959.

Rozwenc, Edwin C., ed. *Slavery as a Cause of the Civil War.* Boston, 1949.

Russel, Robert, *Economic Aspects of Southern Sectionalism, 1840–1861.* New York, 1960.

Saxelby, C. H., ed. *Bolton Survey.* Bolton, 1933.

Schofield, Maurice Merples. *Economic History of Lancaster, 1680–1860.* 2 vols. Lancaster, 1946.

Shepperson, Wilbur Stanley. *The Promotion of British Emigration by Agents for American Lands.* Nevada, 1954.

Silver, Arthur W. *Manchester Men and Indian Cotton, 1847–1872.* Manchester, 1966.

Smelser, Neil J. *Social Change in the Industrial Revolution. An Application of Theory to the Lancashire Cotton Industry, 1770–1840.* London, 1959.

Smith, Wilfrid. *The County of Lancashire. Report of the Canal Utilization Survey Part 45.* London, 1946.

———. *An Economic Geography of Great Britain.* London, 1955.

Stacey, C. P. *Canada and the British Army, 1846-1871: A Study in the Practice of Responsible Government.* Toronto, 1963.

Stampp, Kenneth M. *The Peculiar Institution.* New York, 1956.

Stowe, Harriet Beecher. *Uncle Tom's Cabin. A Tale of Slave Life.* London, 1853.

Thistlethwaite, Frank. *The Anglo-American Connection in the Early Nineteenth Century.* Philadelphia, 1959.

Thomas, John Alun. *The House of Commons, 1832–1901: A Study of Its Economic and Functional Character.* Cardiff, 1939.

Thompson, F. M. L. *English Landed Society in the Nineteenth Century.* London, 1965.

Thompson, S. B. *Confederate Purchasing Operations Abroad.* North Carolina, 1935.

Touzeau, James. *Rise and Progress of Liverpool.* Liverpool, 1910.

Trevelyan, George. *The Life of John Bright.* London, 1913.

Tupling, George Henry. *The Economic History of Rossendale.* Manchester, 1927.

———. *The History of Lancashire and Cheshire.* Manchester, 1934.

Vandiver, Frank E., ed. *Confederate Blockade Running through Bermuda, 1861–1865, Letters and Cargo Manifests.* Austin, Texas, 1947.

The Victoria History of the Counties of England. Vol. 3, *Lancashire,* London, 1908.

Villiers, Brougham, and Chesson, W. H. *Anglo-American Relations, 1861–1865.* London, 1919.

Vincent, J. R. *The Formation of the Liberal Party, 1857–68.* London, 1966.

———. *Pollbooks, How Victorians Voted.* Cambridge, 1967.

Wadsworth, A. P., and Mann, J. De L. *The Cotton Industry and Industrial Lancashire.* Manchester, 1931.

Wearmouth, Robert F. *Methodism and the Working-Class Movements of England, 1800–1850.* London, 1937.

———. *Some Working Class Movements of the Nineteenth Century.* London, 1948.

Williams, W. E. *The Rise of Gladstone to the Leadership of the Liberal Party, 1859–1868.* Cambridge, 1934.

Winks, Robin W. *Canada and the United States. The Civil War Years.* Baltimore, 1960.

Wittke, Carl. *The Irish in America.* Baton Rouge, 1956.

Woodward, Sir Llewellyn. *The Age of Reform, 1815–1870.* Oxford, 1962.

Articles

Bailey, Thomas A. "World Analogues of the Trent Affair." *American Historical Review,* vol. 23 (1933).

Banbury, Philip. "Steamers on the Run." *Sea Breezes,* n.s., vol 34 (December 1962).

Barnes, Melvyn. "Children's Libraries in Manchester: A History." *Manchester Review,* vol. 2 (Winter 1966–67).

Beloff, Max. "Great Britain and the American Civil War." *History,* n.s., vol. 37 (February 1952).

Blaug, M. "The Productivity of Capital in the Lancashire Cotton Industry During the Nineteenth Century." *Economic History Review,* 2d ser., vol. 13 (1960).

Bourne, Kenneth. "British Preparations for War with the North, 1861–1862." English Historical Review, vol. 76 (October 1961).

Brady, E. A. "A Reconstruction of the Lancashire 'Cotton Famine,' " *Agricultural History* (Urbana, Illinois), vol. 37 (1963).

Carnall, Geoffrey. "Dickens, Mrs. Gaskell, and the Preston Strike." *Victorian Studies,* vol. 8 (September 1964).

Chapman, S. J., and Ashton, T. S. "The Size of Business, Mainly in the Textile Industries." *Journal of the Royal Statistical Society,* vol. 27 (1964).

Claussen, Martin P. "Peace Factors in Anglo-American Relations, 1861–1865." *Mississippi Valley Historical Review,* vol. 26 (March 1939).

Conrad, Alfred H. et al. "Slavery as an Obstacle to Economic Growth in the United States: A Panel Discussion." *Journal of Economic History,* vol 27, no. 4 (December 1967).

Du Bois, W. E. B. "The Negro and the Civil War." *Science and Society,* vol. 25, no. 4 (December 1961).

Ellinger, Barnard. "The Cotton Famine of 1860–64." *Economic History,* vol. 3, no. 9 (January 1934).

Erickson, Charlotte. "The Encouragement of Emigration by British

Trade Unions, 1850–1900." *Population Studies,* vol. 3 (1950).

France, R. Sharpe. "The Diary of John Ward of Glitheroe, Weaver, 1860–64." *Transactions of the Historic Society of Lancashire and Cheshire,* vol. 105 (1953).

Genovese, Eugene D. "The Slave South: An Interpretation." *Science and Society,* vol. 25, no. 4 (December 1961).

Greenleaf, R. "British Labour against American Slavery." *Science and Society,* vol 17, no. 1 (January 1953).

Harnetty, Peter. "The Imperialism of Free Trade: Lancashire, India, and the Cotton Supply Question." *Journal of British Studies,* vol. 6, no. 1 (November 1966).

Harrison, Brian. "Religion and Recreation in Nineteenth Century England." *Past and Present,* no. 38 (December 1967).

Harrison, Royden. "British Labour and American Slavery." *Science and Society,* vol. 25, no. 4 (December 1961).

———. "British Labor and the Confederacy." *International Review of Socialist History* (Amsterdam), vol. 2, pt. 1 (1957).

Henderson, W. O. "The Public Works Act, 1863." *Economic History,* vol 2 (1933).

Hernon, Joseph M., Jr. "British Sympathies in the American Civil War." A Reconsideration." *Journal of Southern History,* vol. 33 (August 1967).

Himmelfarb, Gertrude. "The Politics of Democracy: The English Reform Act of 1867." *Journal of British Studies,* vol. 6, no. 1 (1966).

Hopcroft, G. E. L. "Liverpool and the Blockade Runners." *Mersey,* vol. 5 (1929).

Jarvis, Rupert C. "Alabama and the Law." *Transactions of the Historic Society of Lancashire and Chesire,* vol 111 (1959–60).

Jewkes, J. "The Localisation of the Cotton Industry." *Economic History,* vol 2 (1933).

Jones, Wilbur Devereux. "The British Conservatives and the American Civil War." *American Historical Review,* vol. 58, no. 3 (April 1953).

McGready, H. W. "The Cotton Famine in Lancashire, 1863." *Transactions of the Historic Society of Lancashire and Cheshire,* vol. 106 (1955).

Marriner, Sheila. "Rathbones' Trading Activities in the Middle of the Nineteenth Century." *Transactions of the Historic Society of Lancashire and Cheshire,* vol. 108 (1956).

Park, Joseph H. "The English Working Men and the American Civil War." *Political Science Quarterly,* vol. 39 (1924).

Rice, C. Duncan. "The Anti-Slavery Mission of George Thompson to the United States, 1834–1835." *Journal of American Studies,* vol. 2, no. 1 (April 1968).

Searby, P. "Gladstone in West Derby Hundred. The Liberal Campaign in South-West Lancashire in 1868." *Transactions of the Historic Society of Lancashire and Cheshire,* vol. 111 (1959–60).

Sellers, Ian. "Non-Conformist Attitudes in Later Nineteenth Century Liverpool." *Transactions of the Historic Society of Lancashire and Cheshire,* vol 114 (March 1962).

Shortread, Margaret. "The Anti-Slavery Radicals, 1840–1868." *Past and Present,* vol 16 (November 1959).

Taylor, A. J. "Concentration and Specialisation in the Lancashire Cotton Industry, 1825–1850." *Economic History Review,* 2d ser., vol. 1 (1948–49).

Taylor, H. A. "Politics in Famine-Stricken Preston." *Transactions of the Historic Society of Lancashire and Cheshire,* vol. 107 (September 1955).

Wardle, Arthur. "British Built Blockade Runners of the American Civil War." *Transactions of the Nautical Research Society,* vol. 1, no. 7 (1942).

———. "Some Blockade Runners of the American Civil War." *American Neptune* (April 1943).

Dissertations

Bather, Leslie. "The History of the Manchester and Salford Trades Council." Ph.D. dissertation, Manchester, 1956.

Bolt, Christine A. "British Attitudes to Reconstruction in the United States, 1863–1877." Ph.D. dissertation, London, 1966.

Cook, Adrian. "The Way to Geneva: United States Policy and Attitudes towards Great Britain, 1865–1872." Ph.D. dissertation, Cambridge, 1964.

Corke, Margaret Wendy. "Birmingham and the American Civil War." M.A. thesis, Liverpool, 1963.

Courtermanche, Regis. "Vice-Admiral Sir Alexander Milne, K.C.B. and the North American and West Indian Station, 1860–1864." Ph.D. dissertation, London, 1967.

Farnie, D. A. "The English Cotton Industry, 1850–98." Ph.D. dissertation, Manchester, 1953.

Robson, R. "Structure of the Cotton Industry: A Study in Specialization and Integration." Ph.D. dissertation, London, 1950.

Temperley, Howard. "The British and Foreign Anti-Slavery Society, 1839–1868." Ph.D. dissertation, Yale University, 1960.

Van Auken, Sheldon. "English Sympathy for the Southern Confederacy." B. Litt. thesis, Oxford, 1957.

INDEX

Thompson, George, 60, 69, 83, 86, 101;
on Lancashire workers, 59; on
Lincoln, 174, 175, 177; on neu-
trality, 99, 107; visit of, to Amer-
ica, 90
Todd, James, 67
Todmorden, 18, 63, 133
Tories, 13, 14
Trenholm, George A., 170
Trent, 29, 31, 99, 106, 134, 135, 136,
139, 140, 144, 146, 147, 148, 152
Turner, Charles (M.P.), on licenses,
165
Turner, James Aspinall (M.P.), 126,
145
Tuscaloosa, 166

Ulverston Mirror, 54, 107, 133, 152
U.S. Chamber of Commerce, 52
U.S. Oddfellows Society, 44
Uttley, 63

Verity, Rev. A. E., 23, 24, 42, 63, 64,
113, 144; on mediation, 137, 141,
142, 144; on recognition, 115; on
slavery, 173
Vernon, Councillor D., on recognition,
123
Vincent, Henry, 11, 70, 98, 101

Wall, Thomas, on causes of war, 45
Ward, Thomas, 70

Warneford, Lieutenant, on blockade
running, 162
Warrington, 94, 108, 120, 132, 133,
142, 147
Warrington Advertiser, 107, 186
Warrington Guardian, 53, 93
Warrington Standard, 53, 152
Watts, John, 81, 83
Weaving, 18–22
Wesleyans, 13
West Ham, 170
West Indies, 165, 167, 168
White, Joseph, 41
Whitty, J. M., 50, 51, 87
Wigan, 22, 23, 24, 25, 116, 123, 159,
179, 181
Wigan Examiner, 44, 72
Wigan Observer, 45, 72, 116, 139, 158,
160, 178
Wild Dayrell, 168
Wilkes, Captain, 150; and seizure of
Trent, 29
Williams, Rev. H., 74; on recognition,
123, 124
Wilson and Chambers, of Liverpool,
157
Wilson, H. J., 101
Wilson, Rev. F., 75; on emancipation,
77, 78
Wolstencroft, J., on Lincoln, 177
Working class. *See* Labor, attitudes of
Wren, 169